BOOK TWO

ALEXIS DEACON

A GAME WITHOUT RULES

NOBROW

London | New York

geis / ˈgɛʃ /

Geis, pronounced *gesh*, is a Gaelic
word for a taboo or curse. When a geis
is placed upon you, it is like a spell that
cannot be broken and certain rules must
be obeyed. You might be prohibited from
trampling mushrooms, for example,
or from sitting down on the stairs.
If you ignore or break a geis,
the consequences are dire.

But a geis is always broken.

As soon as it is spoken or written,
your fate is set.

The first test to find
the new chief has ended.
The second is about to begin.

Of the fifty souls who entered,
only the girl, Io and
the young man, Nemas
know the truth:
The sorceress plans
to kill them all.
All that is, save one.

For the contest must
have a winner.

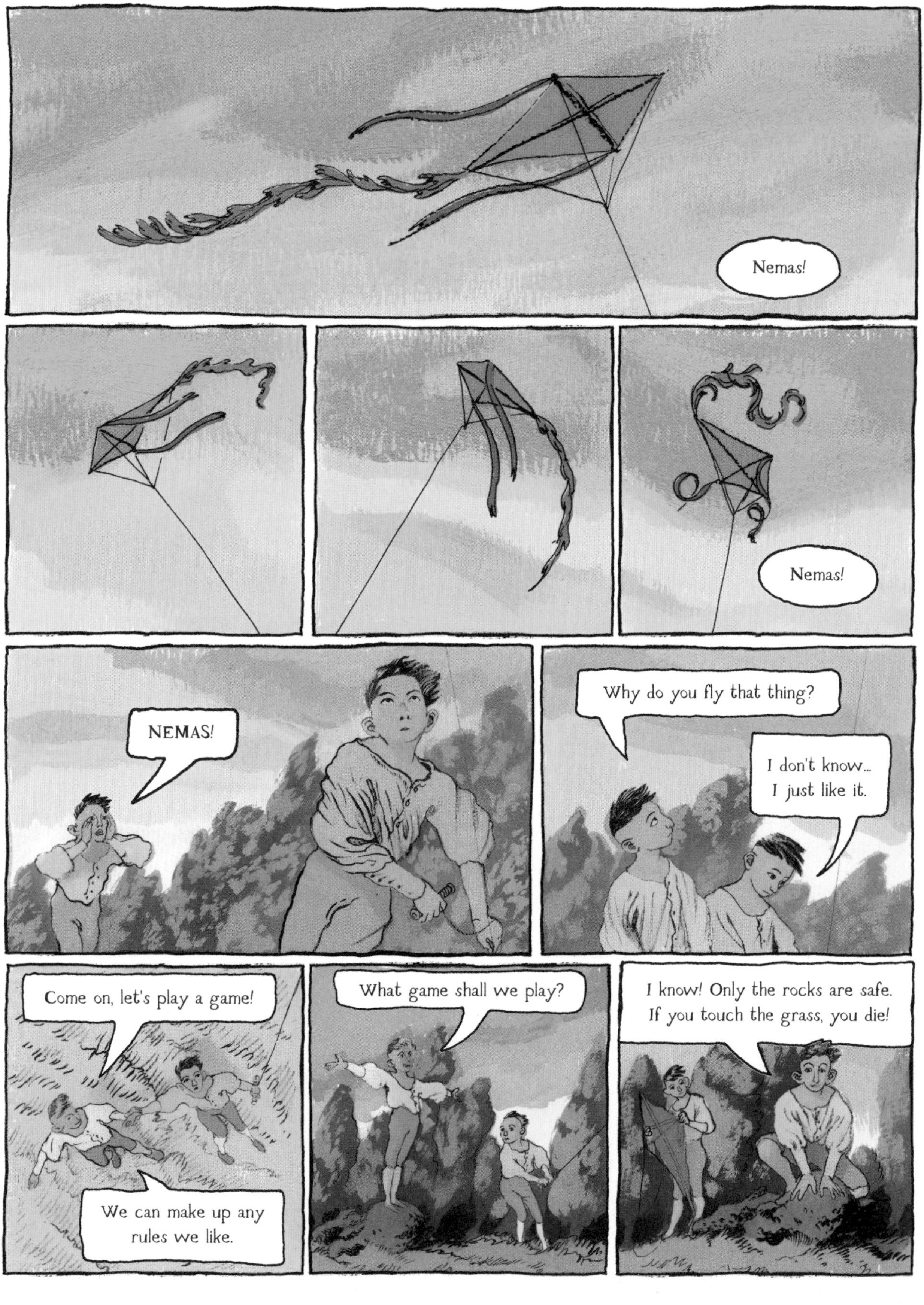
Nemas!
Nemas!
NEMAS!
Why do you fly that thing?
I don't know... I just like it.
Come on, let's play a game!
We can make up any rules we like.
What game shall we play?
I know! Only the rocks are safe. If you touch the grass, you die!

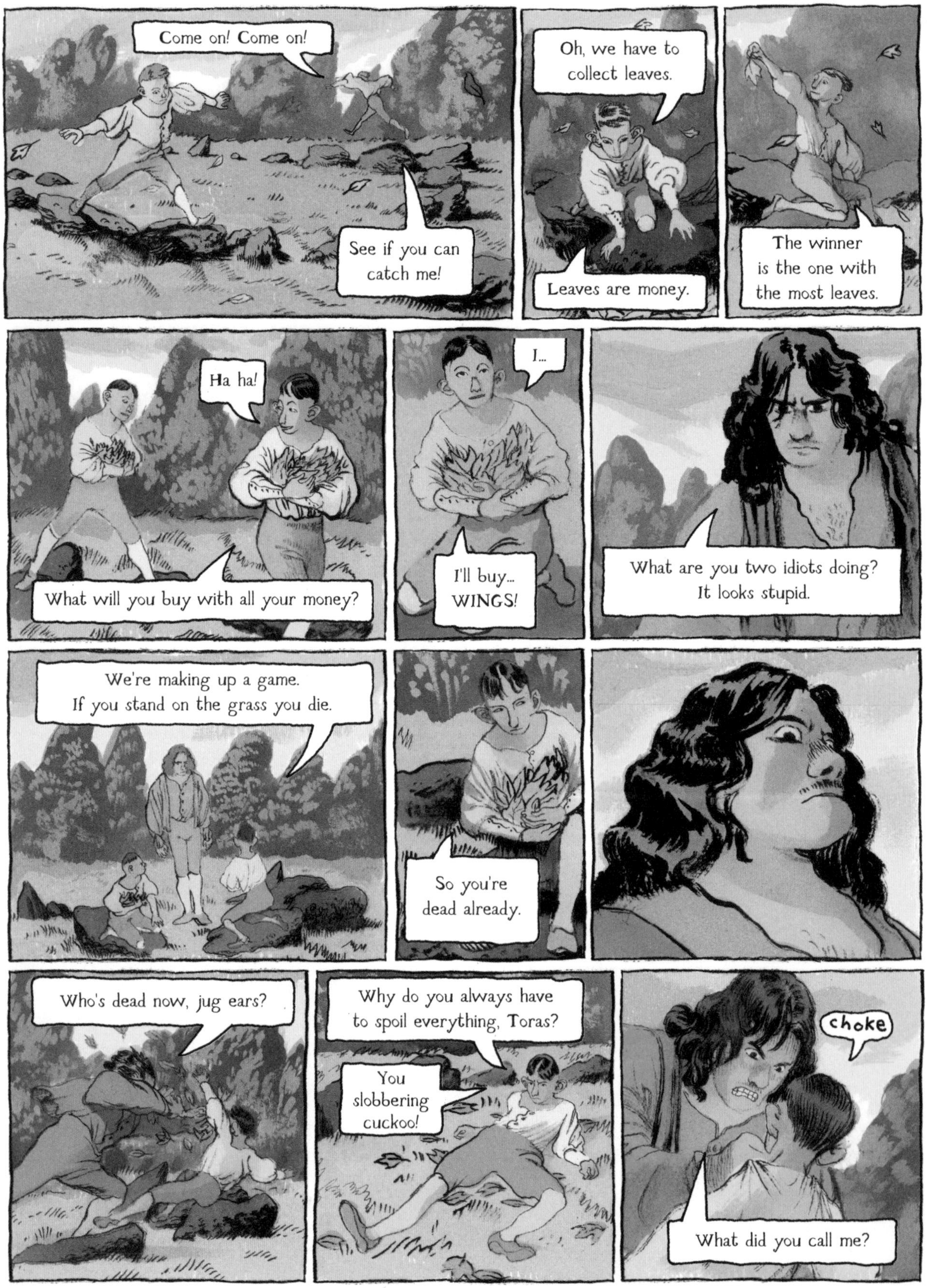

Come on! Come on!
See if you can catch me!
Oh, we have to collect leaves.
Leaves are money.
The winner is the one with the most leaves.
Ha ha!
What will you buy with all your money?
I...
I'll buy... WINGS!
What are you two idiots doing? It looks stupid.
We're making up a game. If you stand on the grass you die.
So you're dead already.
Who's dead now, jug ears?
Why do you always have to spoil everything, Toras?
You slobbering cuckoo!
choke
What did you call me?

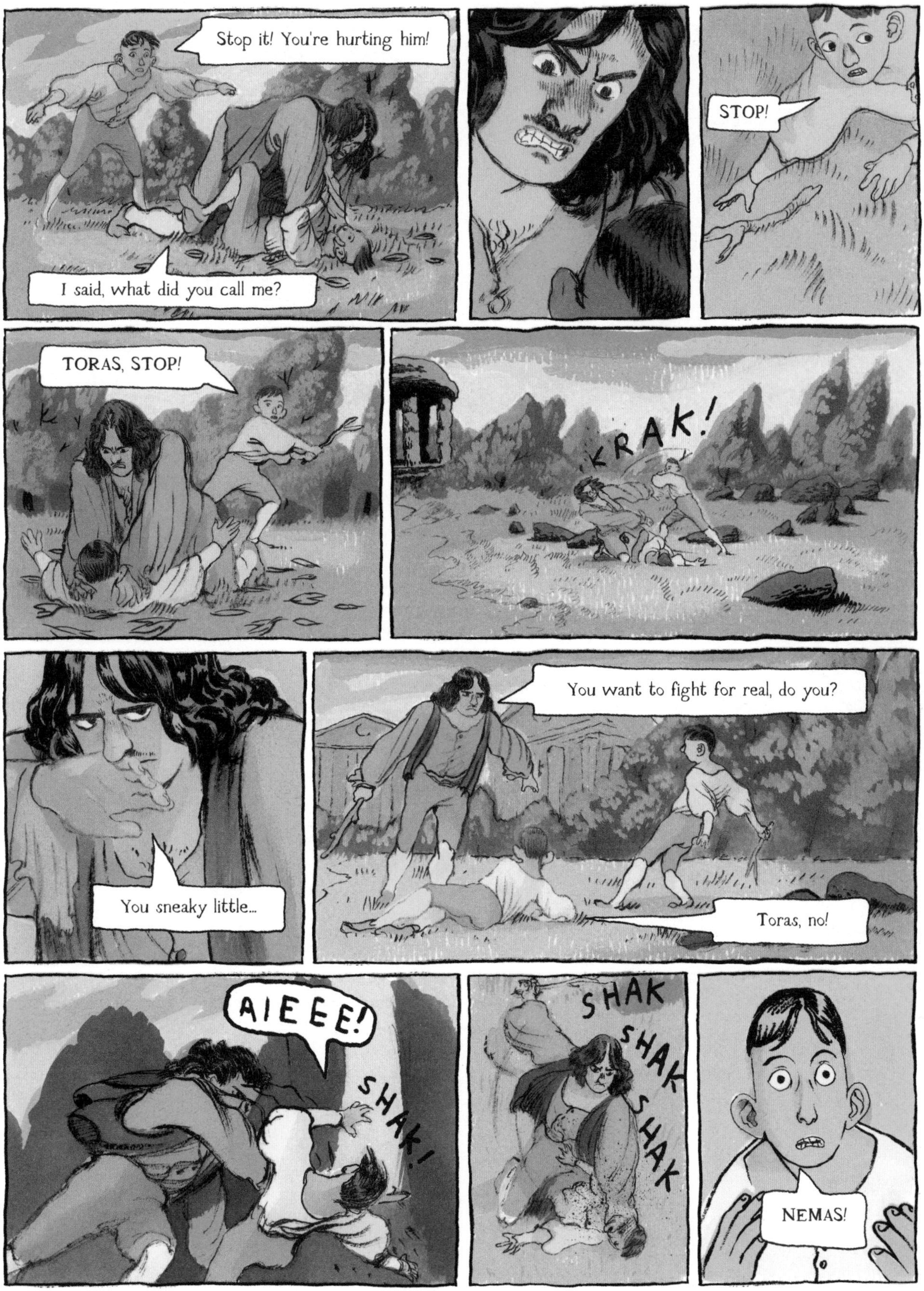
Stop it! You're hurting him!
I said, what did you call me?
STOP!
TORAS, STOP!
KRAK!
You sneaky little...
You want to fight for real, do you?
Toras, no!
AIEEE!
SHAK!
SHAK
SHAK
SHAK
SHAK
NEMAS!

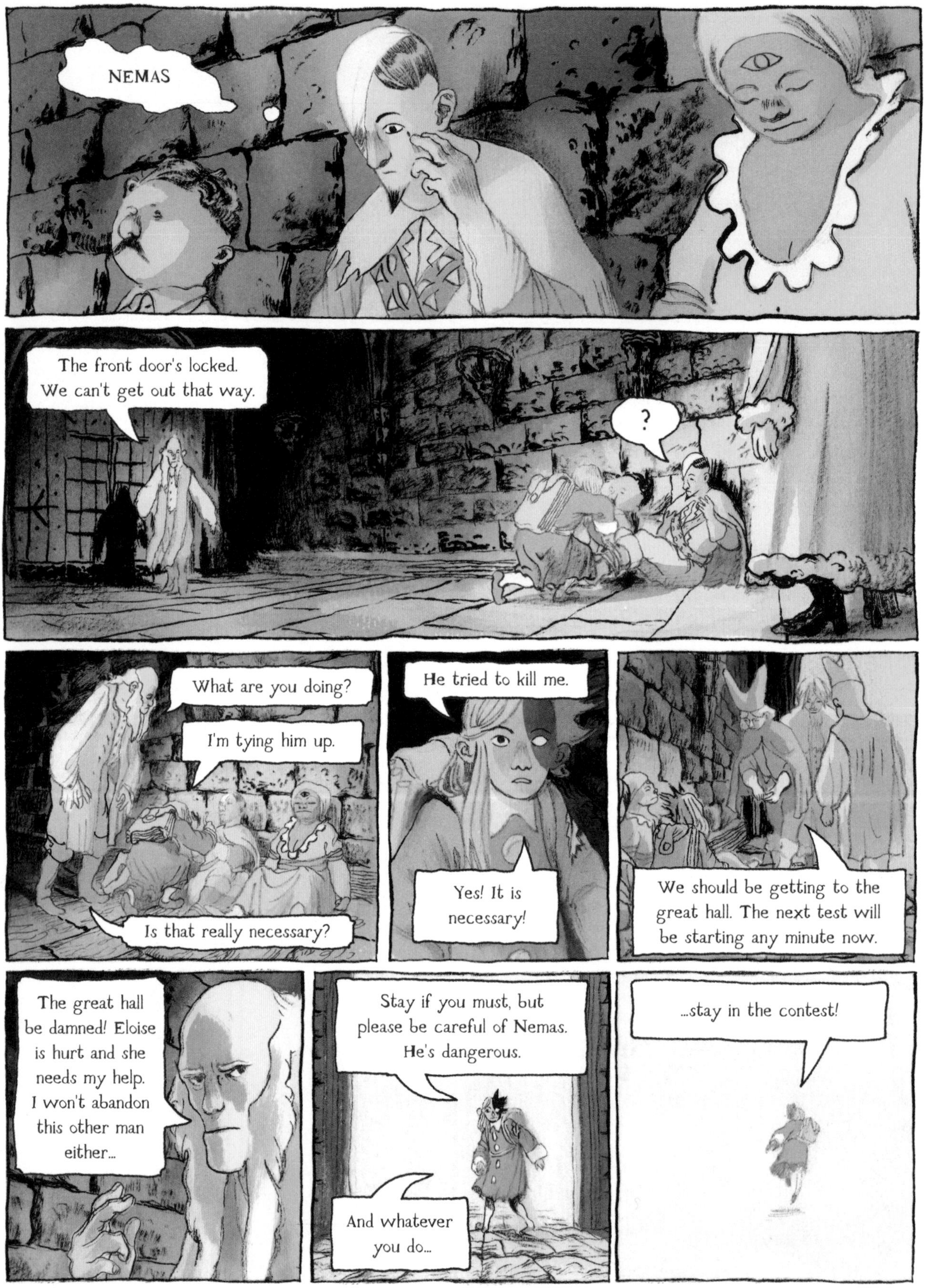
NEMAS
The front door's locked. We can't get out that way.
?
What are you doing?
I'm tying him up.
Is that really necessary?
He tried to kill me.
Yes! It is necessary!
We should be getting to the great hall. The next test will be starting any minute now.
The great hall be damned! Eloise is hurt and she needs my help. I won't abandon this other man either...
Stay if you must, but please be careful of Nemas. He's dangerous.
And whatever you do...
...stay in the contest!

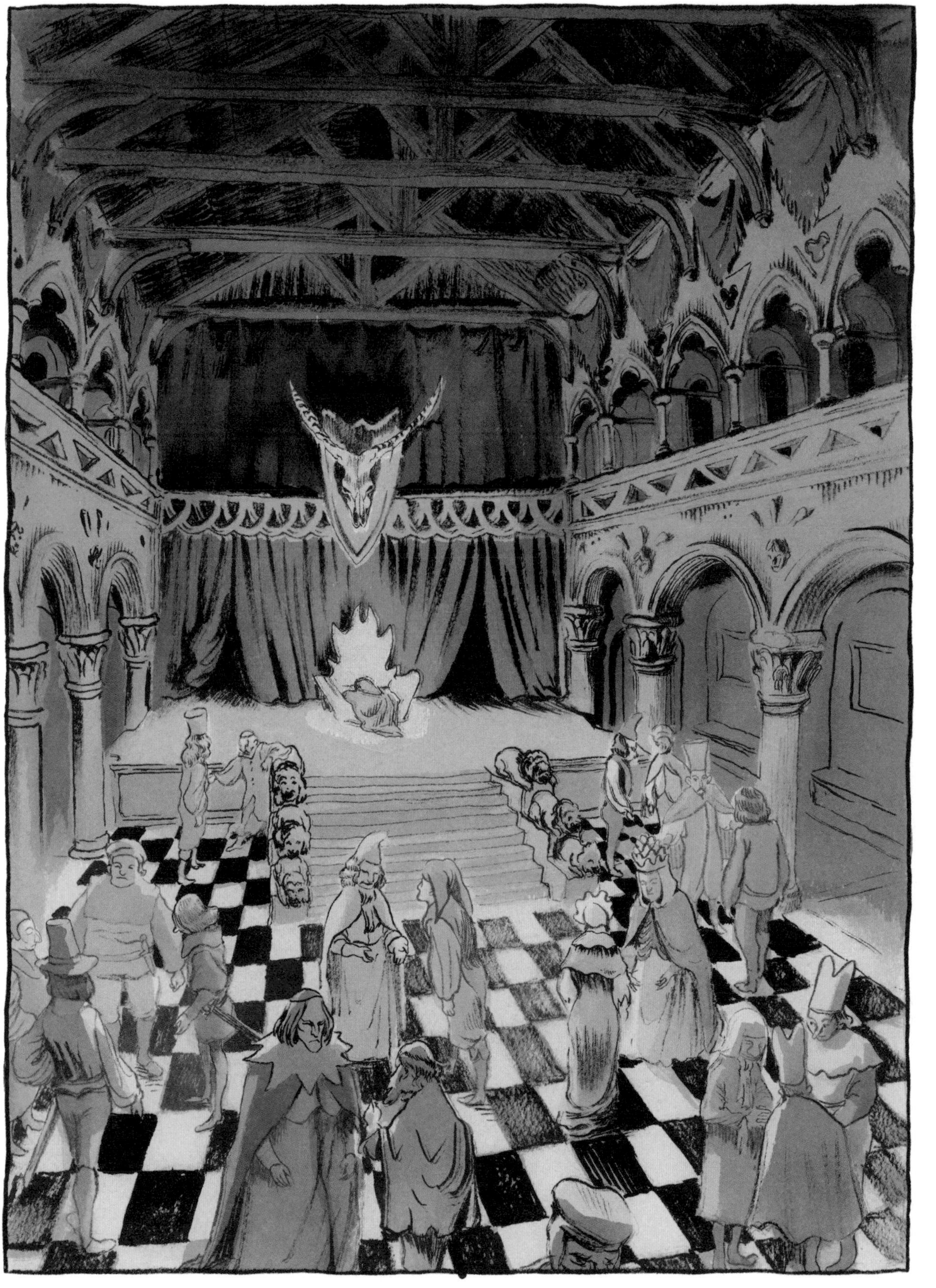

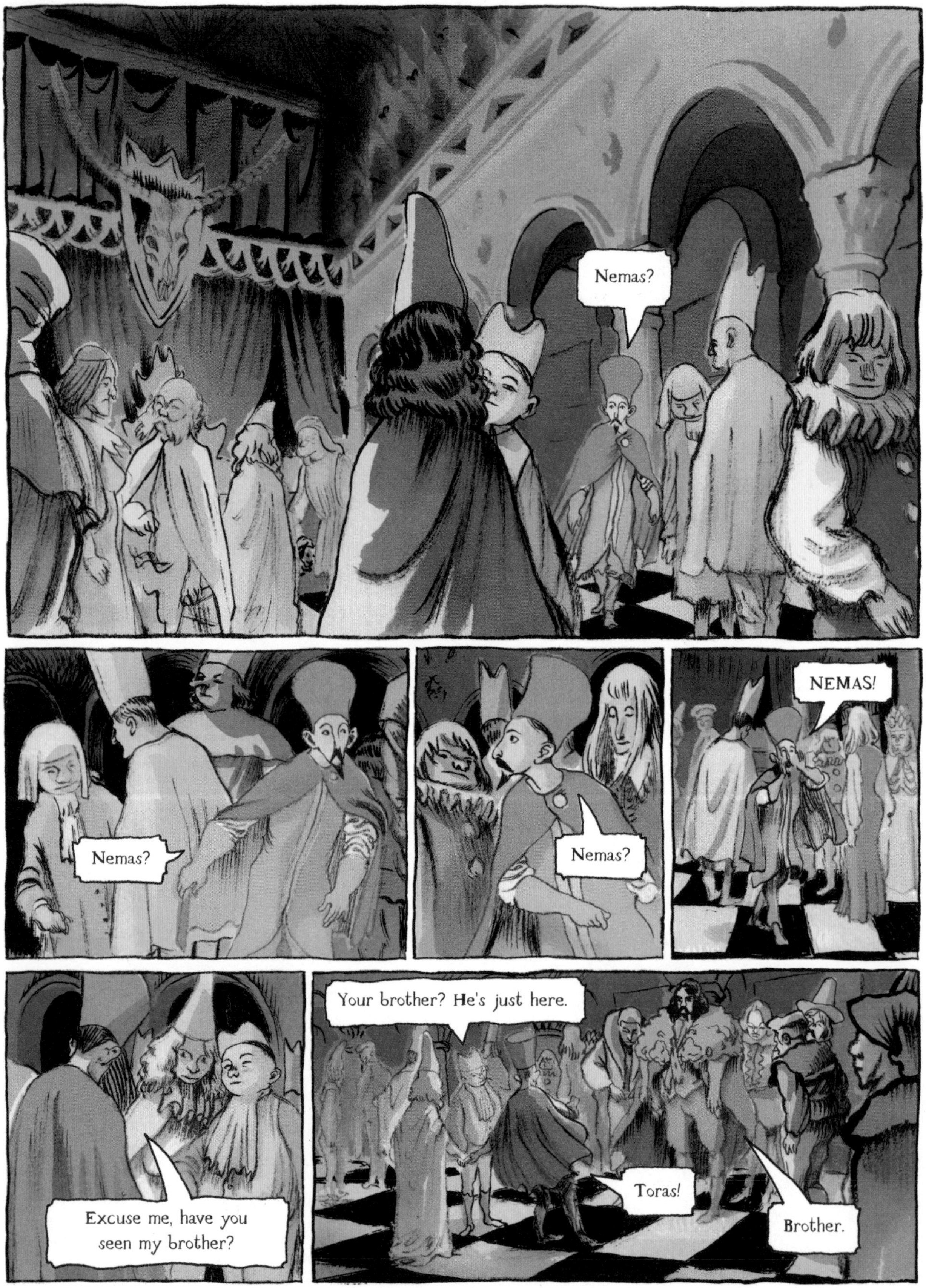
Nemas?
Nemas?
Nemas?
NEMAS!
Excuse me, have you seen my brother?
Your brother? He's just here.
Toras!
Brother.

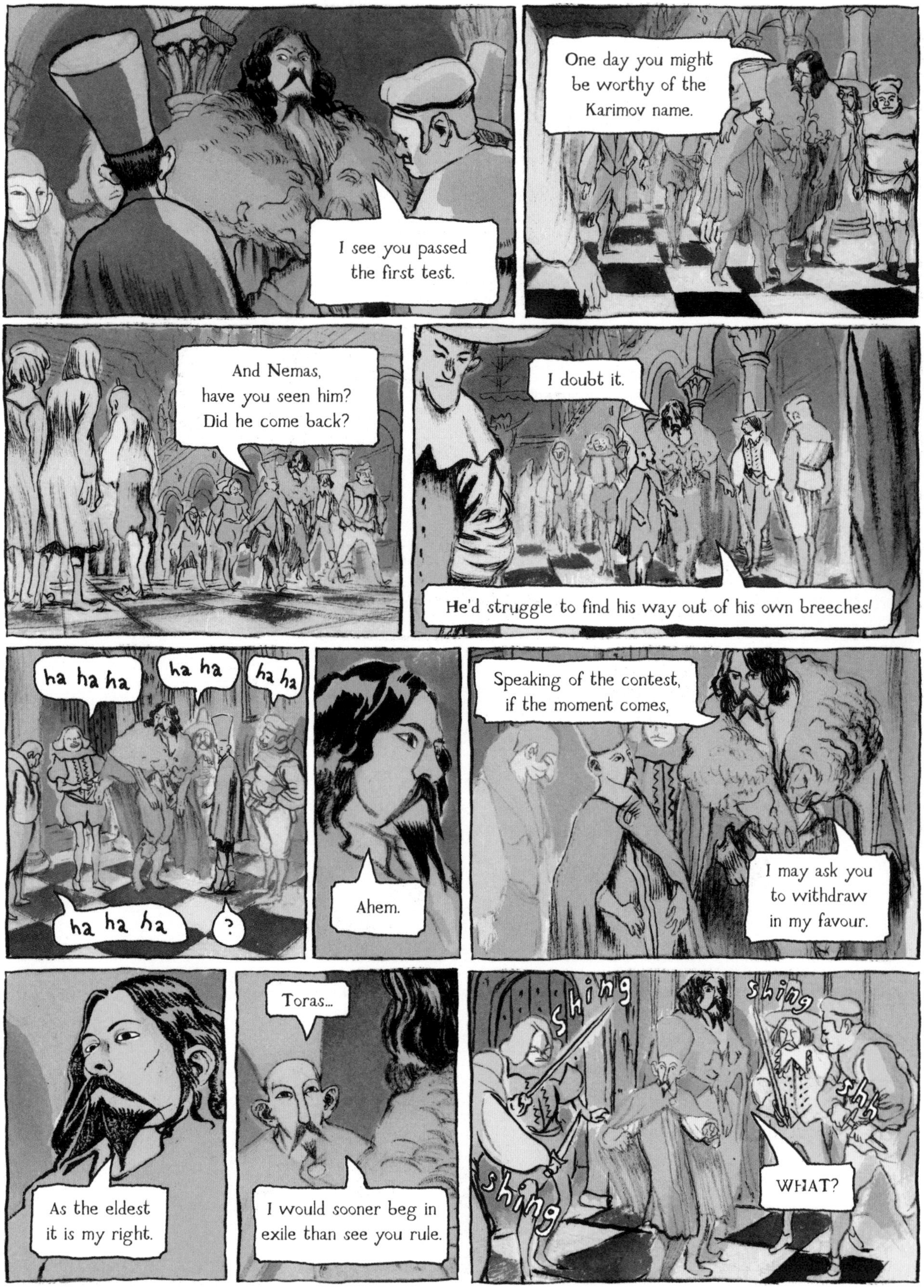
I see you passed the first test.
One day you might be worthy of the Karimov name.
And Nemas, have you seen him? Did he come back?
I doubt it.
He'd struggle to find his way out of his own breeches!
ha ha ha
ha ha
ha ha
ha ha ha
?
Ahem.
Speaking of the contest, if the moment comes,
I may ask you to withdraw in my favour.
As the eldest it is my right.
Toras...
I would sooner beg in exile than see you rule.
shing
shing
shing
shh
WHAT?

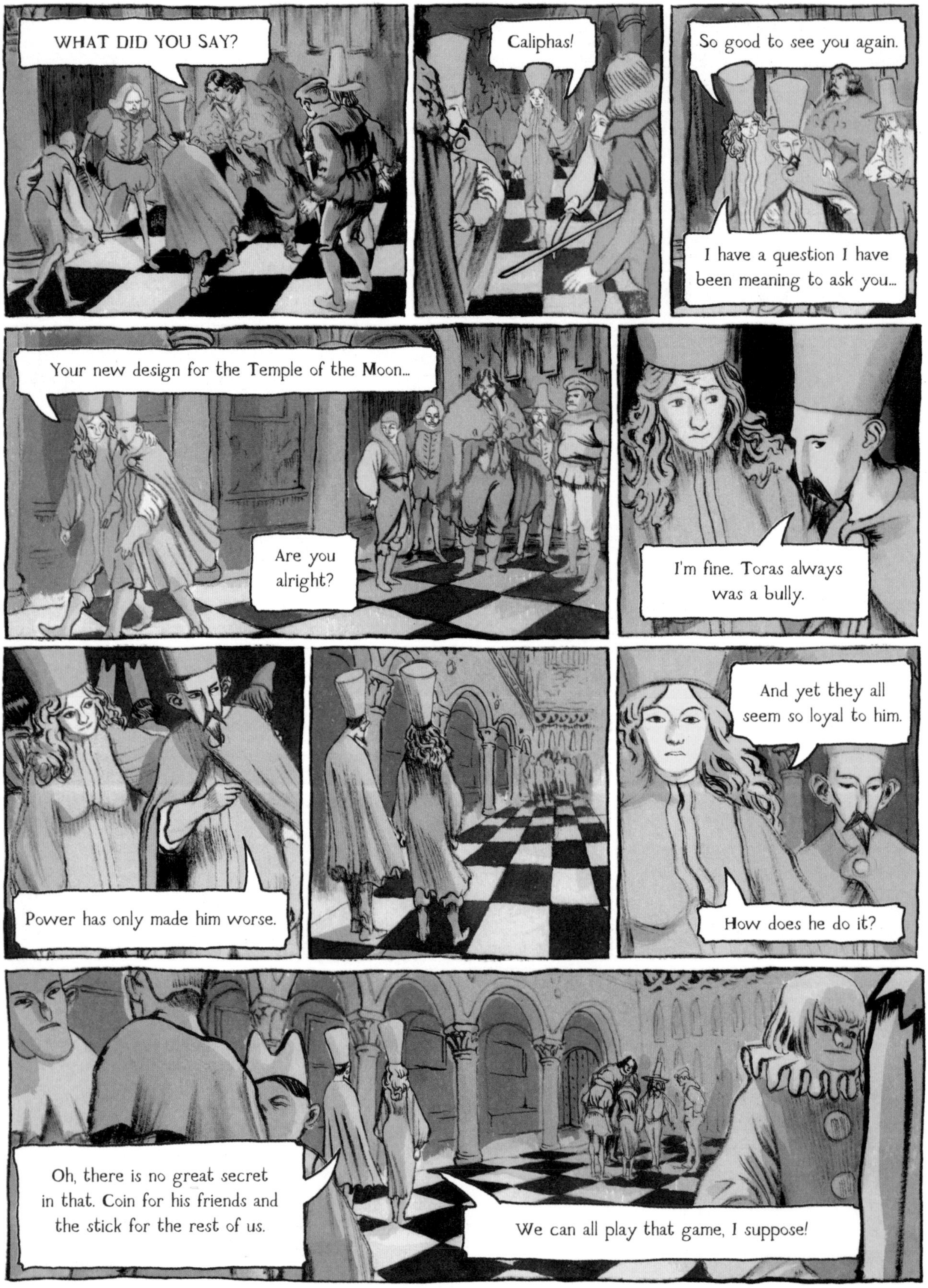
WHAT DID YOU SAY?
Caliphas!
So good to see you again.
I have a question I have been meaning to ask you...
Your new design for the Temple of the Moon...
Are you alright?
I'm fine. Toras always was a bully.
Power has only made him worse.
And yet they all seem so loyal to him.
How does he do it?
Oh, there is no great secret in that. Coin for his friends and the stick for the rest of us.
We can all play that game, I suppose!

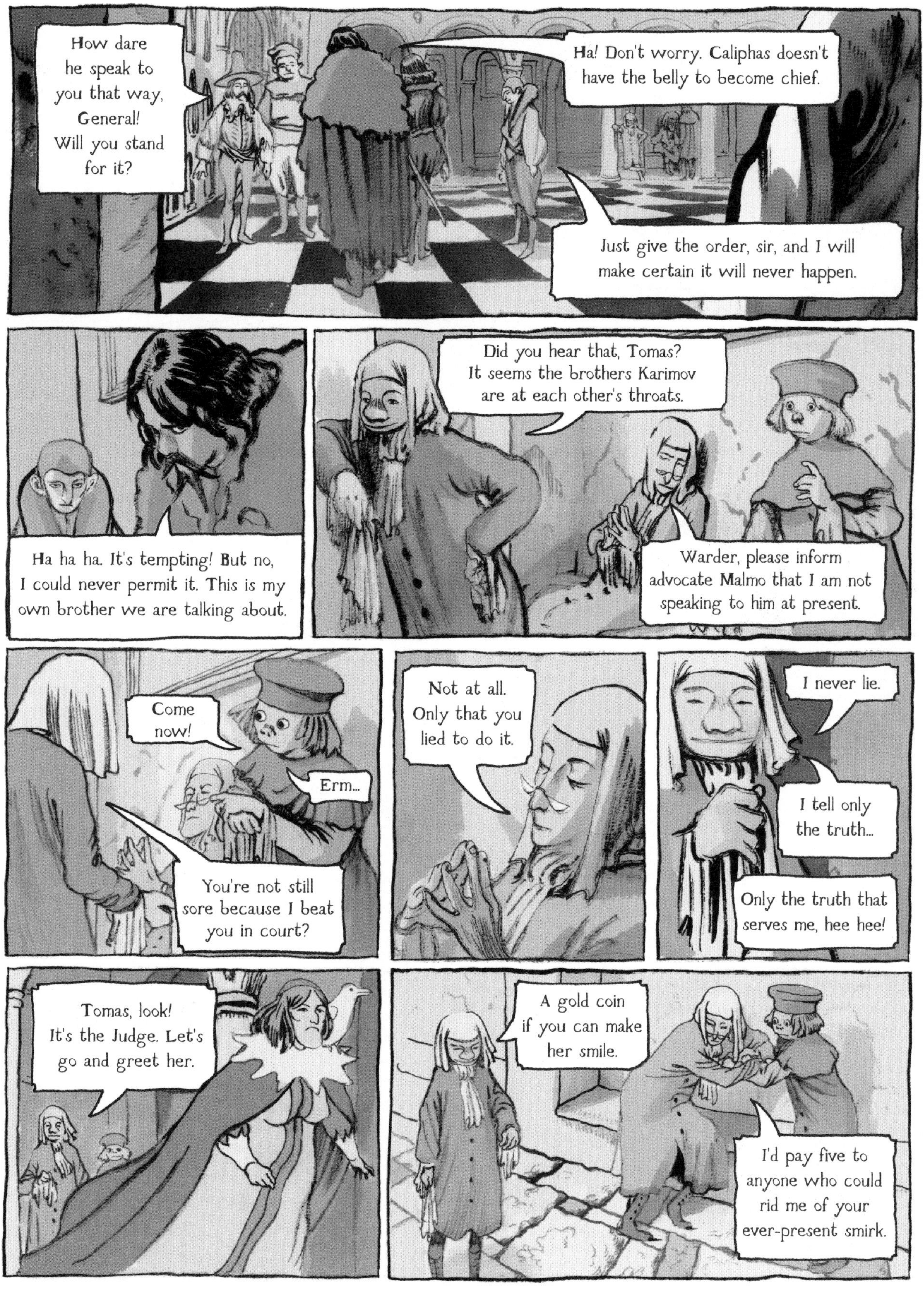

How dare he speak to you that way, General! Will you stand for it?
Ha! Don't worry. Caliphas doesn't have the belly to become chief.
Just give the order, sir, and I will make certain it will never happen.
Ha ha ha. It's tempting! But no, I could never permit it. This is my own brother we are talking about.
Did you hear that, Tomas? It seems the brothers Karimov are at each other's throats.
Warder, please inform advocate Malmo that I am not speaking to him at present.
Come now!
Erm...
You're not still sore because I beat you in court?
Not at all. Only that you lied to do it.
I never lie.
I tell only the truth...
Only the truth that serves me, hee hee!
Tomas, look! It's the Judge. Let's go and greet her.
A gold coin if you can make her smile.
I'd pay five to anyone who could rid me of your ever-present smirk.

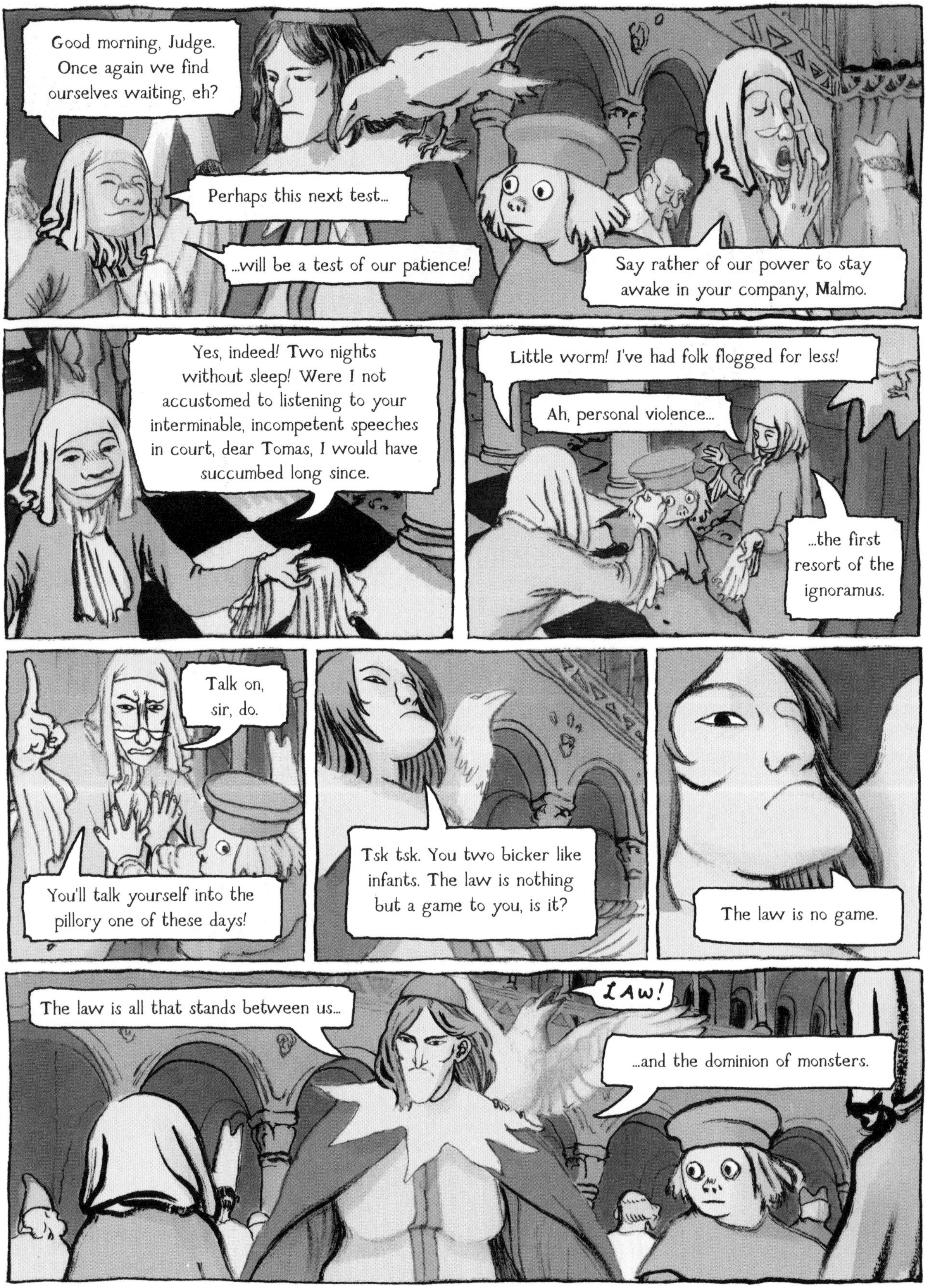
Good morning, Judge. Once again we find ourselves waiting, eh?
Perhaps this next test...
...will be a test of our patience!
Say rather of our power to stay awake in your company, Malmo.
Yes, indeed! Two nights without sleep! Were I not accustomed to listening to your interminable, incompetent speeches in court, dear Tomas, I would have succumbed long since.
Little worm! I've had folk flogged for less!
Ah, personal violence...
...the first resort of the ignoramus.
Talk on, sir, do.
You'll talk yourself into the pillory one of these days!
Tsk tsk. You two bicker like infants. The law is nothing but a game to you, is it?
The law is no game.
The law is all that stands between us...
LAW!
...and the dominion of monsters.

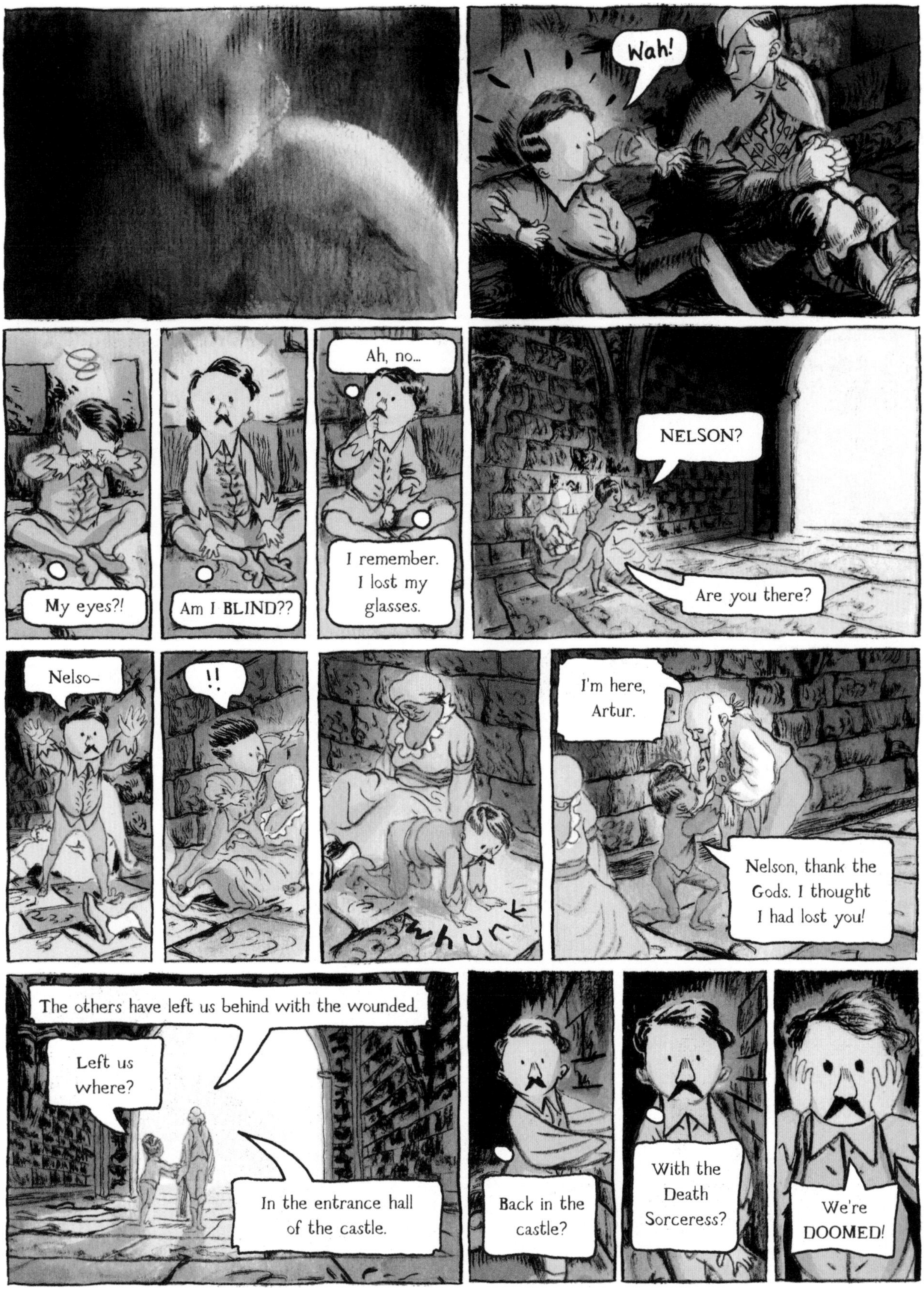
Wah!
My eyes?!
Am I BLIND??
Ah, no...
I remember. I lost my glasses.
NELSON?
Are you there?
Nelso-
!!
whunk
I'm here, Artur.
Nelson, thank the Gods. I thought I had lost you!
The others have left us behind with the wounded.
Left us where?
In the entrance hall of the castle.
Back in the castle?
With the Death Sorceress?
We're DOOMED!

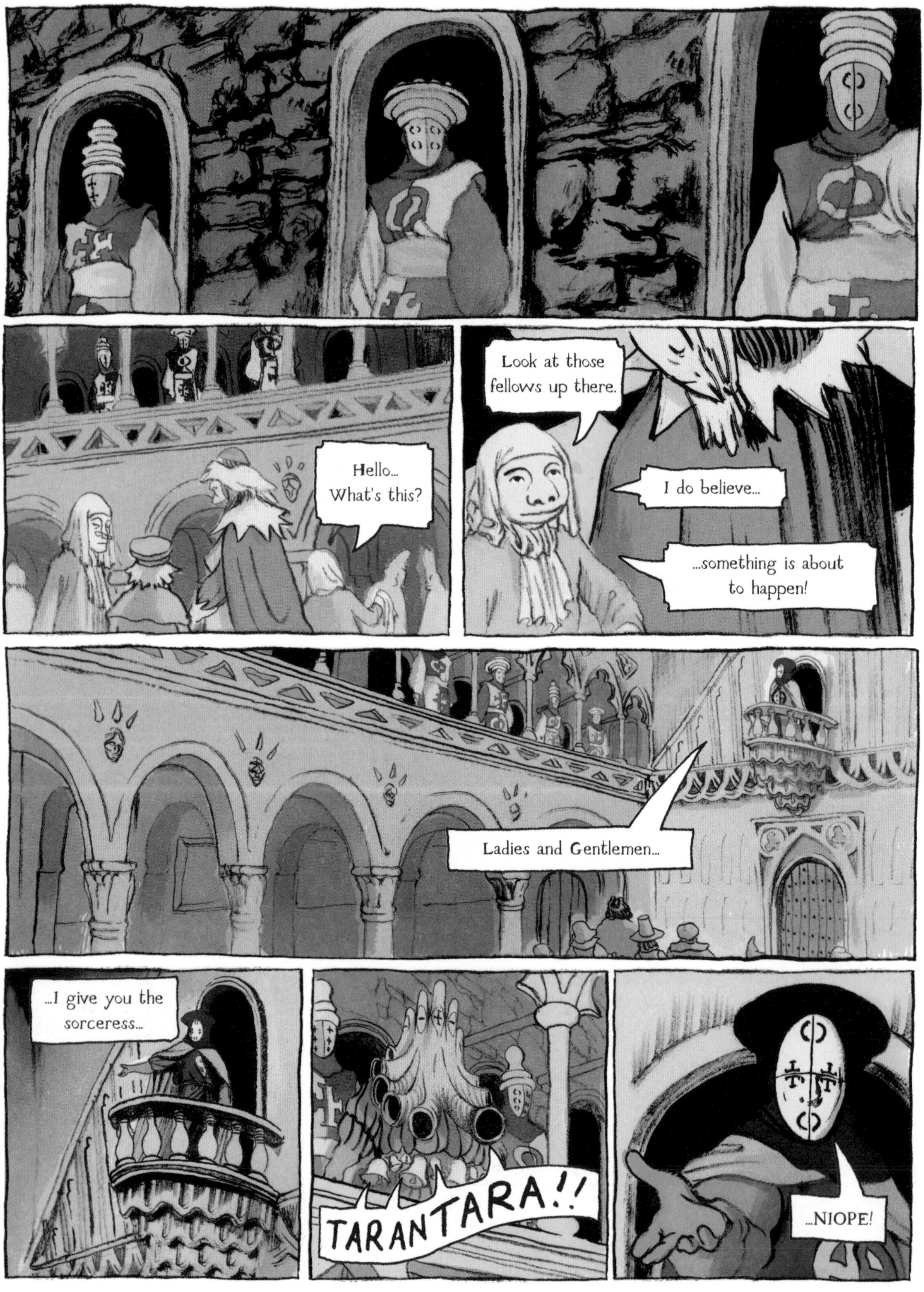
Hello... What's this?
Look at those fellows up there.
I do believe...
...something is about to happen!
Ladies and Gentlemen...
...I give you the sorceress...
TARANTARA!!
...NIOPE!

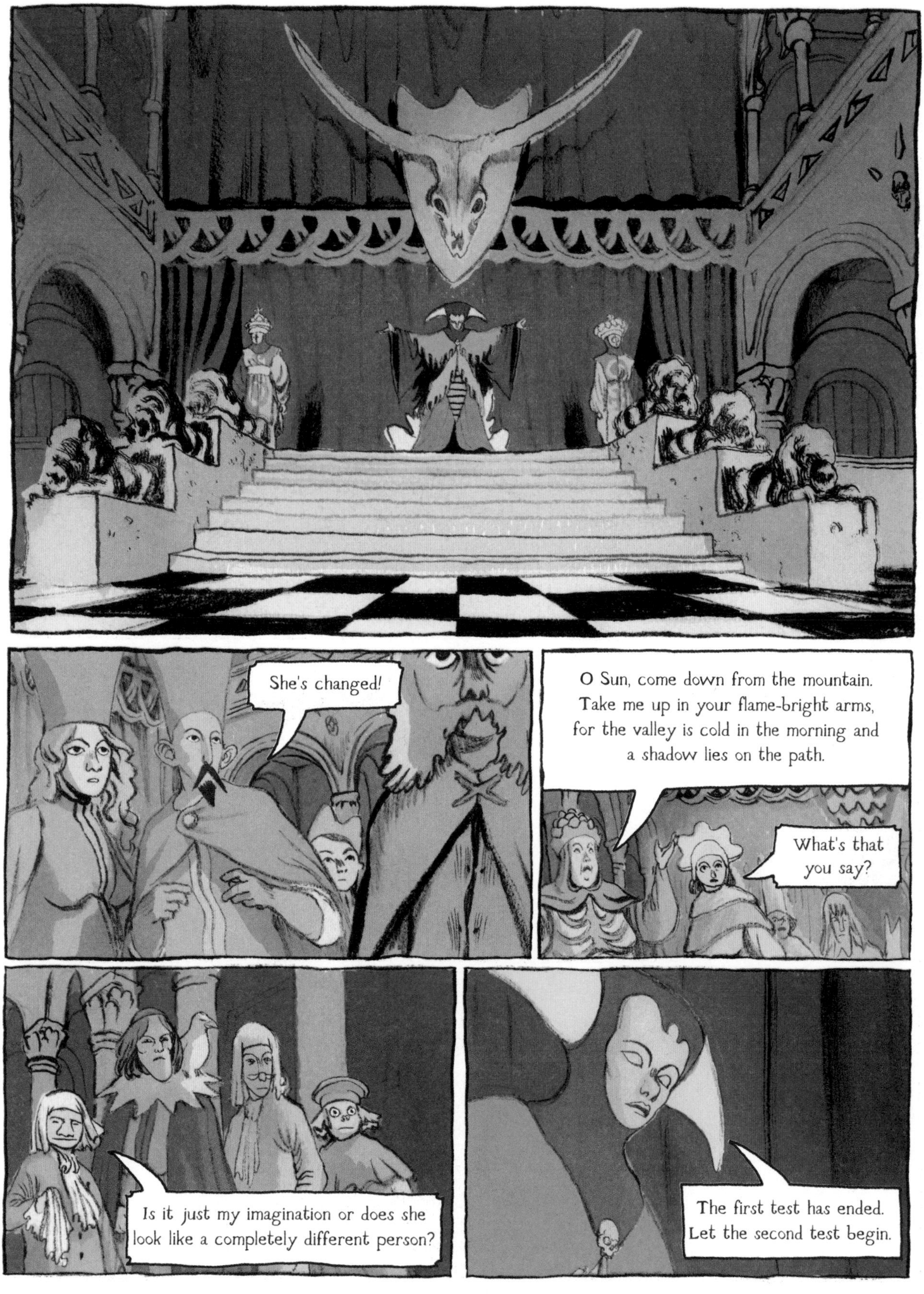
She's changed!
O Sun, come down from the mountain. Take me up in your flame-bright arms, for the valley is cold in the morning and a shadow lies on the path.
What's that you say?
Is it just my imagination or does she look like a completely different person?
The first test has ended. Let the second test begin.

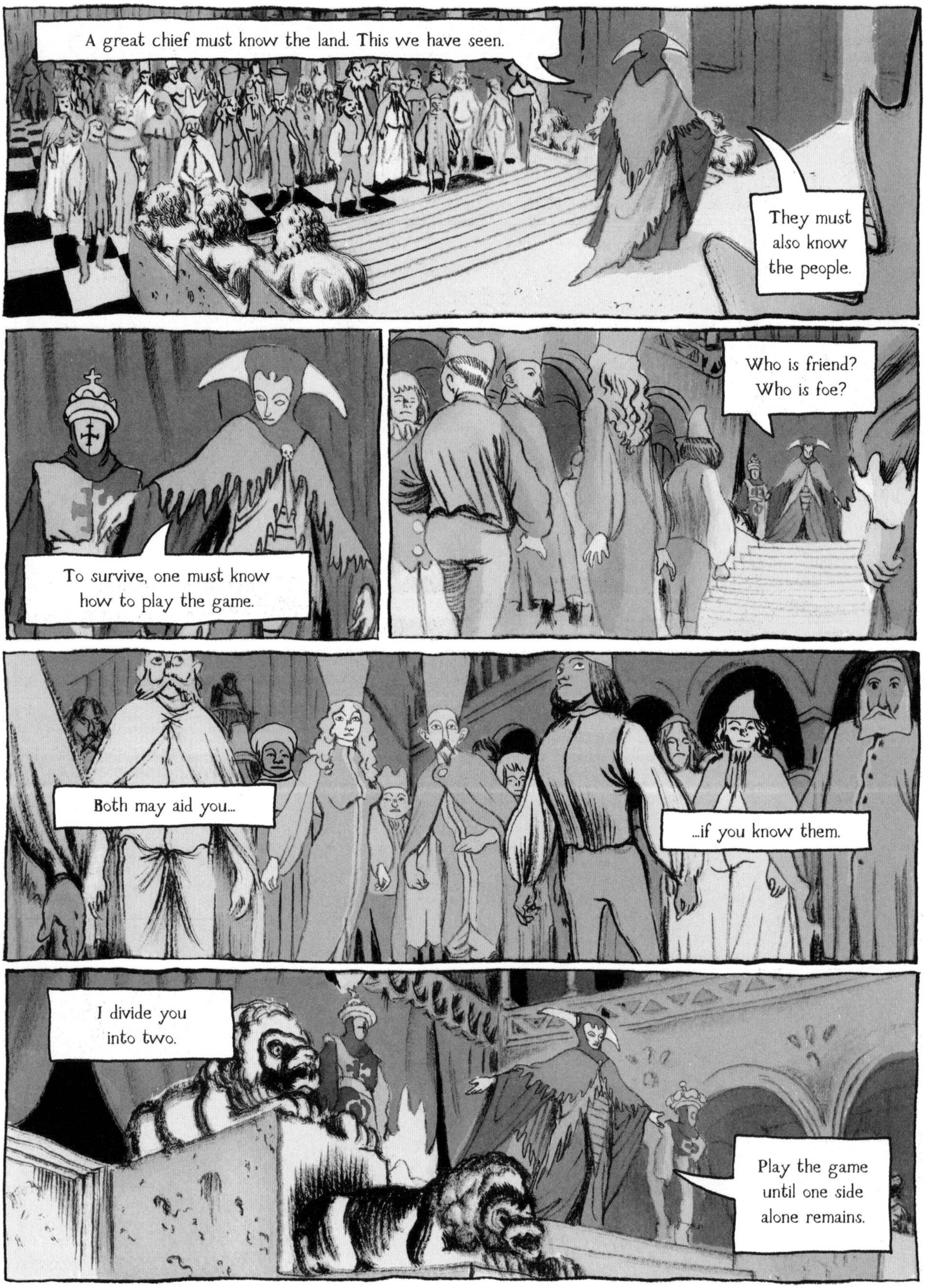
A great chief must know the land. This we have seen.
They must also know the people.
To survive, one must know how to play the game.
Who is friend? Who is foe?
Both may aid you...
...if you know them.
I divide you into two.
Play the game until one side alone remains.

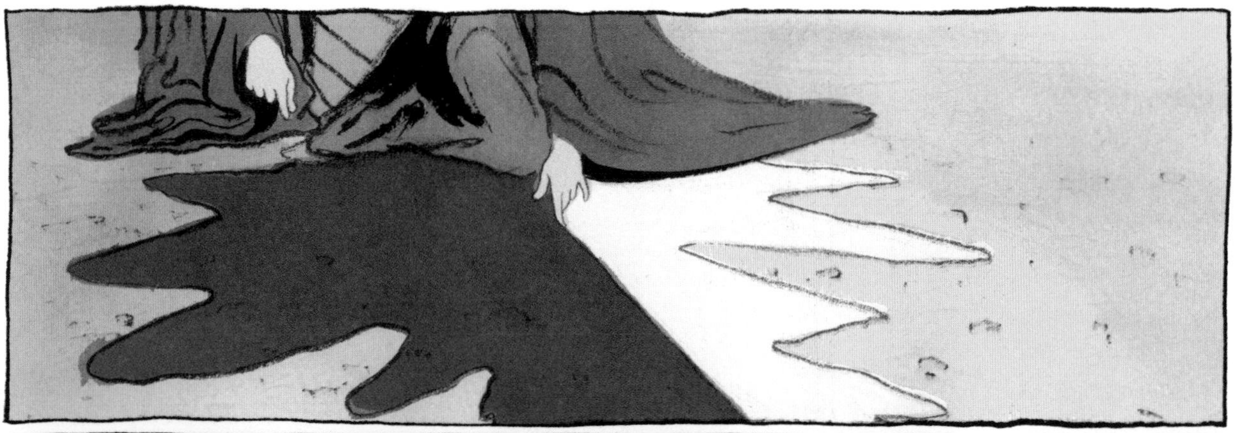

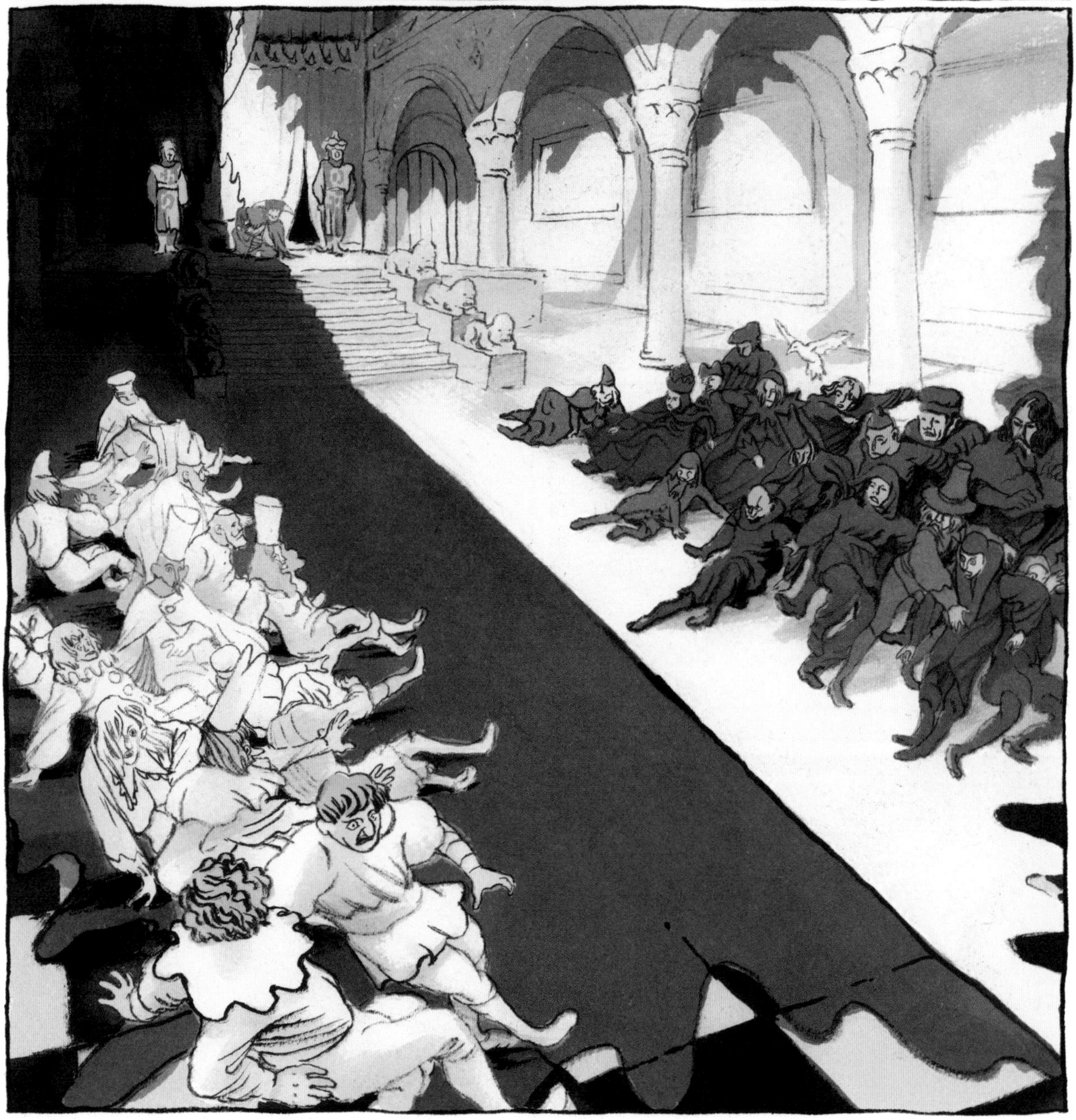

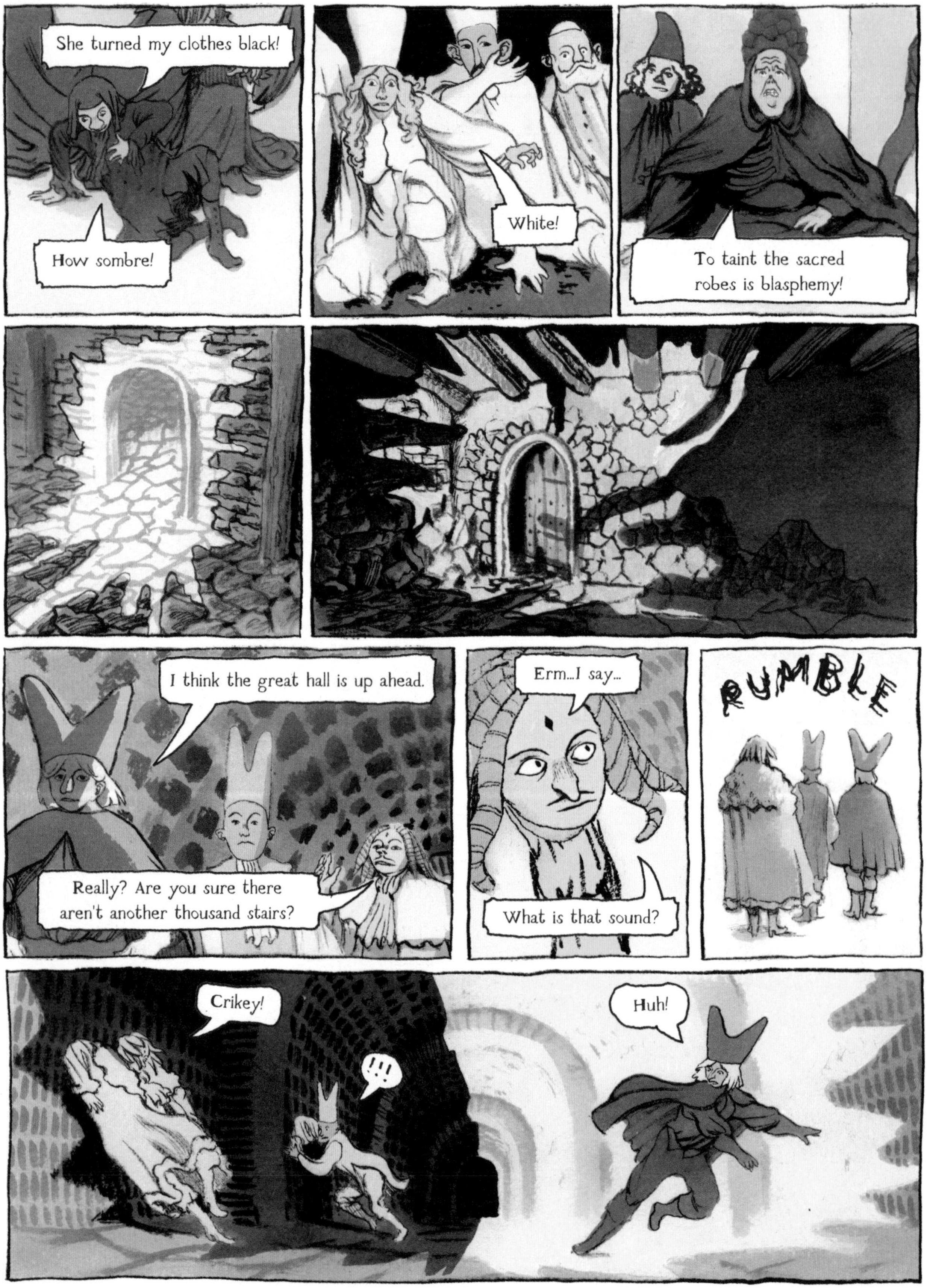
She turned my clothes black!
How sombre!
White!
To taint the sacred robes is blasphemy!
I think the great hall is up ahead.
Really? Are you sure there aren't another thousand stairs?
Erm...I say...
What is that sound?
RUMBLE
Crikey!
!!!
Huh!

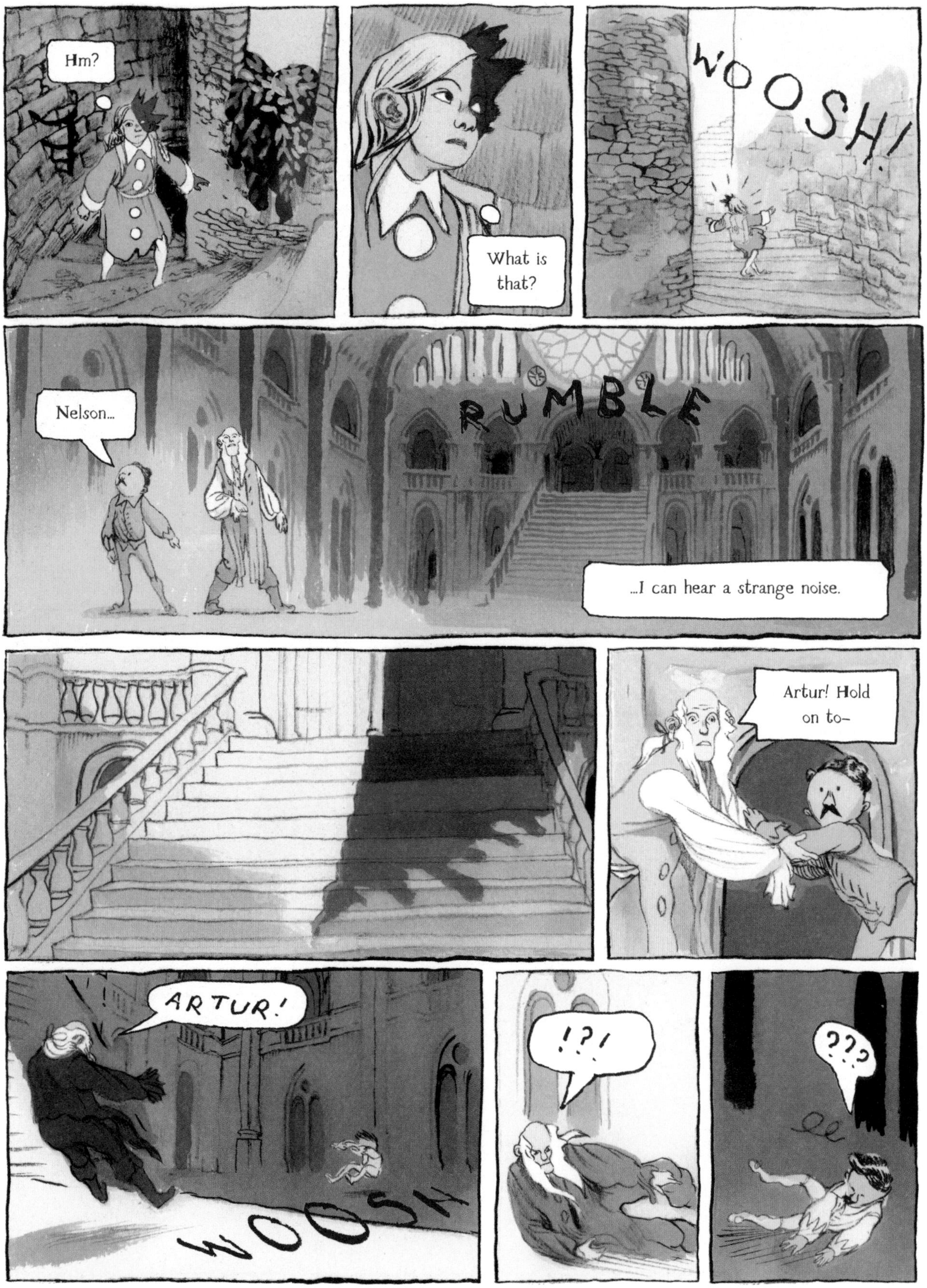
Hm?
What is that?
WOOSH!
Nelson...
RUMBLE
...I can hear a strange noise.
Artur! Hold on to-
ARTUR!
WOOSH
!?!
???

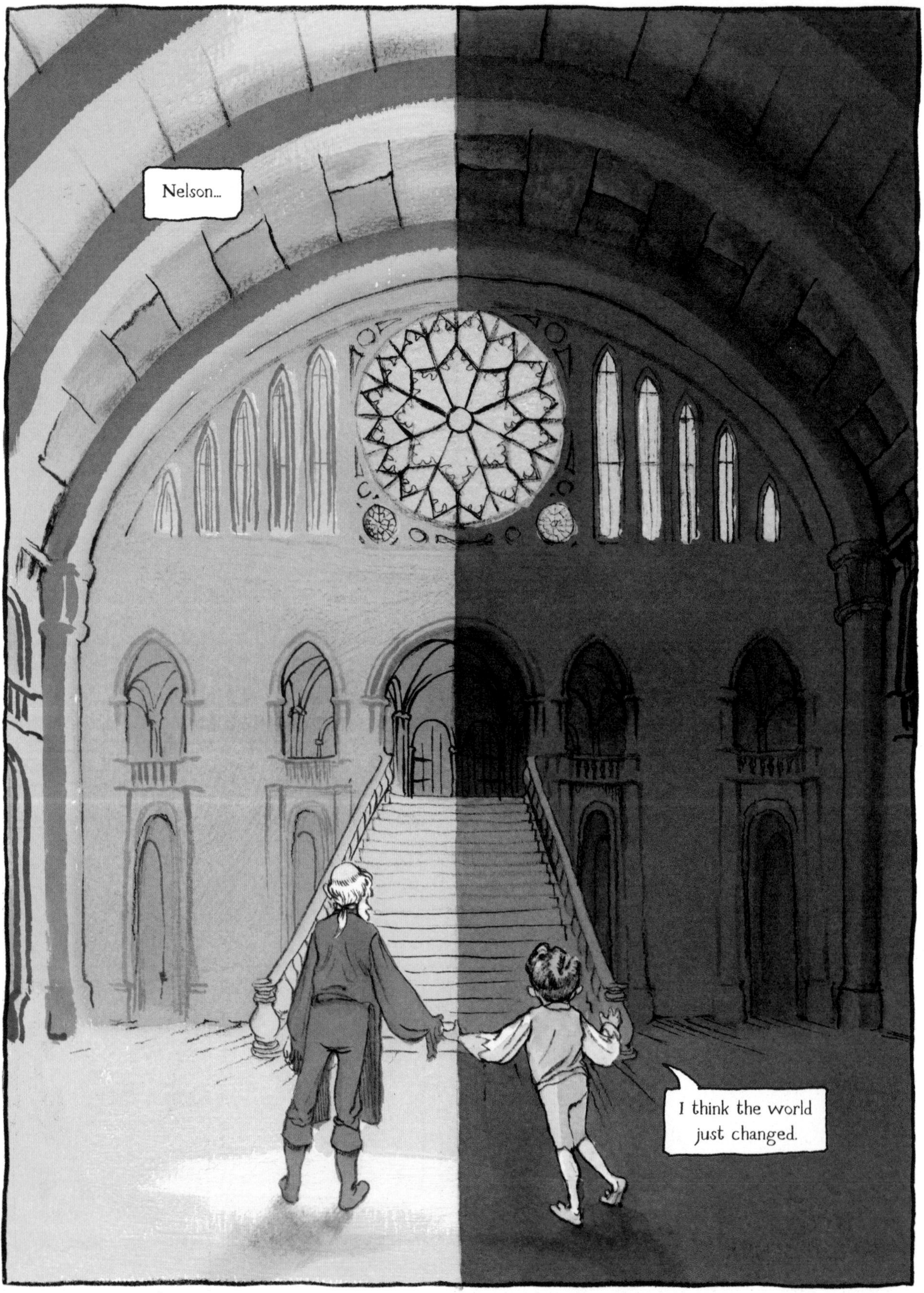
Nelson...
I think the world just changed.

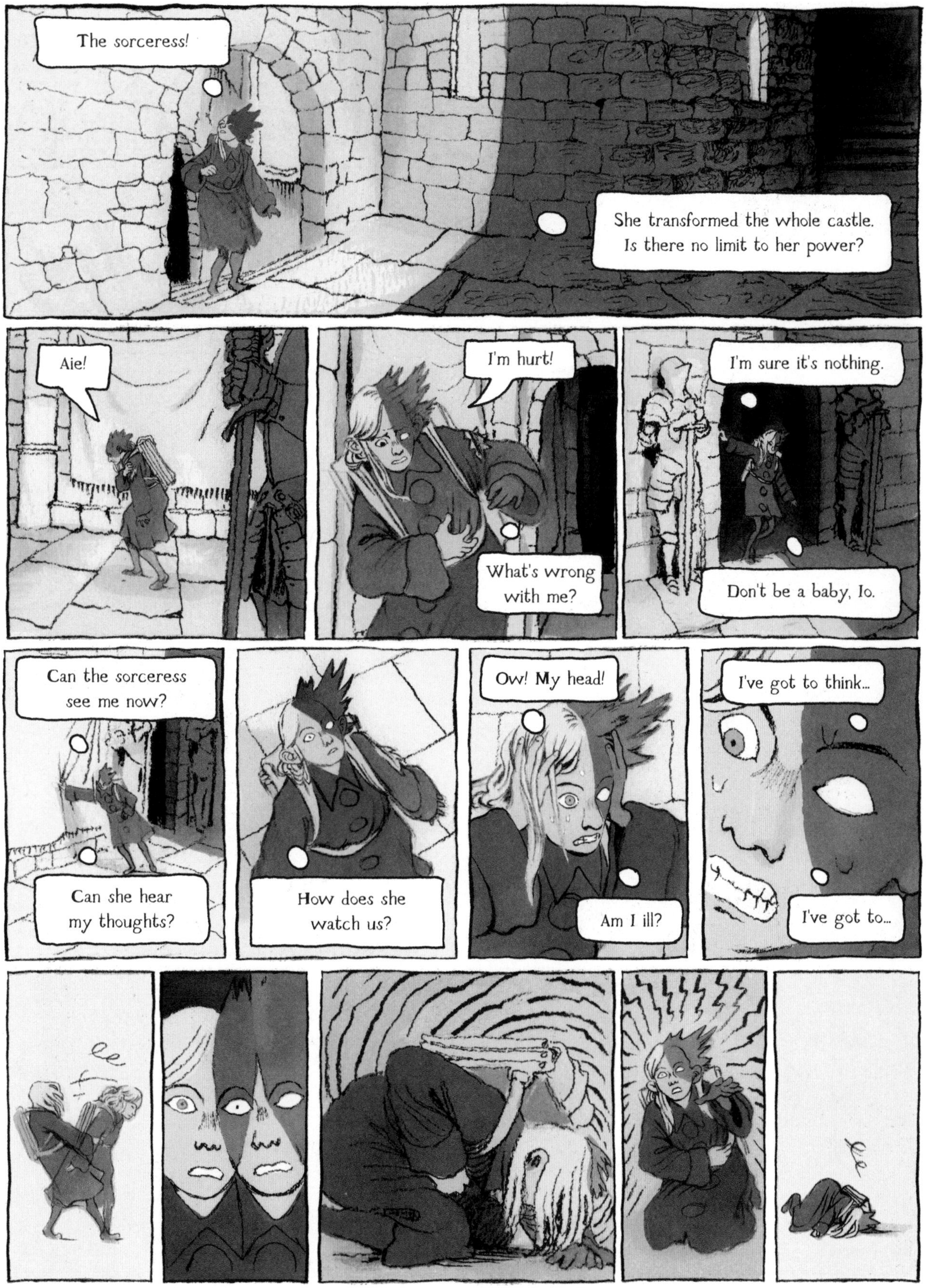
The sorceress!
She transformed the whole castle. Is there no limit to her power?
Aie!
I'm hurt!
What's wrong with me?
I'm sure it's nothing.
Don't be a baby, Io.
Can the sorceress see me now?
Can she hear my thoughts?
How does she watch us?
Ow! My head!
Am I ill?
I've got to think...
I've got to...

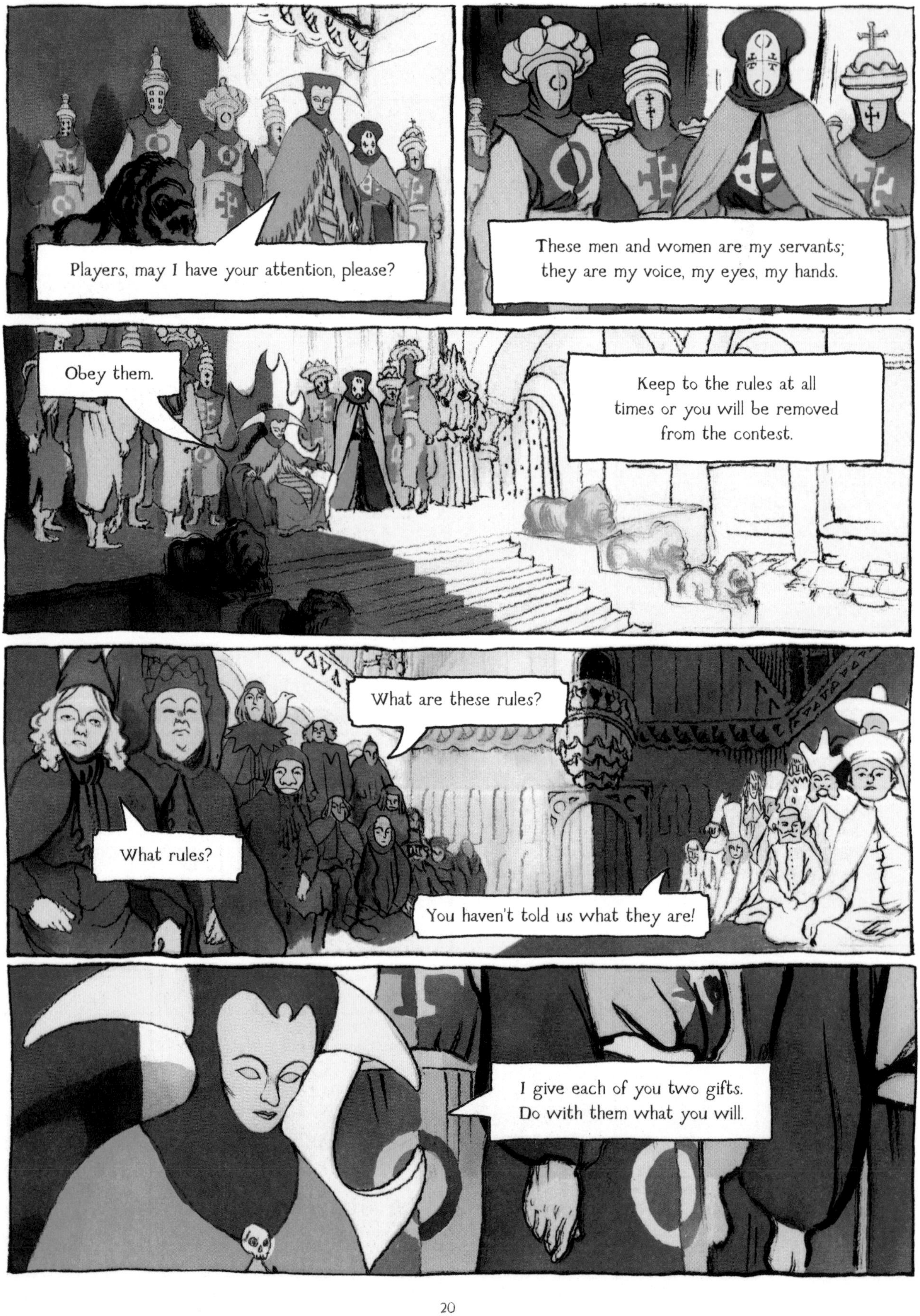
Players, may I have your attention, please?
These men and women are my servants; they are my voice, my eyes, my hands.
Obey them.
Keep to the rules at all times or you will be removed from the contest.
What are these rules?
What rules?
You haven't told us what they are!
I give each of you two gifts. Do with them what you will.

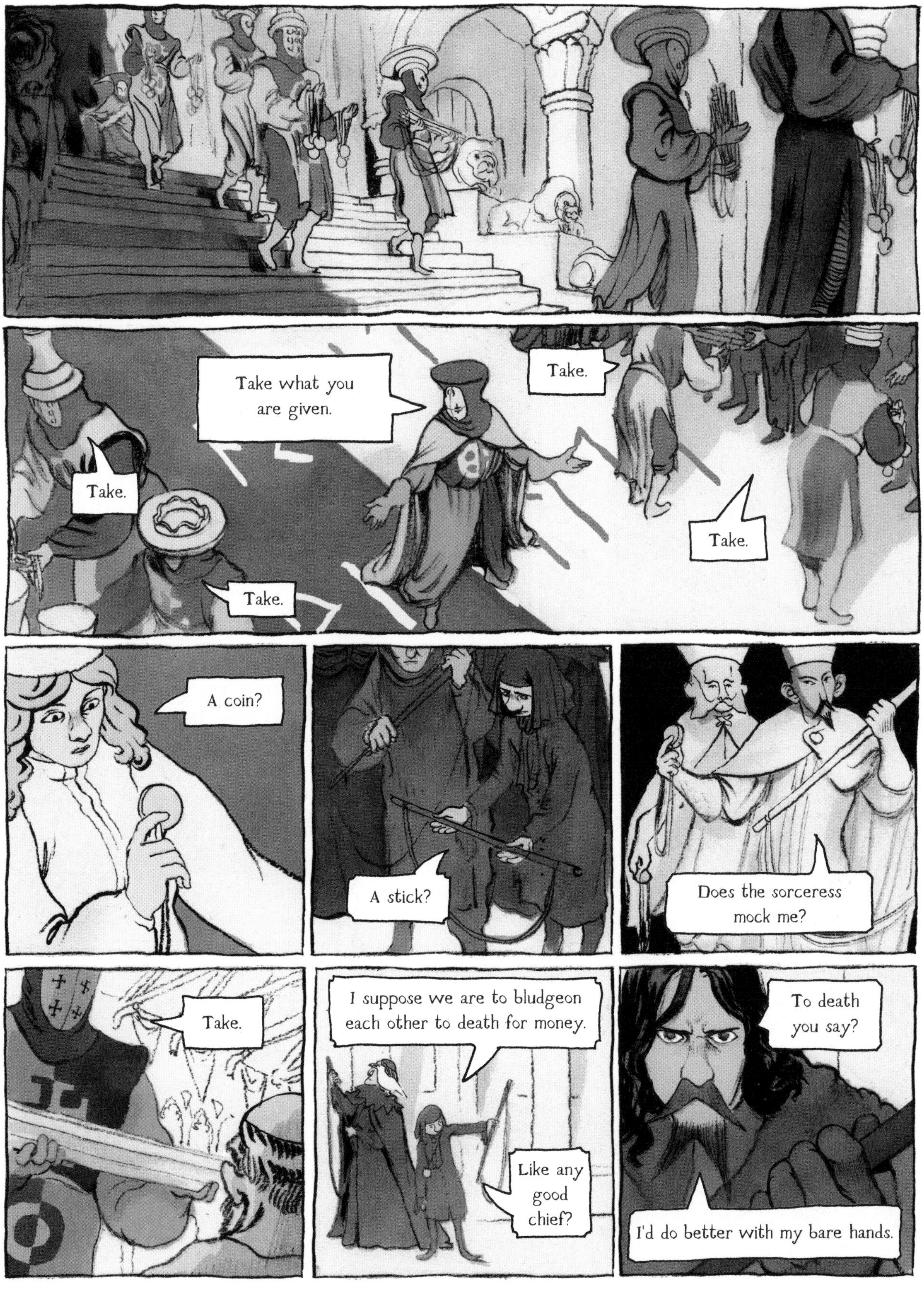
Take what you are given.
Take.
Take.
Take.
Take.
A coin?
A stick?
Does the sorceress mock me?
Take.
I suppose we are to bludgeon each other to death for money.
Like any good chief?
To death you say?
I'd do better with my bare hands.

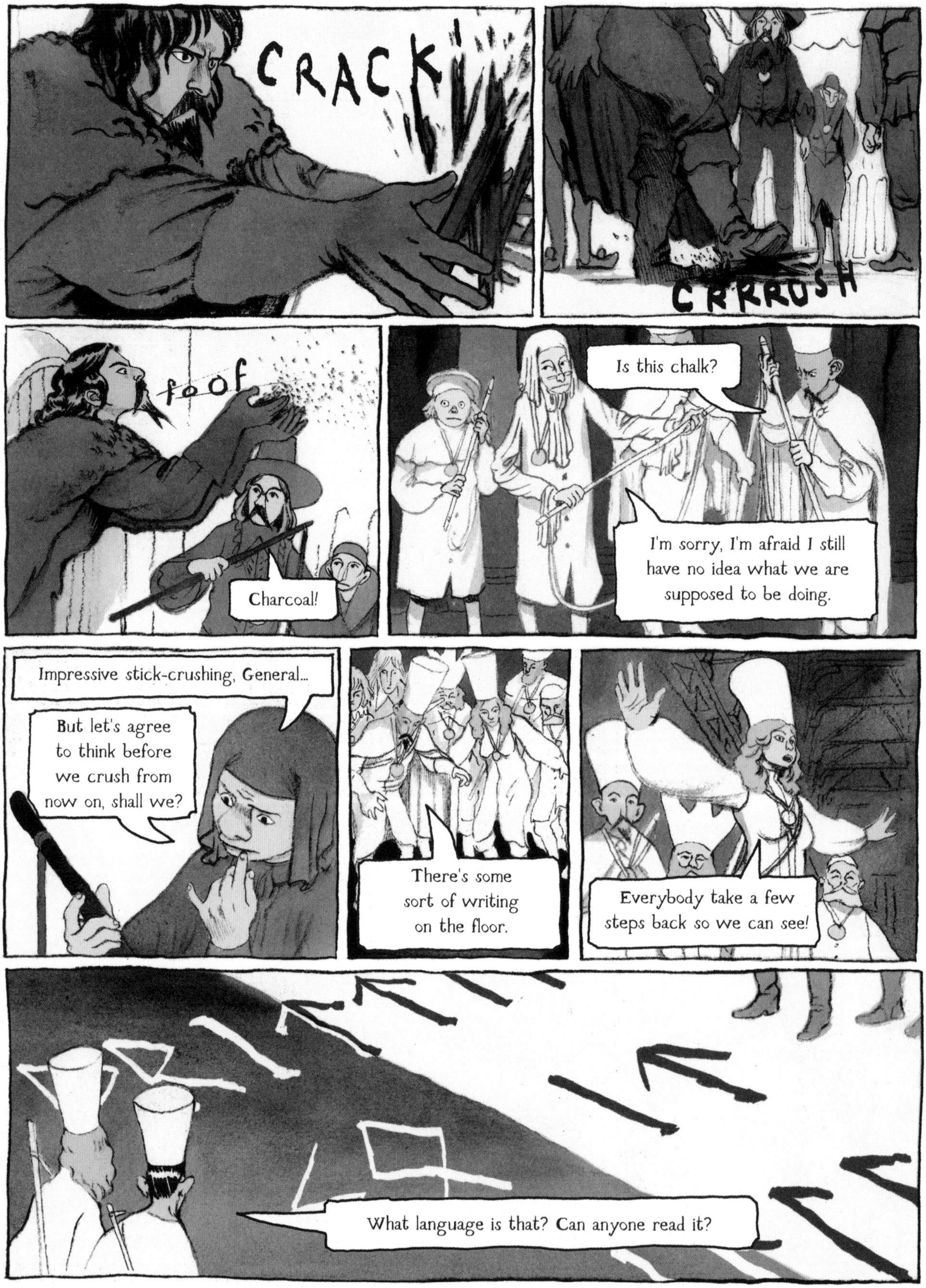
CRACK!
CRRRUSH
fooF
Charcoal!
Is this chalk?
I'm sorry, I'm afraid I still have no idea what we are supposed to be doing.
Impressive stick-crushing, General...
But let's agree to think before we crush from now on, shall we?
There's some sort of writing on the floor.
Everybody take a few steps back so we can see!
What language is that? Can anyone read it?

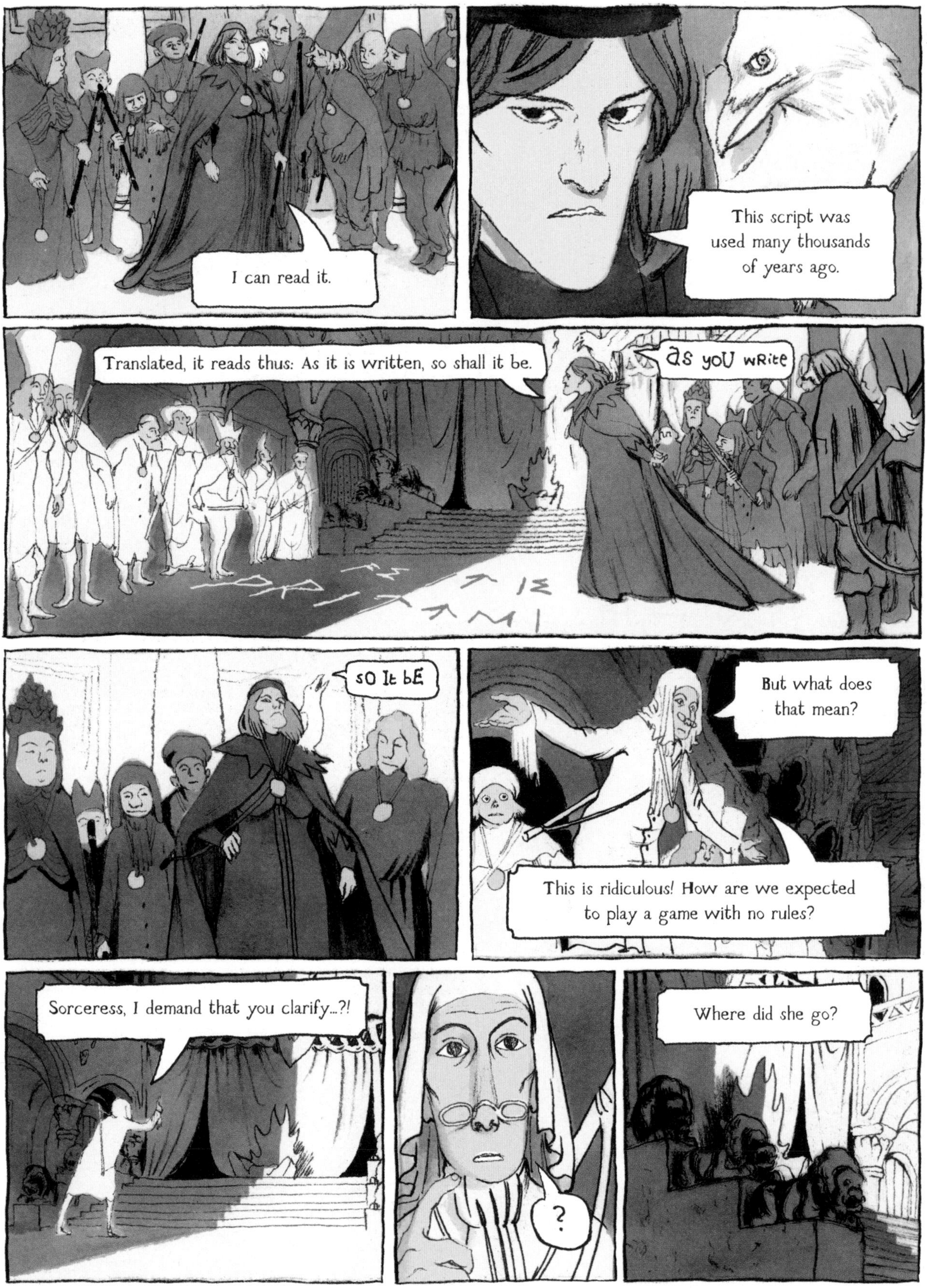
I can read it.
This script was used many thousands of years ago.
Translated, it reads thus: As it is written, so shall it be.
as you write
so it be
But what does that mean?
This is ridiculous! How are we expected to play a game with no rules?
Sorceress, I demand that you clarify...?!
?
Where did she go?

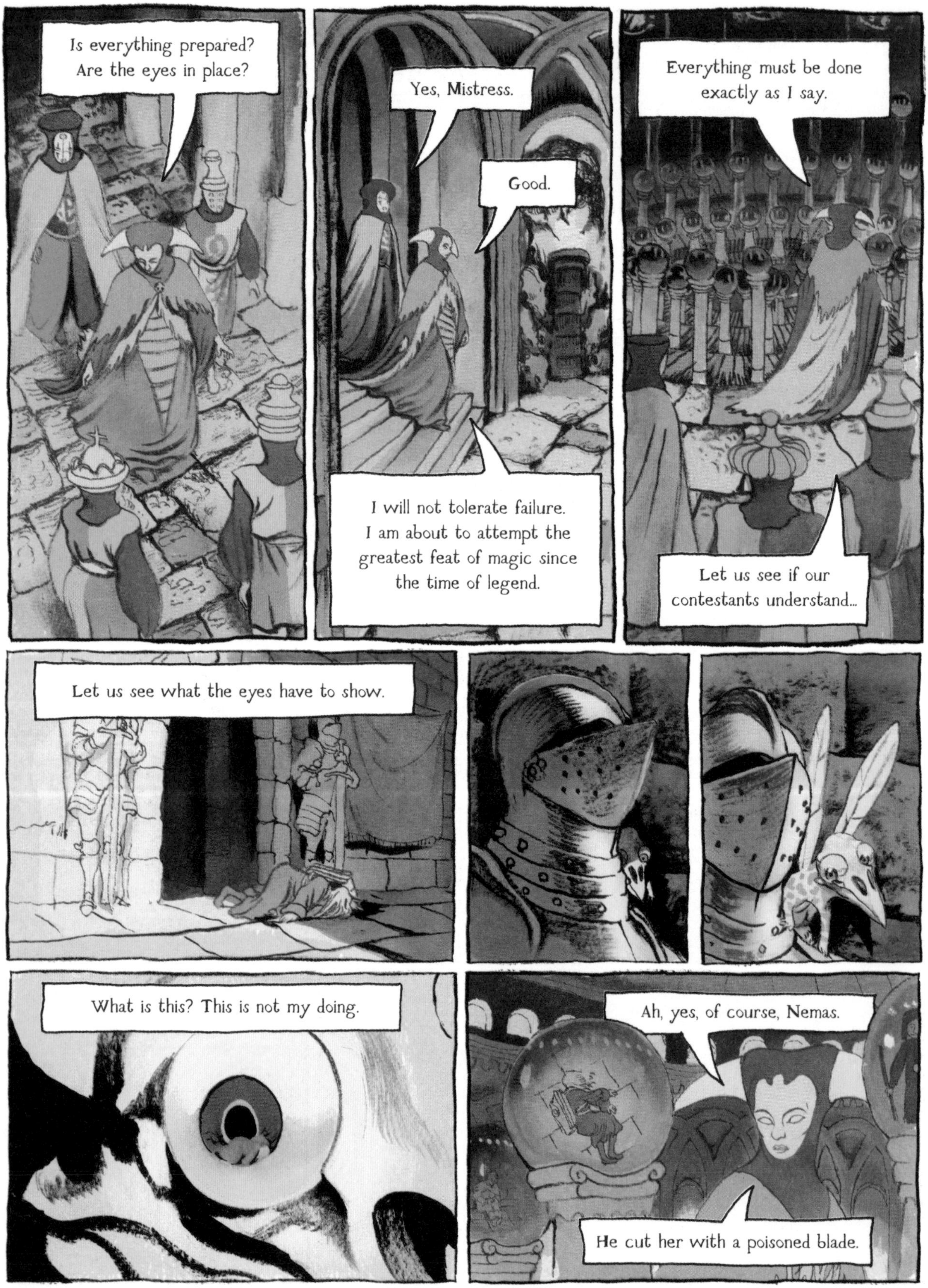
Is everything prepared? Are the eyes in place?
Yes, Mistress.
Good.
I will not tolerate failure. I am about to attempt the greatest feat of magic since the time of legend.
Everything must be done exactly as I say.
Let us see if our contestants understand...
Let us see what the eyes have to show.
What is this? This is not my doing.
Ah, yes, of course, Nemas.
He cut her with a poisoned blade.

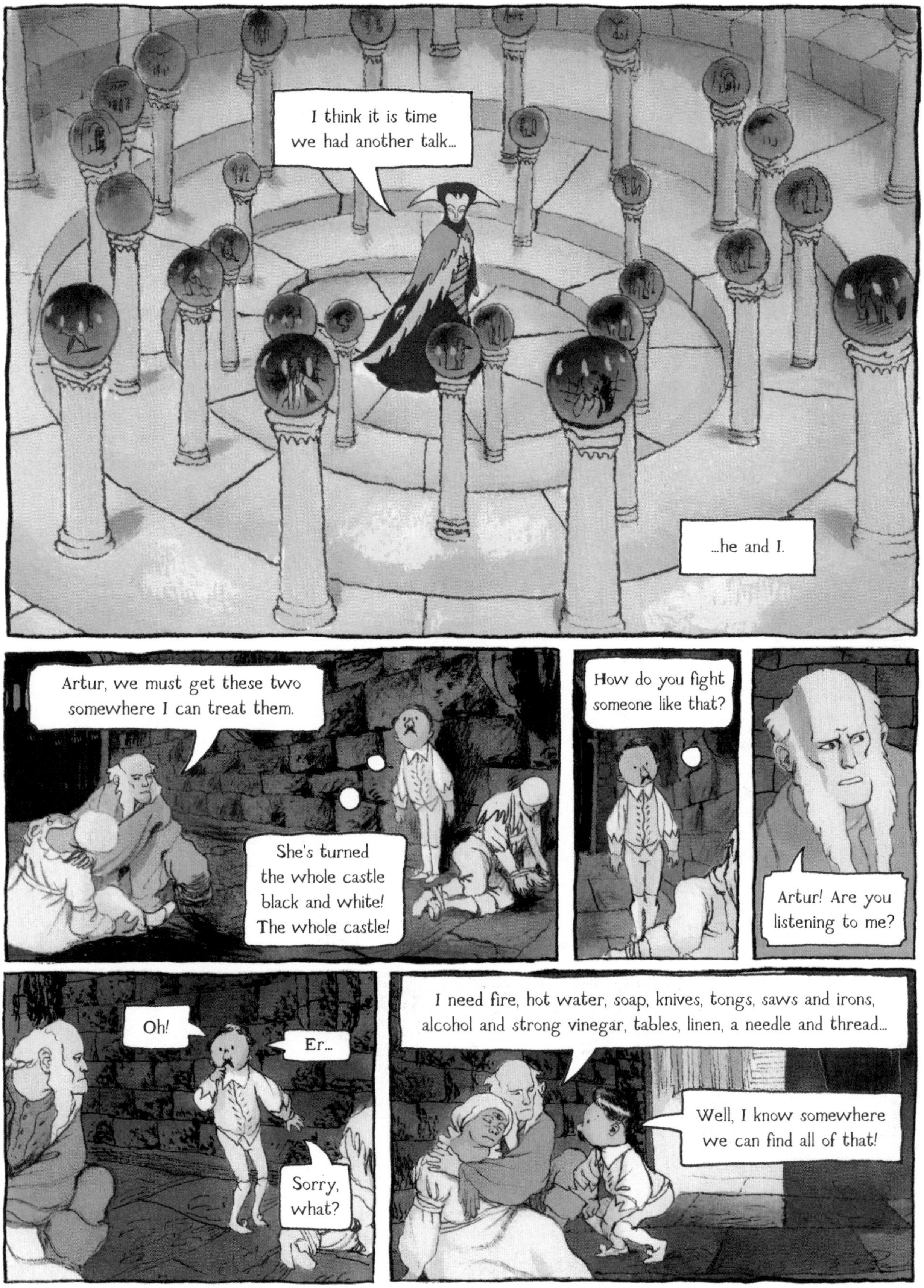
I think it is time we had another talk...
...he and I.
Artur, we must get these two somewhere I can treat them.
She's turned the whole castle black and white! The whole castle!
How do you fight someone like that?
Artur! Are you listening to me?
Oh!
Er...
Sorry, what?
I need fire, hot water, soap, knives, tongs, saws and irons, alcohol and strong vinegar, tables, linen, a needle and thread...
Well, I know somewhere we can find all of that!

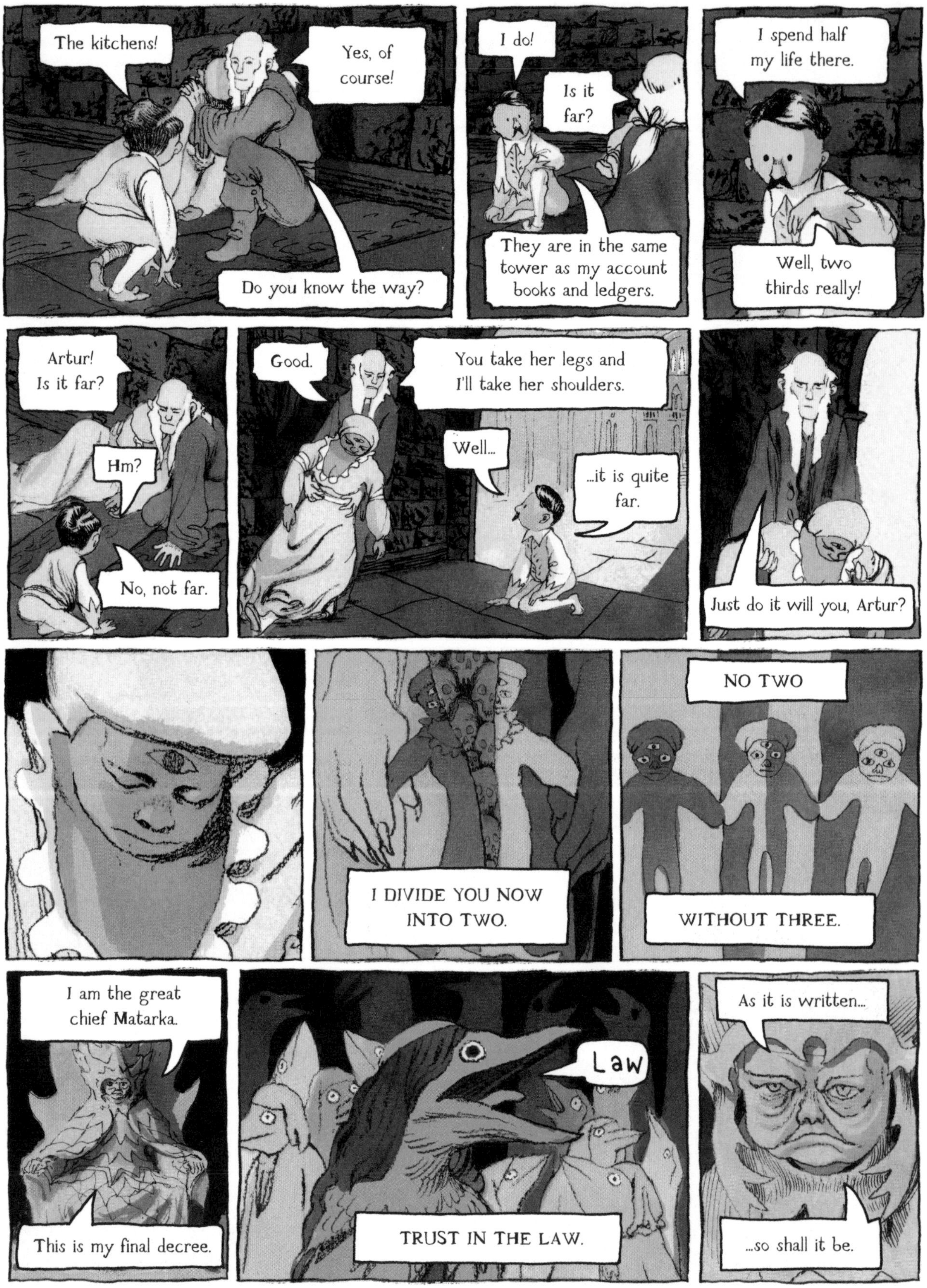
The kitchens!
Yes, of course!
Do you know the way?
I do!
Is it far?
They are in the same tower as my account books and ledgers.
I spend half my life there.
Well, two thirds really!
Artur! Is it far?
Hm?
No, not far.
Good.
You take her legs and I'll take her shoulders.
Well...
...it is quite far.
Just do it will you, Artur?
I DIVIDE YOU NOW INTO TWO.
NO TWO
WITHOUT THREE.
I am the great chief Matarka.
This is my final decree.
Law
TRUST IN THE LAW.
As it is written...
...so shall it be.

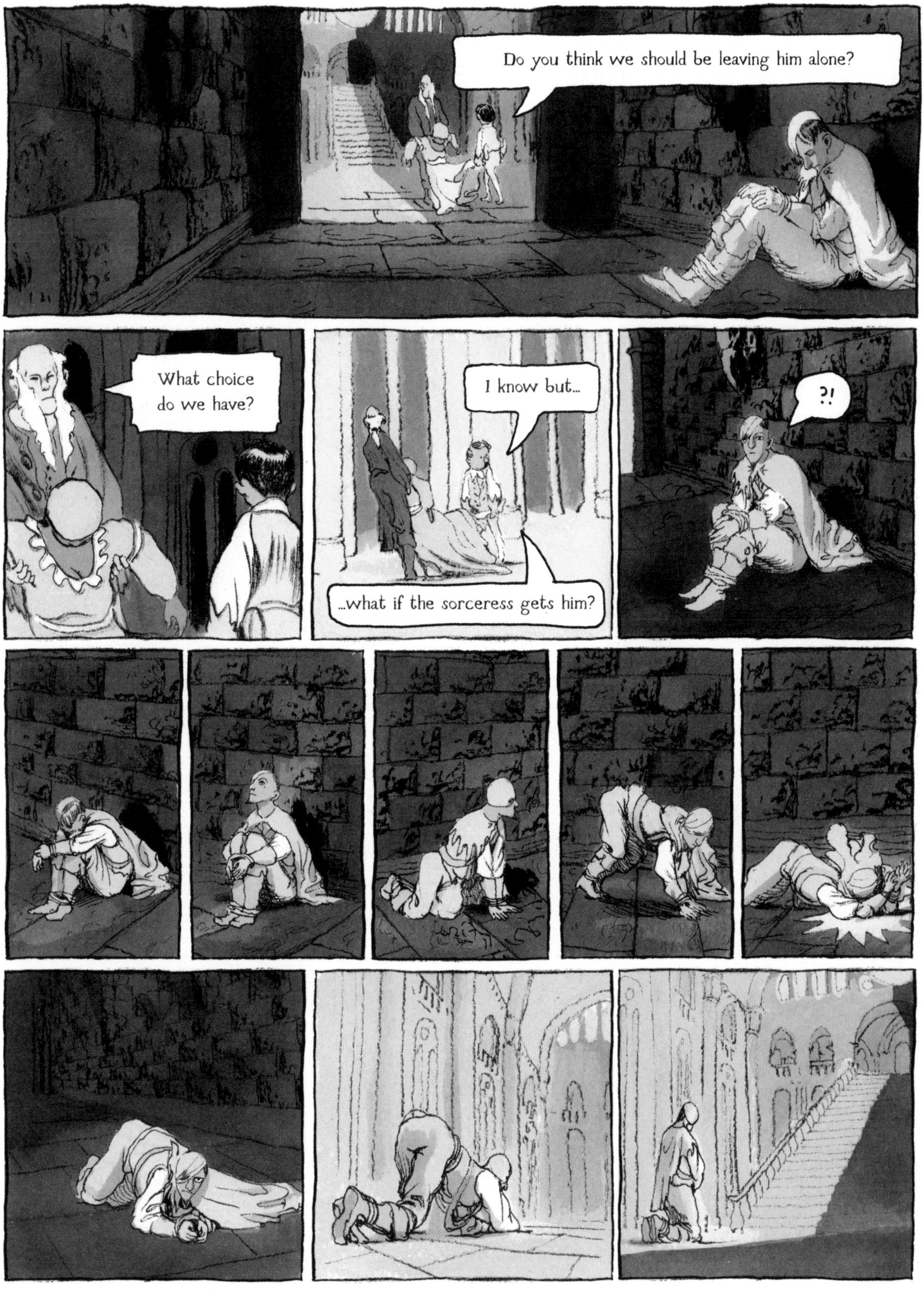

Do you think we should be leaving him alone?
What choice do we have?
I know but...
...what if the sorceress gets him?
?!

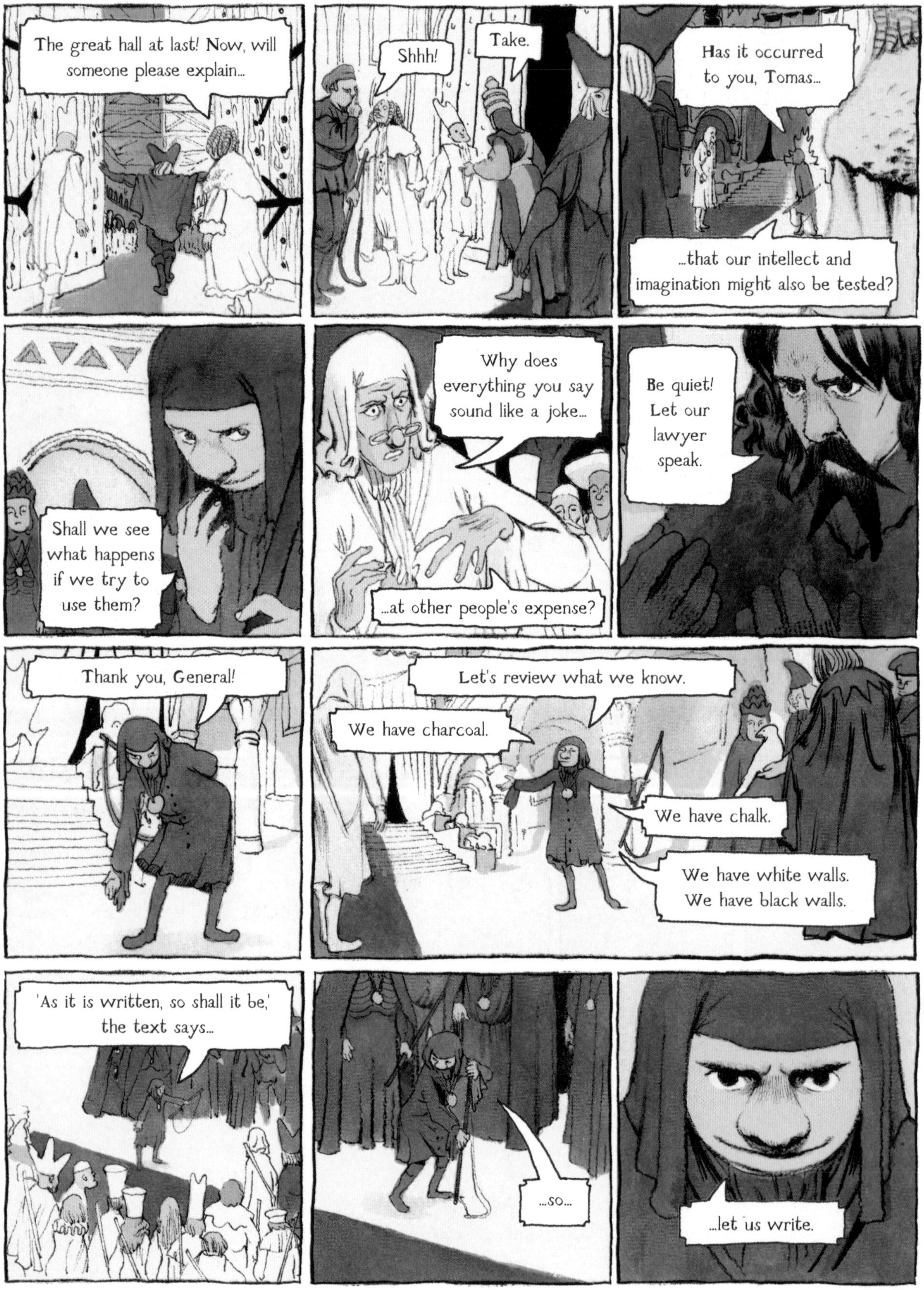
The great hall at last! Now, will someone please explain...
Shhh!
Take.
Has it occurred to you, Tomas...
...that our intellect and imagination might also be tested?
Shall we see what happens if we try to use them?
Why does everything you say sound like a joke...
...at other people's expense?
Be quiet! Let our lawyer speak.
Thank you, General!
Let's review what we know.
We have charcoal.
We have chalk.
We have white walls. We have black walls.
'As it is written, so shall it be,' the text says...
...so...
...let us write.

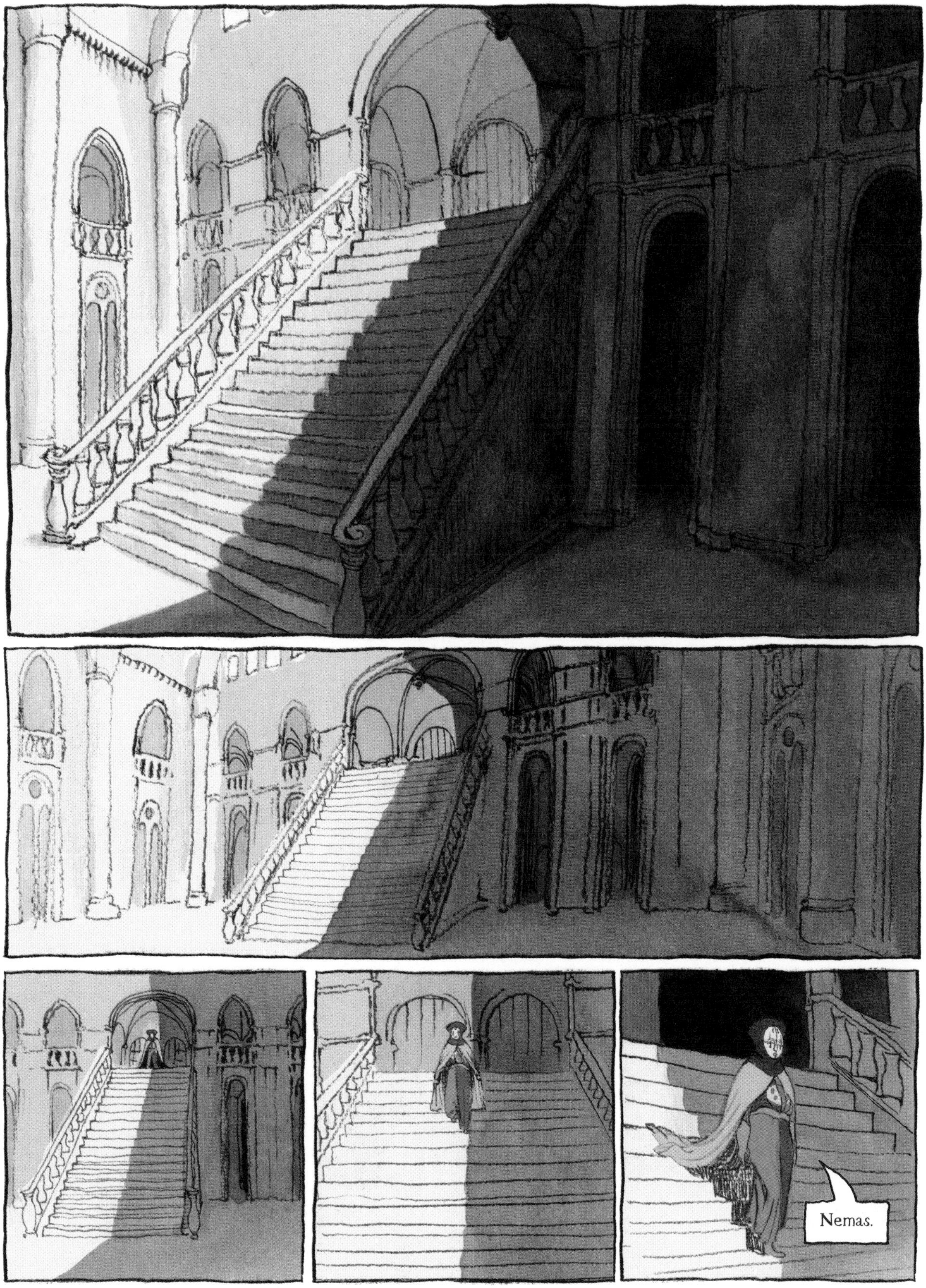
Nemas.

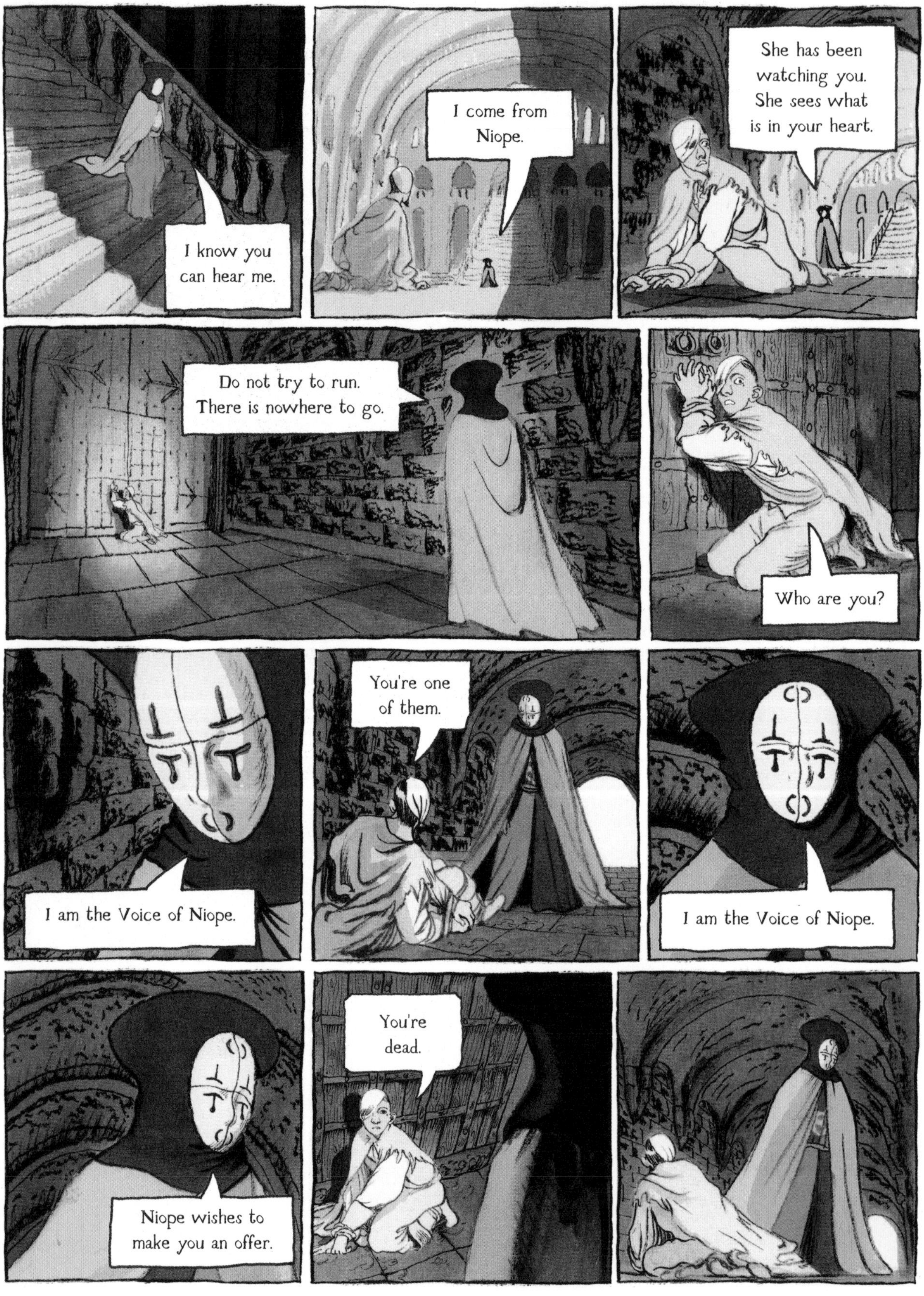
I know you can hear me.
I come from Niope.
She has been watching you. She sees what is in your heart.
Do not try to run. There is nowhere to go.
Who are you?
I am the Voice of Niope.
You're one of them.
I am the Voice of Niope.
Niope wishes to make you an offer.
You're dead.

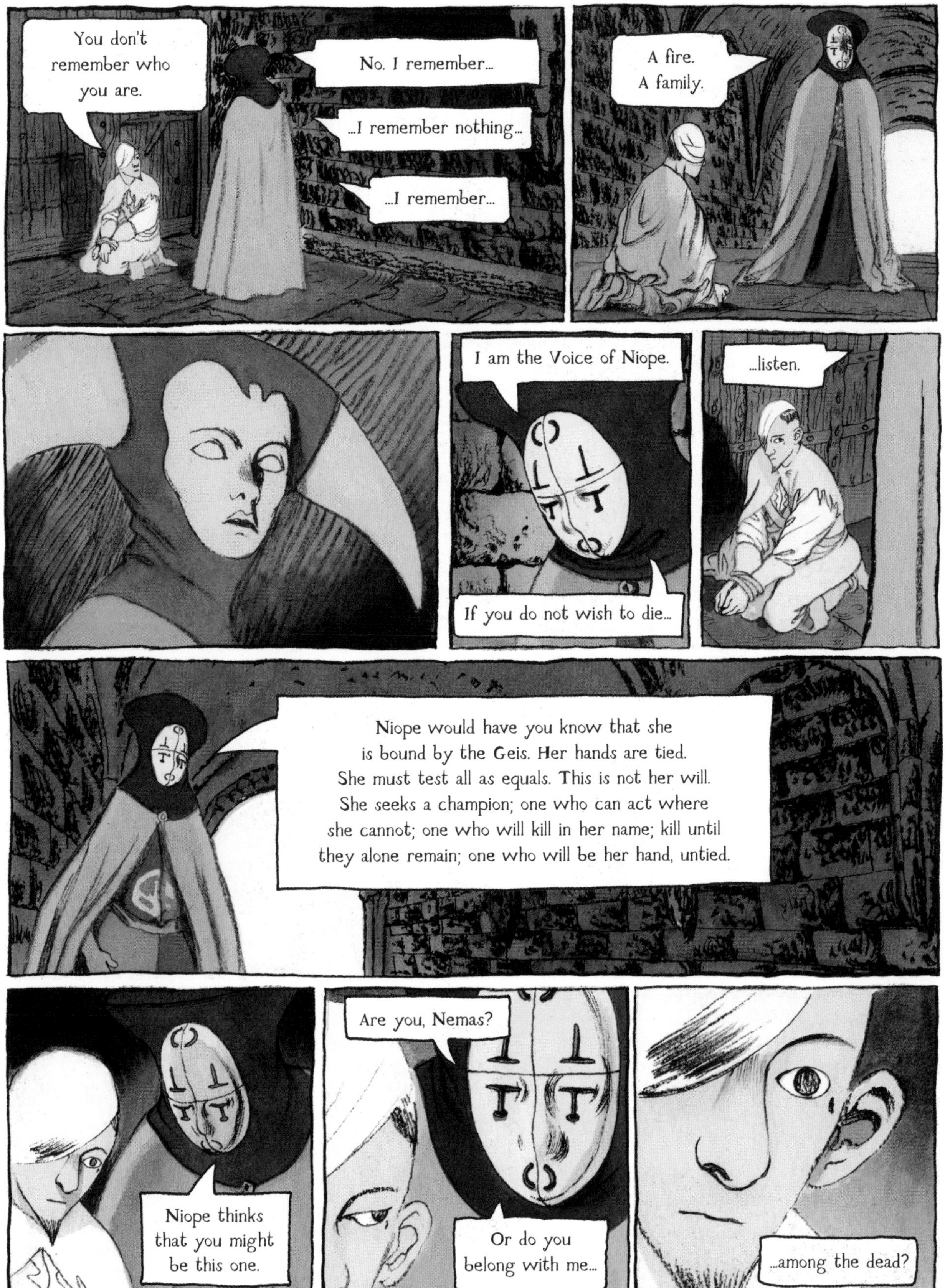

You don't remember who you are.
No. I remember...
...I remember nothing...
...I remember...
A fire. A family.
I am the Voice of Niope.
If you do not wish to die...
...listen.
Niope would have you know that she is bound by the Geis. Her hands are tied. She must test all as equals. This is not her will. She seeks a champion; one who can act where she cannot; one who will kill in her name; kill until they alone remain; one who will be her hand, untied.
Niope thinks that you might be this one.
Are you, Nemas?
Or do you belong with me...
...among the dead?

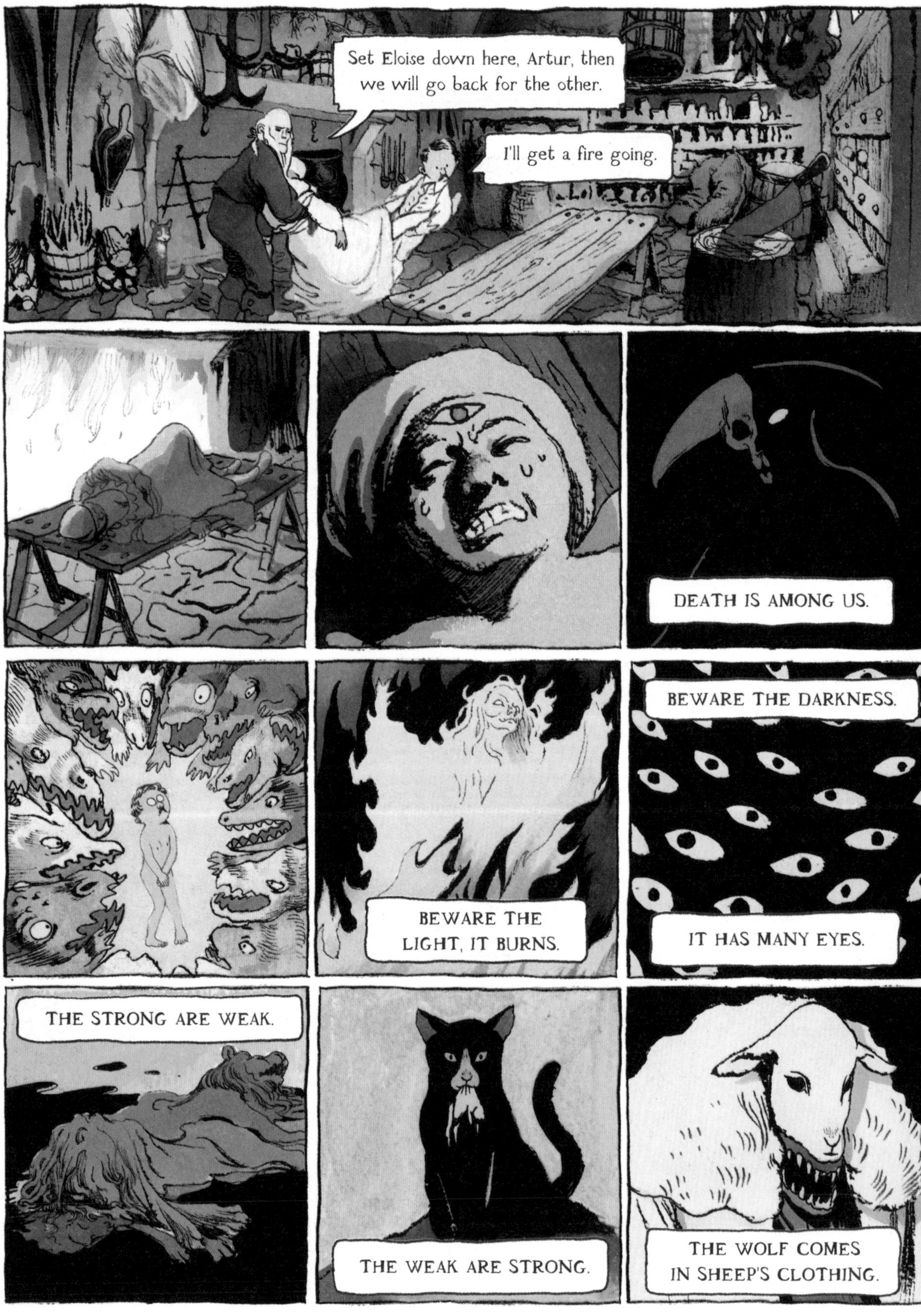
Set Eloise down here, Artur, then we will go back for the other.
I'll get a fire going.
DEATH IS AMONG US.
BEWARE THE LIGHT, IT BURNS.
BEWARE THE DARKNESS.
IT HAS MANY EYES.
THE STRONG ARE WEAK.
THE WEAK ARE STRONG.
THE WOLF COMES IN SHEEP'S CLOTHING.

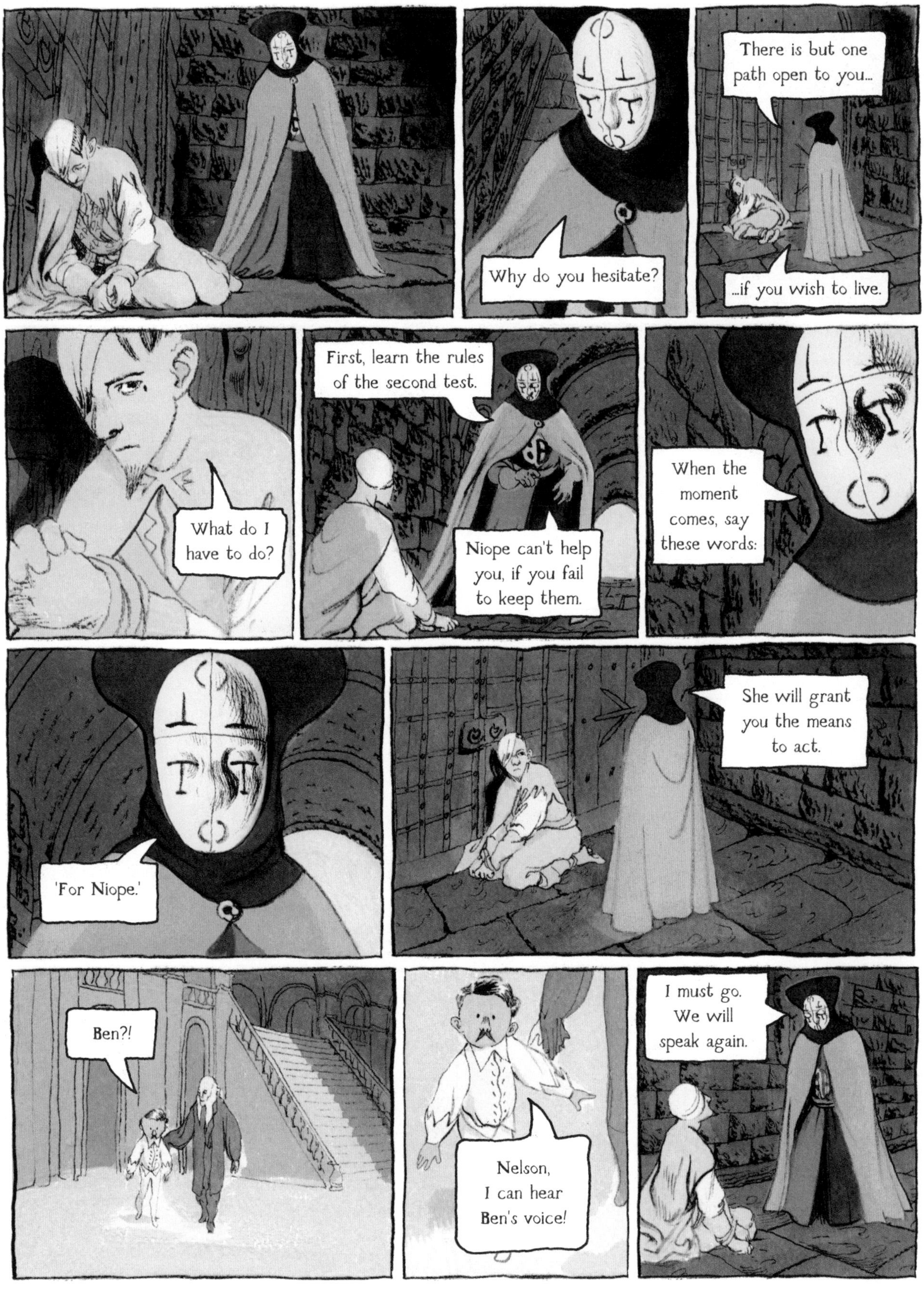
Why do you hesitate?
There is but one path open to you...
...if you wish to live.
What do I have to do?
First, learn the rules of the second test.
Niope can't help you, if you fail to keep them.
When the moment comes, say these words:
'For Niope.'
She will grant you the means to act.
Ben?!
Nelson, I can hear Ben's voice!
I must go. We will speak again.

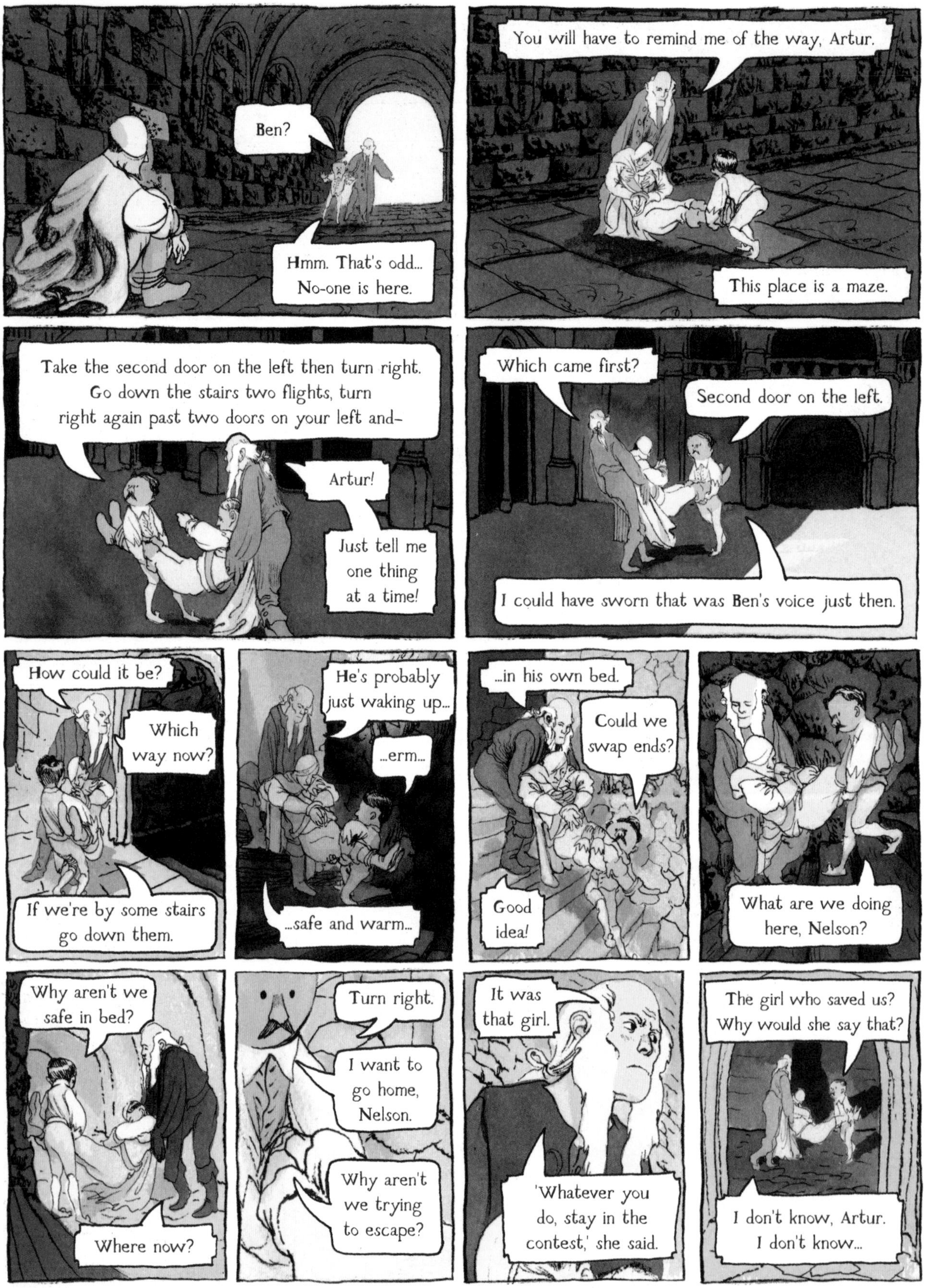
Ben?
Hmm. That's odd... No-one is here.
You will have to remind me of the way, Artur.
This place is a maze.
Take the second door on the left then turn right. Go down the stairs two flights, turn right again past two doors on your left and–
Artur!
Just tell me one thing at a time!
Which came first?
Second door on the left.
I could have sworn that was Ben's voice just then.
How could it be?
Which way now?
If we're by some stairs go down them.
He's probably just waking up...
...erm...
...safe and warm...
...in his own bed.
Could we swap ends?
Good idea!
What are we doing here, Nelson?
Why aren't we safe in bed?
Where now?
Turn right.
I want to go home, Nelson.
Why aren't we trying to escape?
It was that girl.
'Whatever you do, stay in the contest,' she said.
The girl who saved us? Why would she say that?
I don't know, Artur. I don't know...

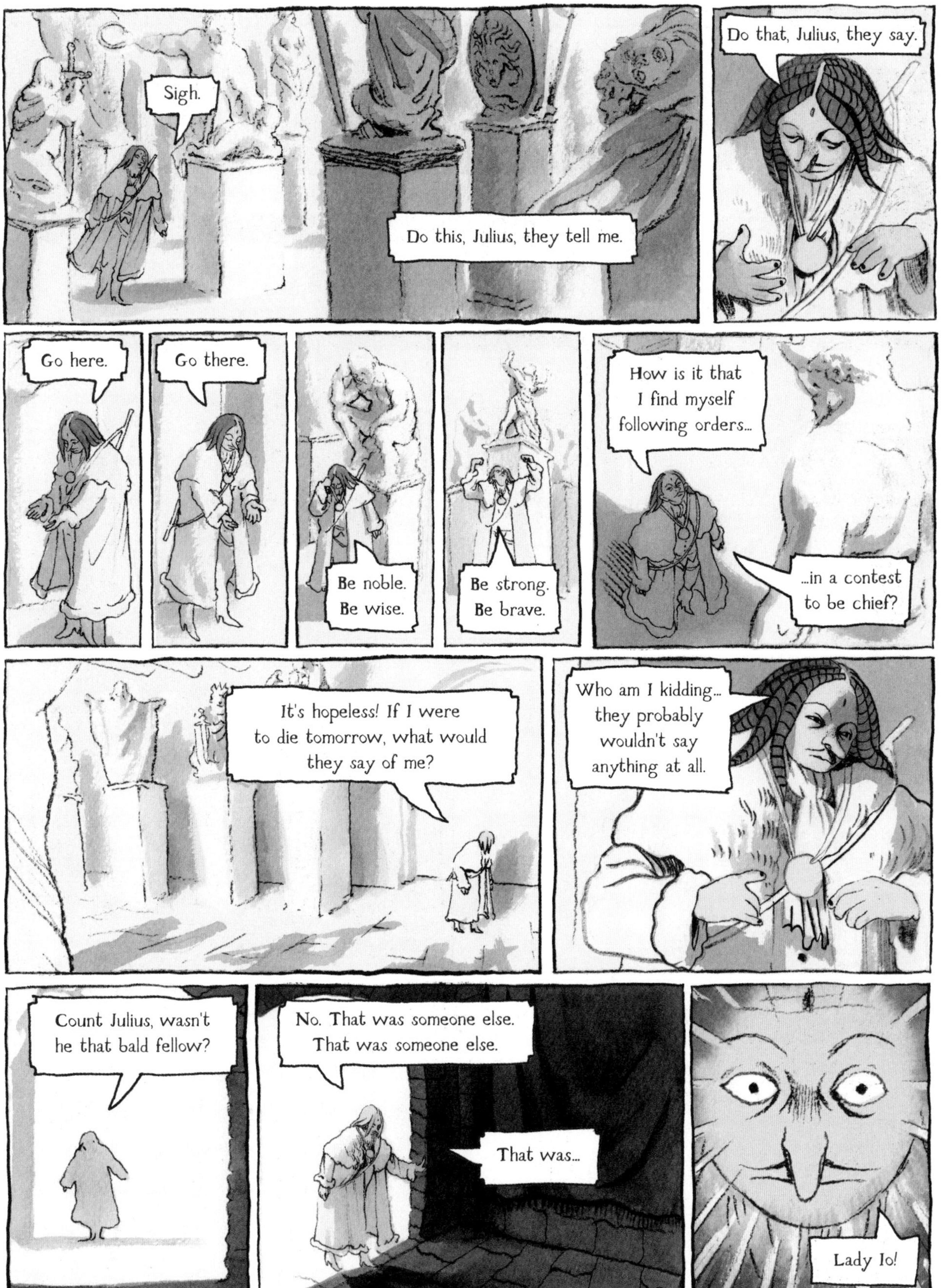
Sigh.
Do this, Julius, they tell me.
Do that, Julius, they say.
Go here.
Go there.
Be noble. Be wise.
Be strong. Be brave.
How is it that I find myself following orders...
...in a contest to be chief?
It's hopeless! If I were to die tomorrow, what would they say of me?
Who am I kidding... they probably wouldn't say anything at all.
Count Julius, wasn't he that bald fellow?
No. That was someone else. That was someone else.
That was...
Lady Io!

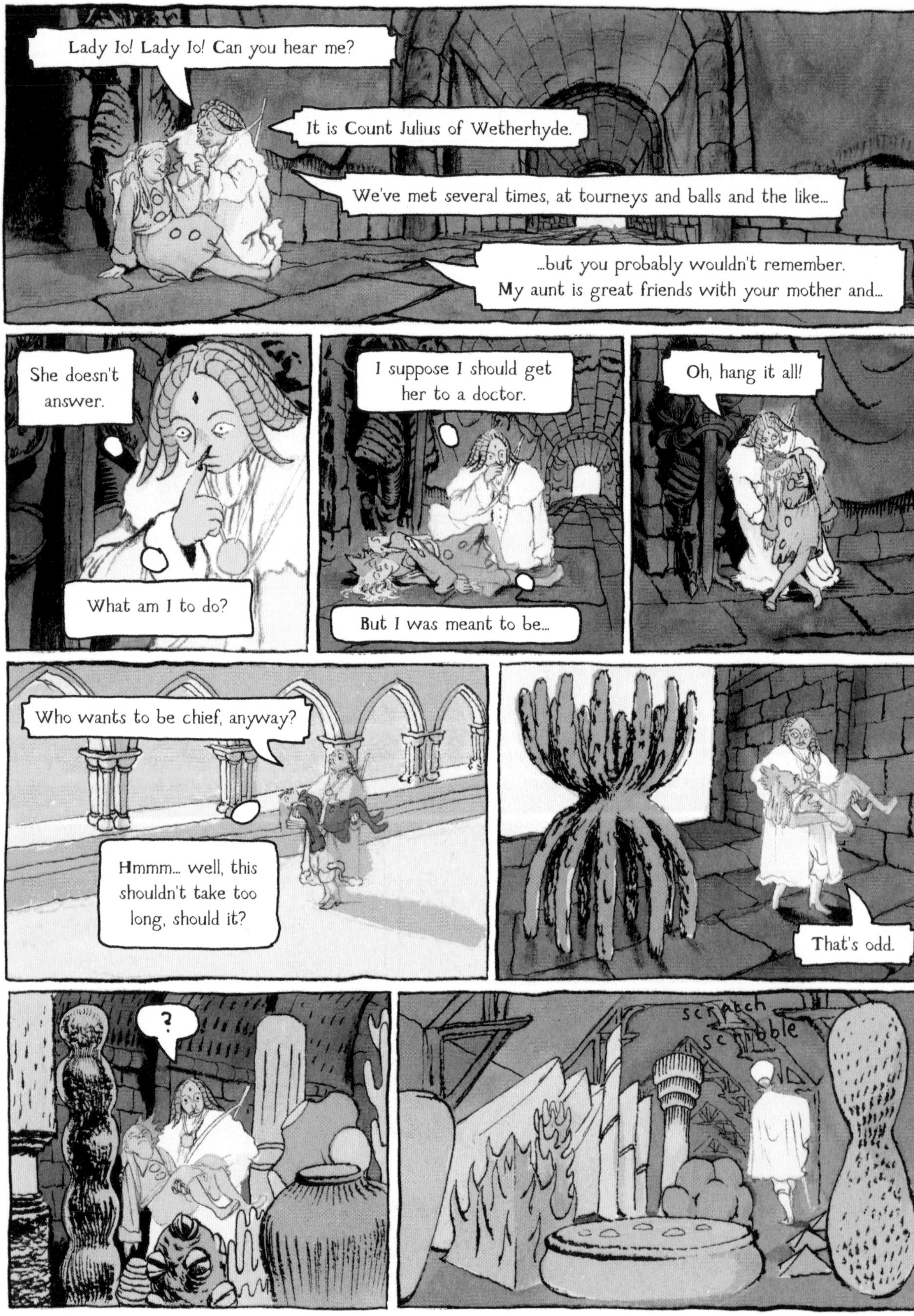
Lady Io! Lady Io! Can you hear me?
It is Count Julius of Wetherhyde.
We've met several times, at tourneys and balls and the like...
...but you probably wouldn't remember. My aunt is great friends with your mother and...
She doesn't answer.
What am I to do?
I suppose I should get her to a doctor.
But I was meant to be...
Oh, hang it all!
Who wants to be chief, anyway?
Hmmm... well, this shouldn't take too long, should it?
That's odd.
?
scratch
scribble

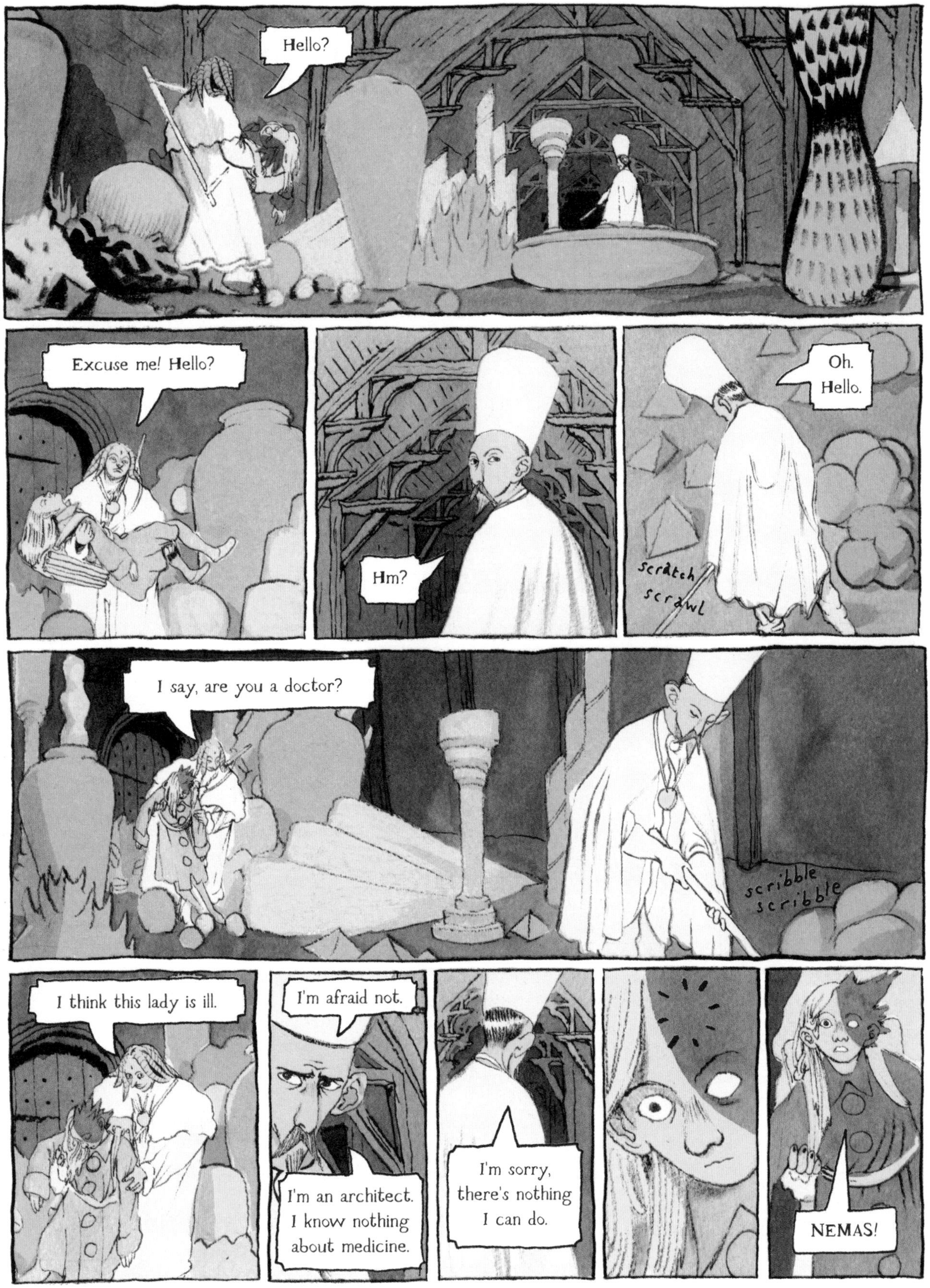
Hello?
Excuse me! Hello?
Hm?
Oh. Hello.
scratch scrawl
I say, are you a doctor?
scribble scribble
I think this lady is ill.
I'm afraid not.
I'm an architect. I know nothing about medicine.
I'm sorry, there's nothing I can do.
NEMAS!

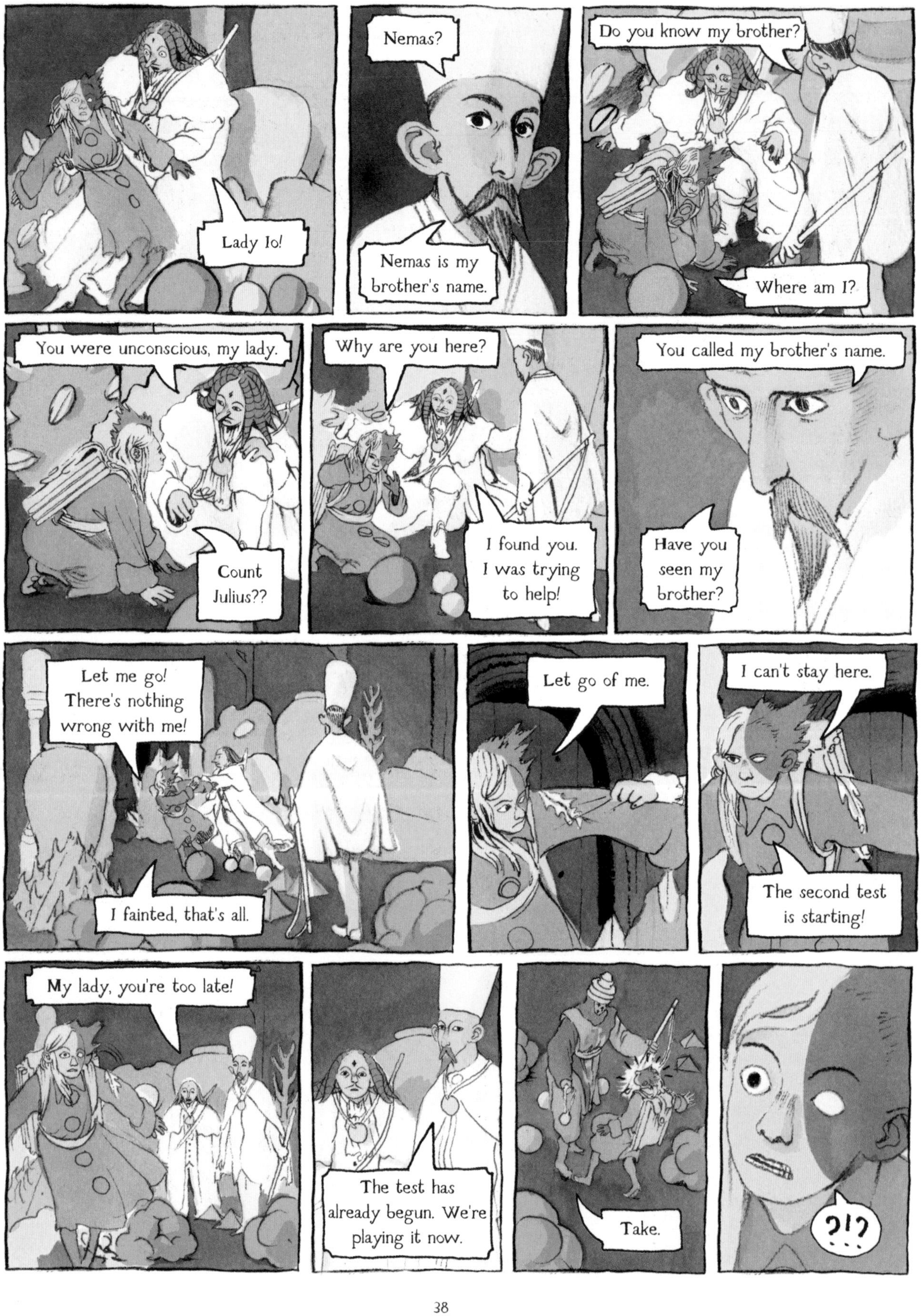
Lady Io!
Nemas?
Nemas is my brother's name.
Do you know my brother?
Where am I?
You were unconscious, my lady.
Count Julius??
Why are you here?
I found you. I was trying to help!
You called my brother's name.
Have you seen my brother?
Let me go! There's nothing wrong with me!
I fainted, that's all.
Let go of me.
I can't stay here.
The second test is starting!
My lady, you're too late!
The test has already begun. We're playing it now.
Take.
?!?

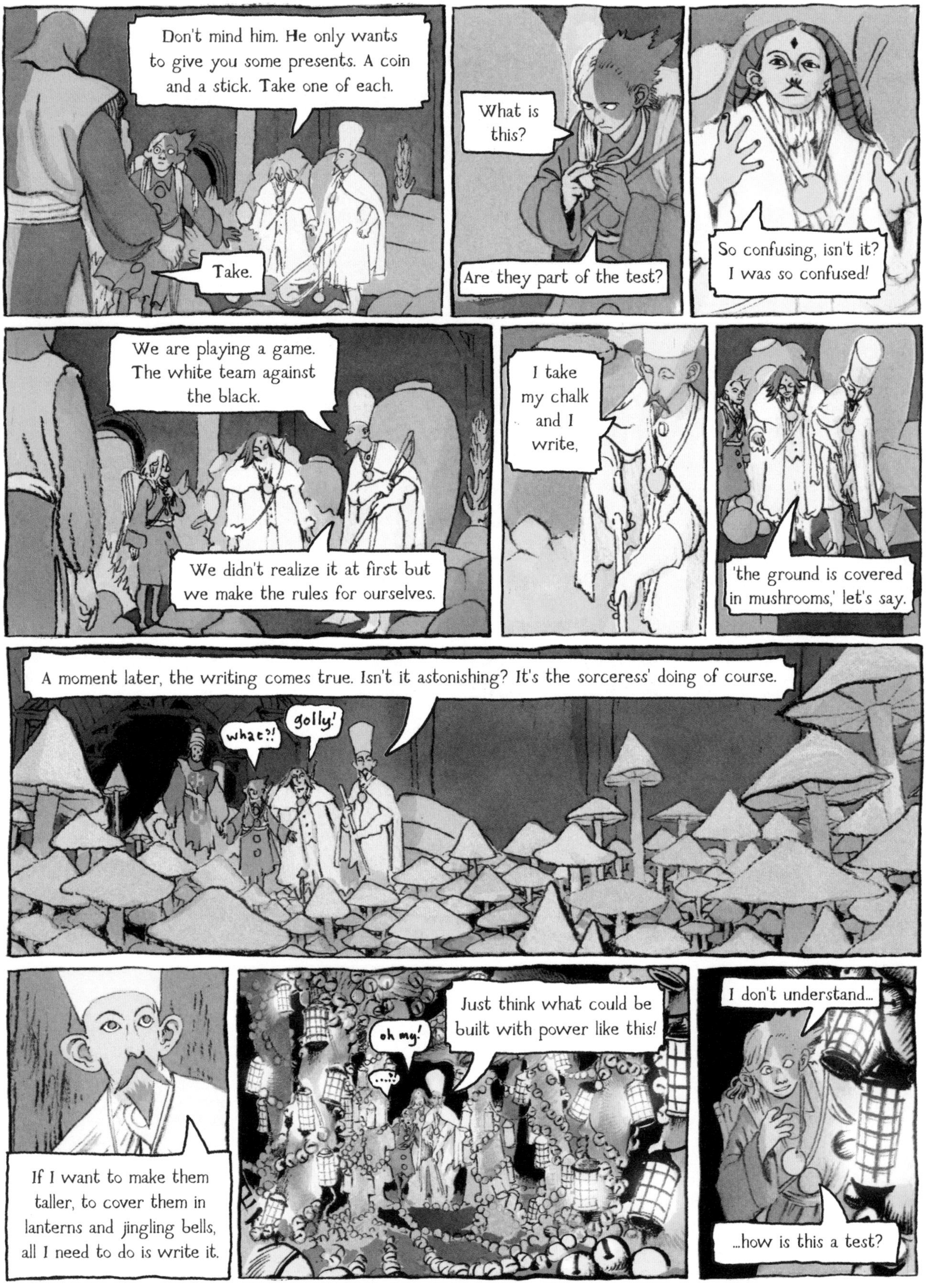
Don't mind him. He only wants to give you some presents. A coin and a stick. Take one of each.
Take.
What is this?
Are they part of the test?
So confusing, isn't it? I was so confused!
We are playing a game. The white team against the black.
We didn't realize it at first but we make the rules for ourselves.
I take my chalk and I write,
'the ground is covered in mushrooms,' let's say.
A moment later, the writing comes true. Isn't it astonishing? It's the sorceress' doing of course.
whac?!
golly!
If I want to make them taller, to cover them in lanterns and jingling bells, all I need to do is write it.
oh my!
Just think what could be built with power like this!
I don't understand...
...how is this a test?

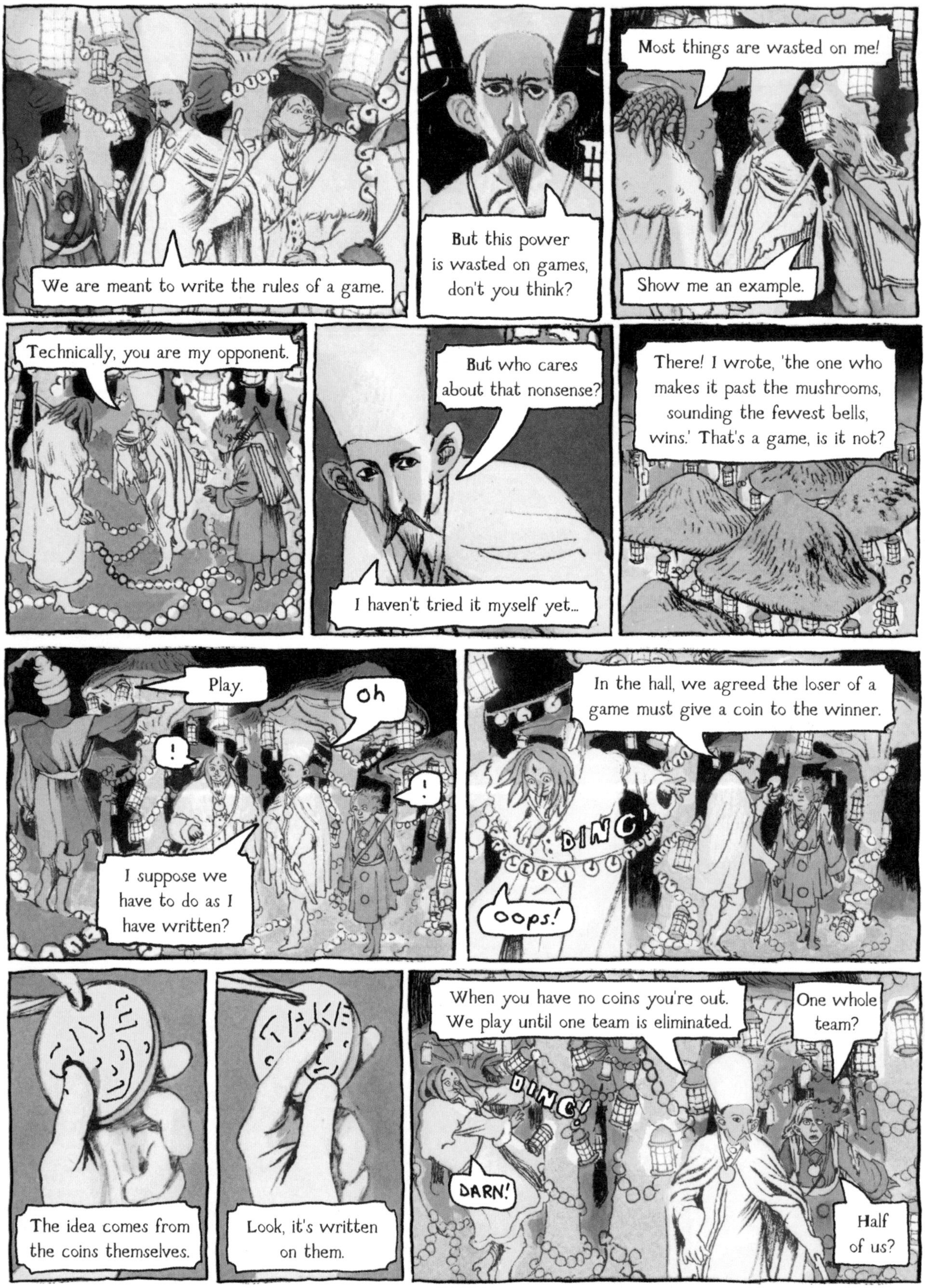

We are meant to write the rules of a game.
But this power is wasted on games, don't you think?
Most things are wasted on me!
Show me an example.
Technically, you are my opponent.
But who cares about that nonsense?
I haven't tried it myself yet...
There! I wrote, 'the one who makes it past the mushrooms, sounding the fewest bells, wins.' That's a game, is it not?
Play.
Oh
!
!
I suppose we have to do as I have written?
In the hall, we agreed the loser of a game must give a coin to the winner.
DING!
Oops!
The idea comes from the coins themselves.
Look, it's written on them.
When you have no coins you're out. We play until one team is eliminated.
One whole team?
DING!
DARN!
Half of us?

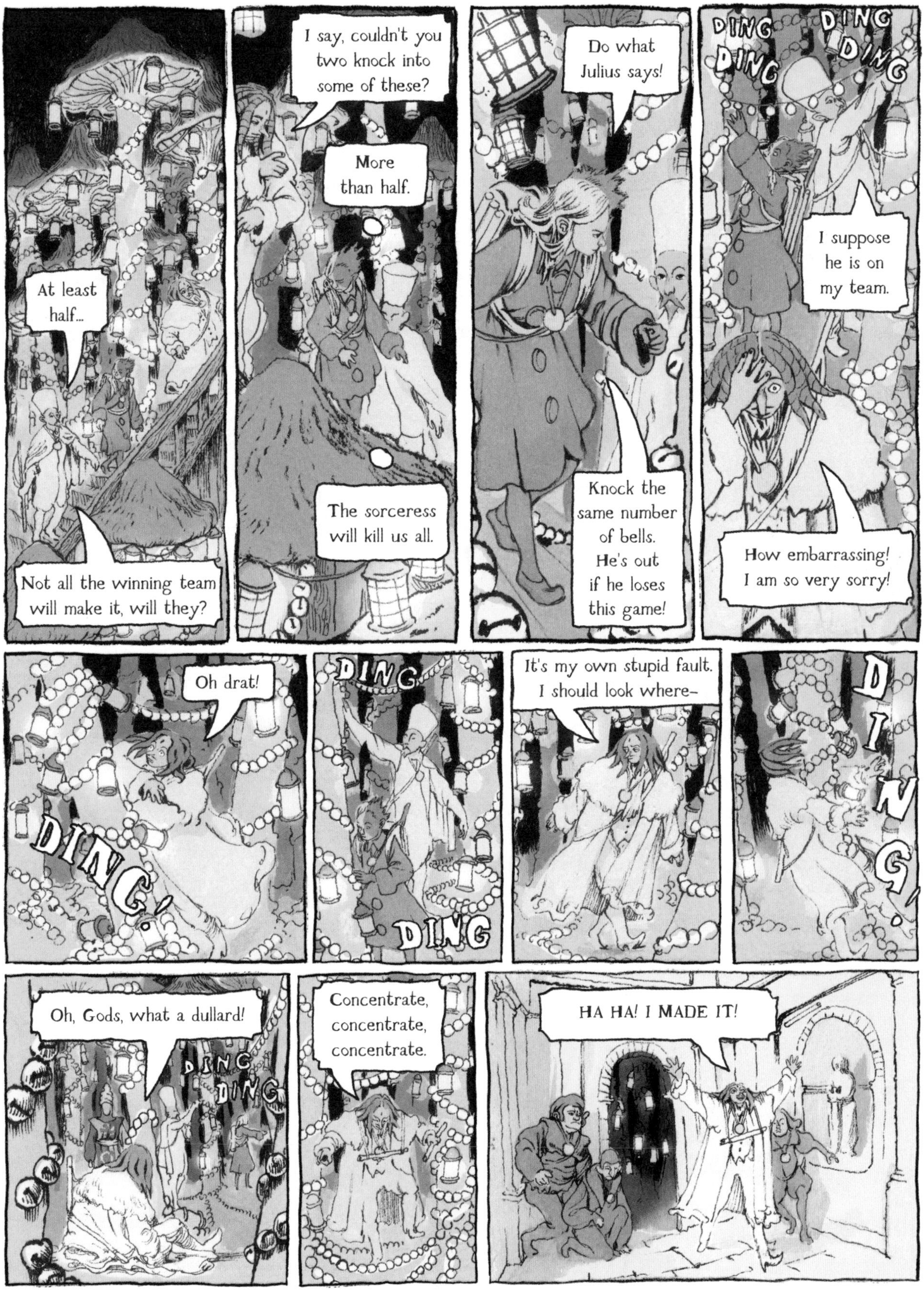
At least half...
Not all the winning team will make it, will they?
I say, couldn't you two knock into some of these?
More than half.
The sorceress will kill us all.
Do what Julius says!
Knock the same number of bells. He's out if he loses this game!
DING DING DING DING
I suppose he is on my team.
How embarrassing! I am so very sorry!
Oh drat!
DING!
DING
DING
It's my own stupid fault. I should look where–
DING!
Oh, Gods, what a dullard!
DING DING
Concentrate, concentrate, concentrate.
HA HA! I MADE IT!

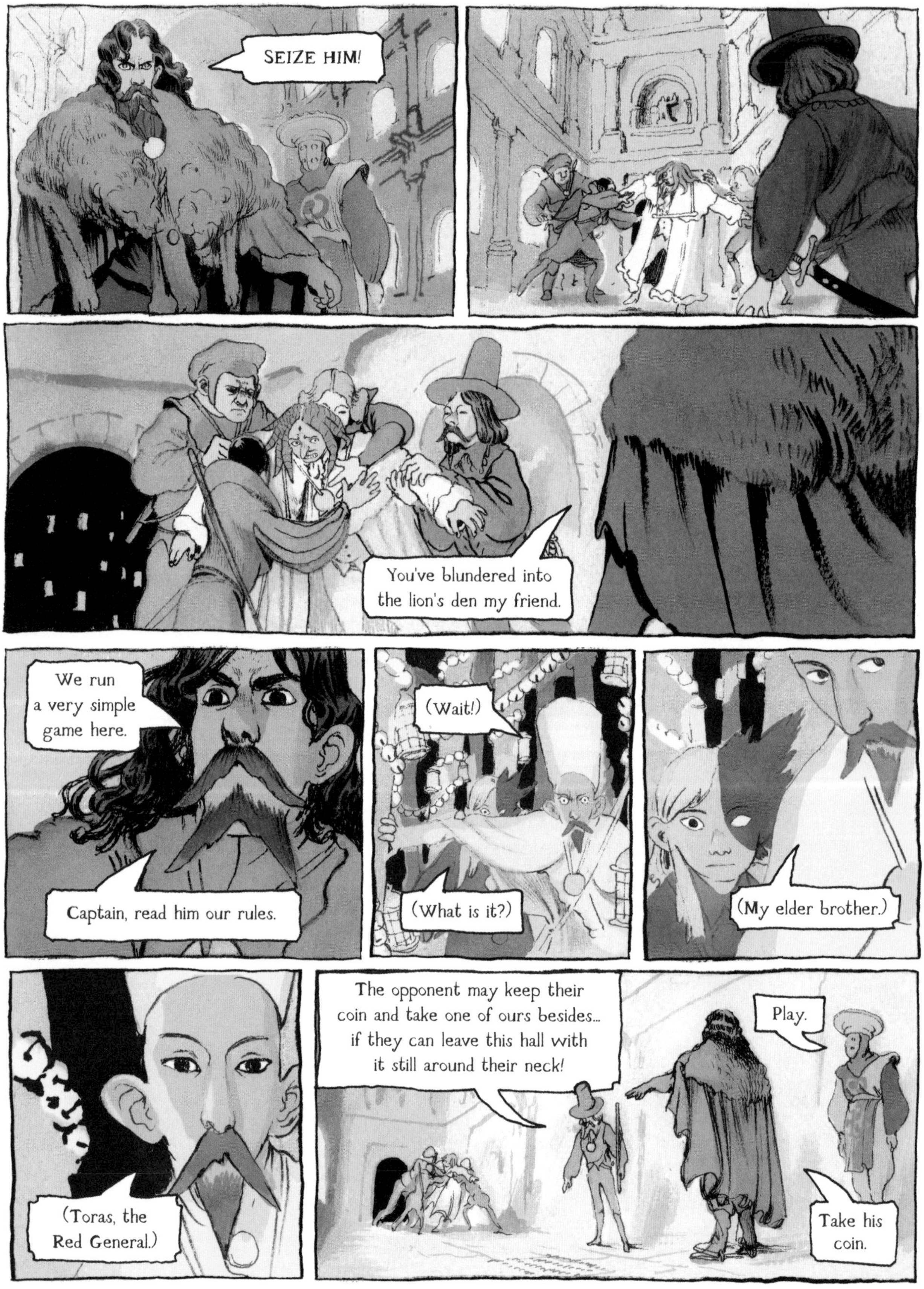

SEIZE HIM!
You've blundered into the lion's den my friend.
We run a very simple game here.
Captain, read him our rules.
(Wait!)
(What is it?)
(My elder brother.)
(Toras, the Red General.)
The opponent may keep their coin and take one of ours besides... if they can leave this hall with it still around their neck!
Play.
Take his coin.

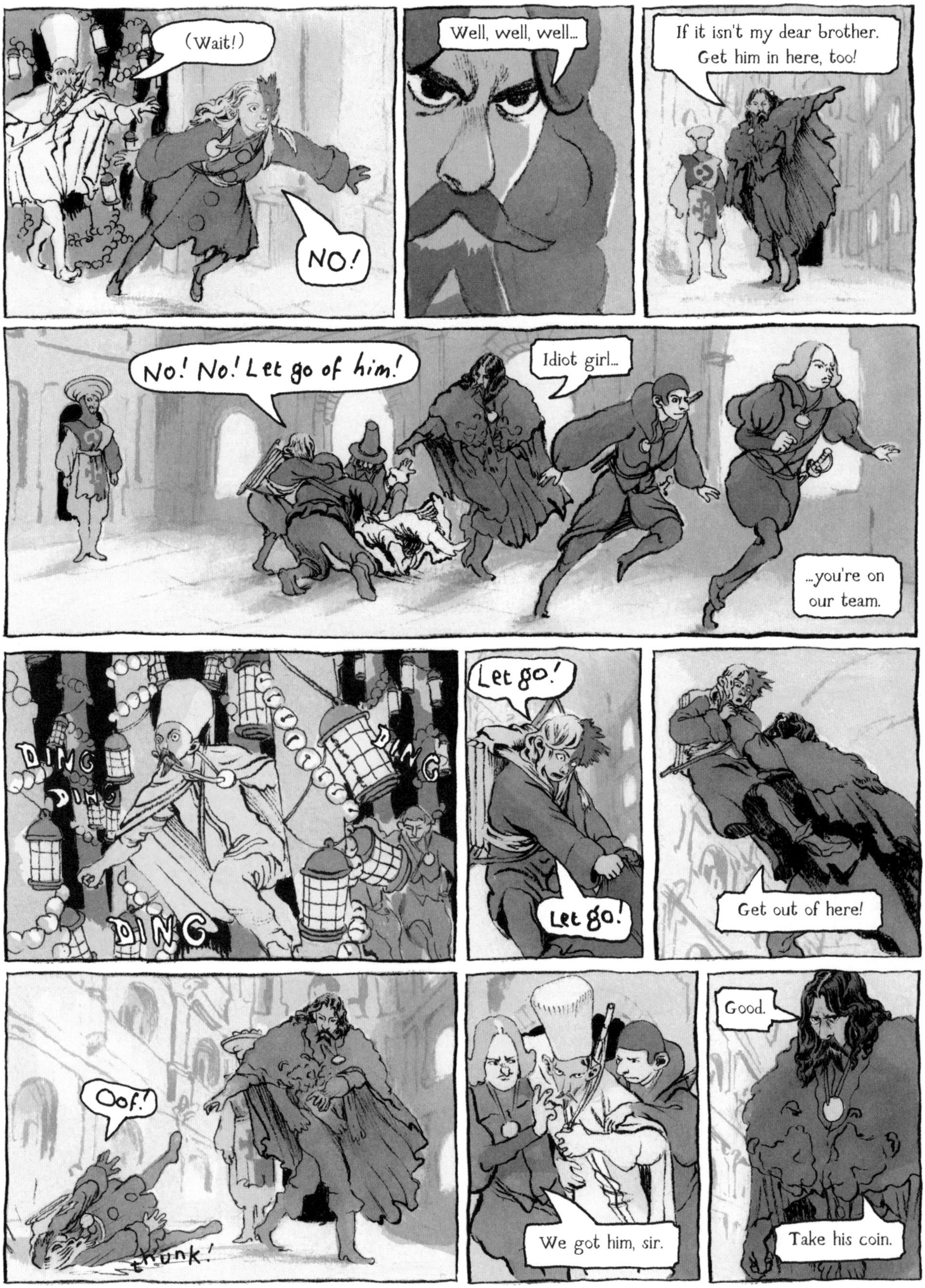
(Wait!)
NO!
Well, well, well...
If it isn't my dear brother. Get him in here, too!
No! No! Let go of him!
Idiot girl...
...you're on our team.
DING
DING
DING
DING
Let go!
Let go!
Get out of here!
Oof!
thunk!
We got him, sir.
Good.
Take his coin.

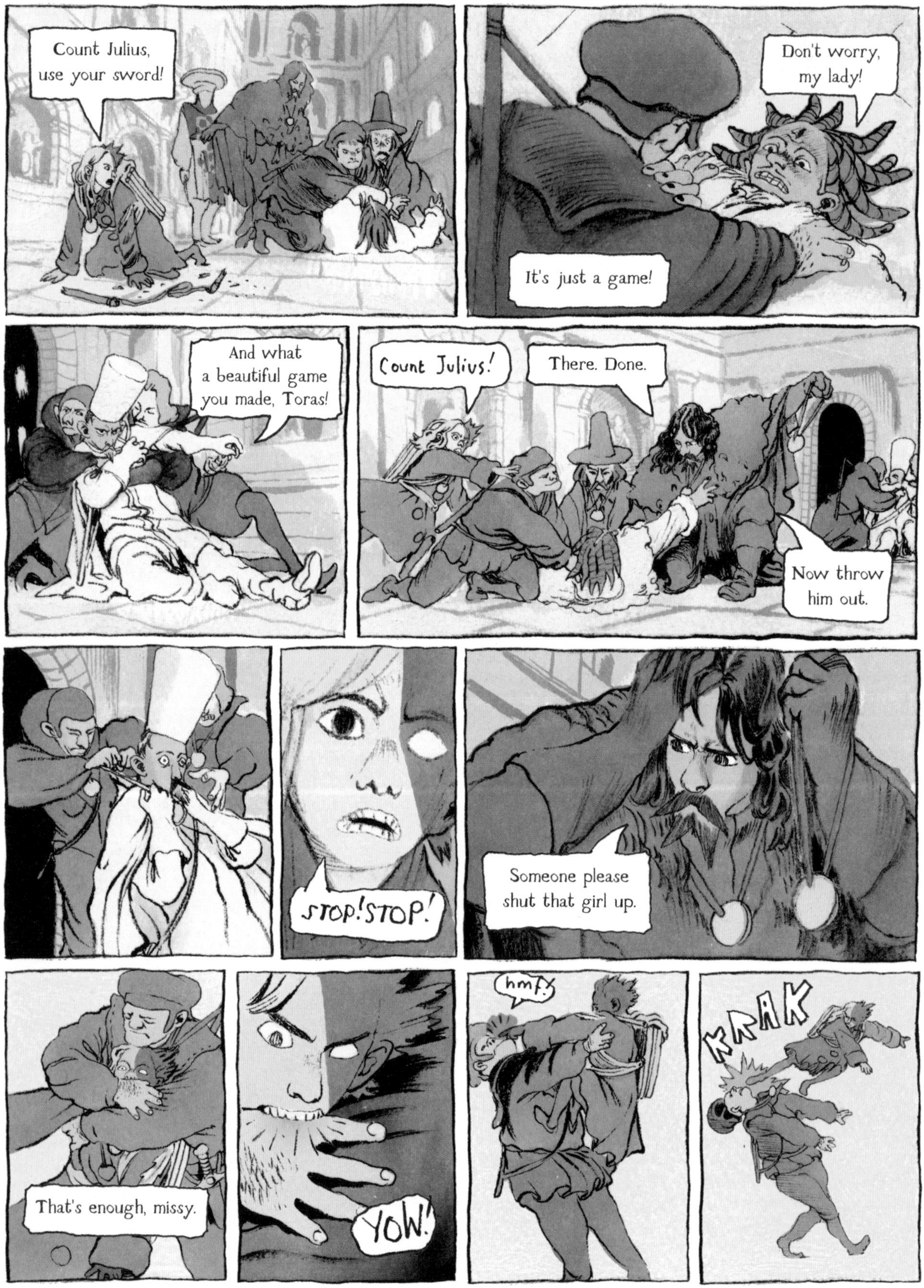

Count Julius, use your sword!
Don't worry, my lady!
It's just a game!
And what a beautiful game you made, Toras!
Count Julius!
There. Done.
Now throw him out.
STOP! STOP!
Someone please shut that girl up.
That's enough, missy.
YOW!
hmf.
KRAK

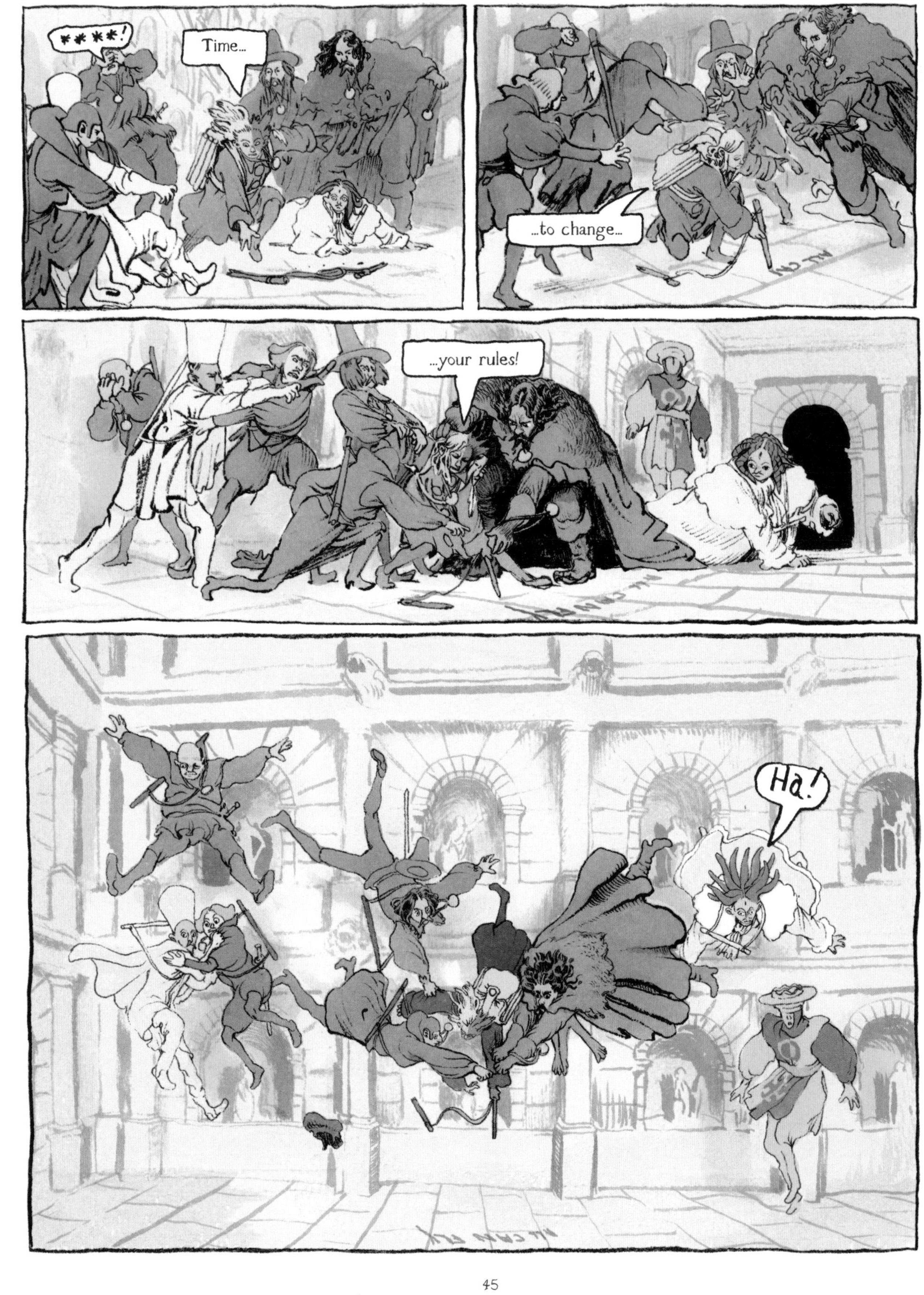
****!
Time...
...to change...
...your rules!
Ha!

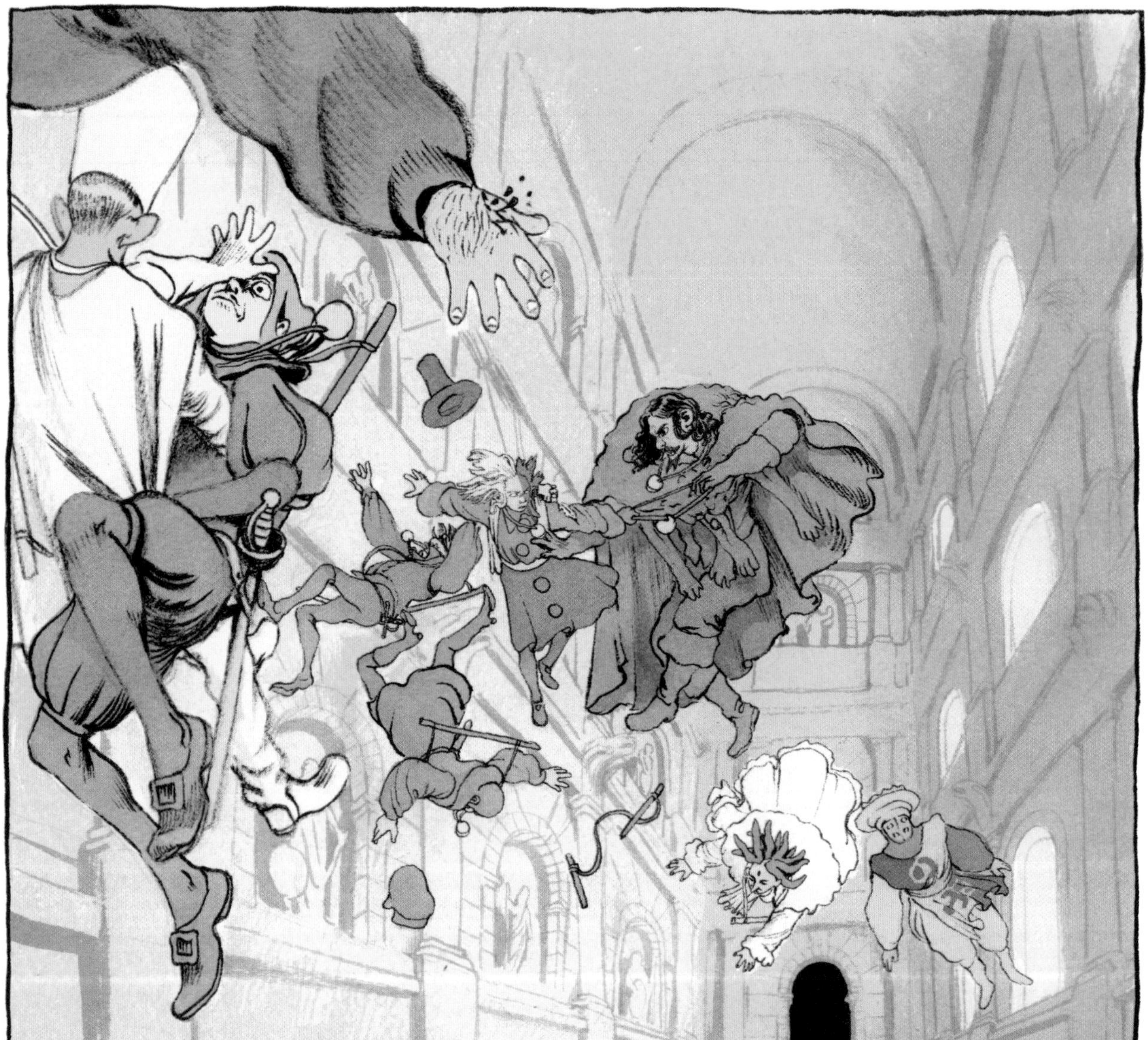

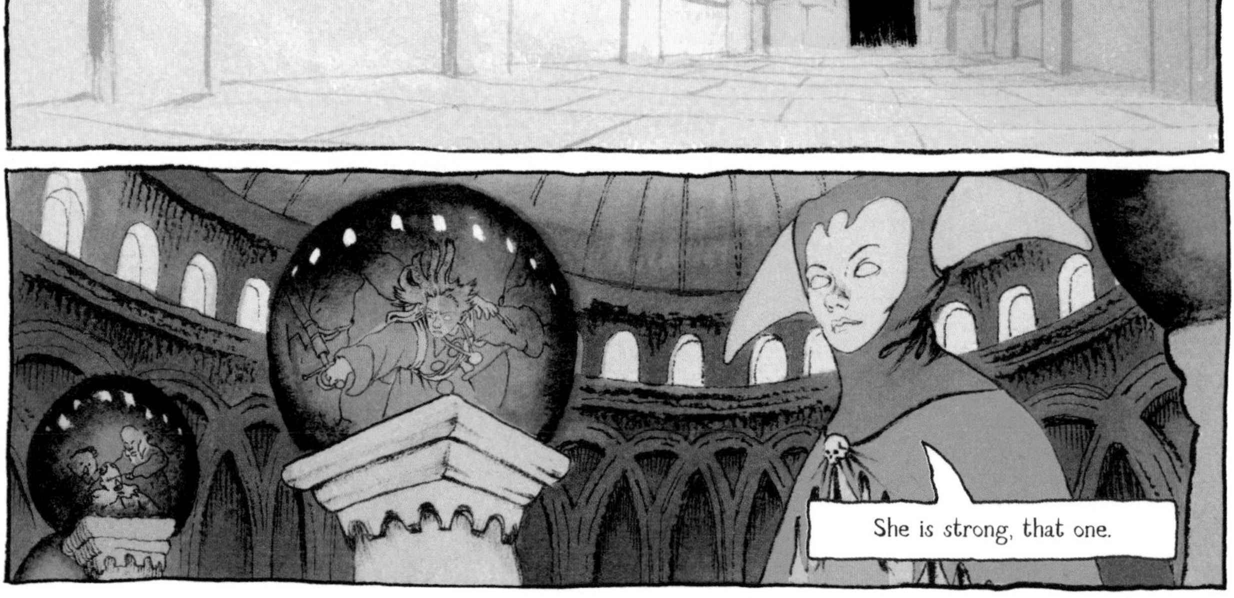
She is strong, that one.

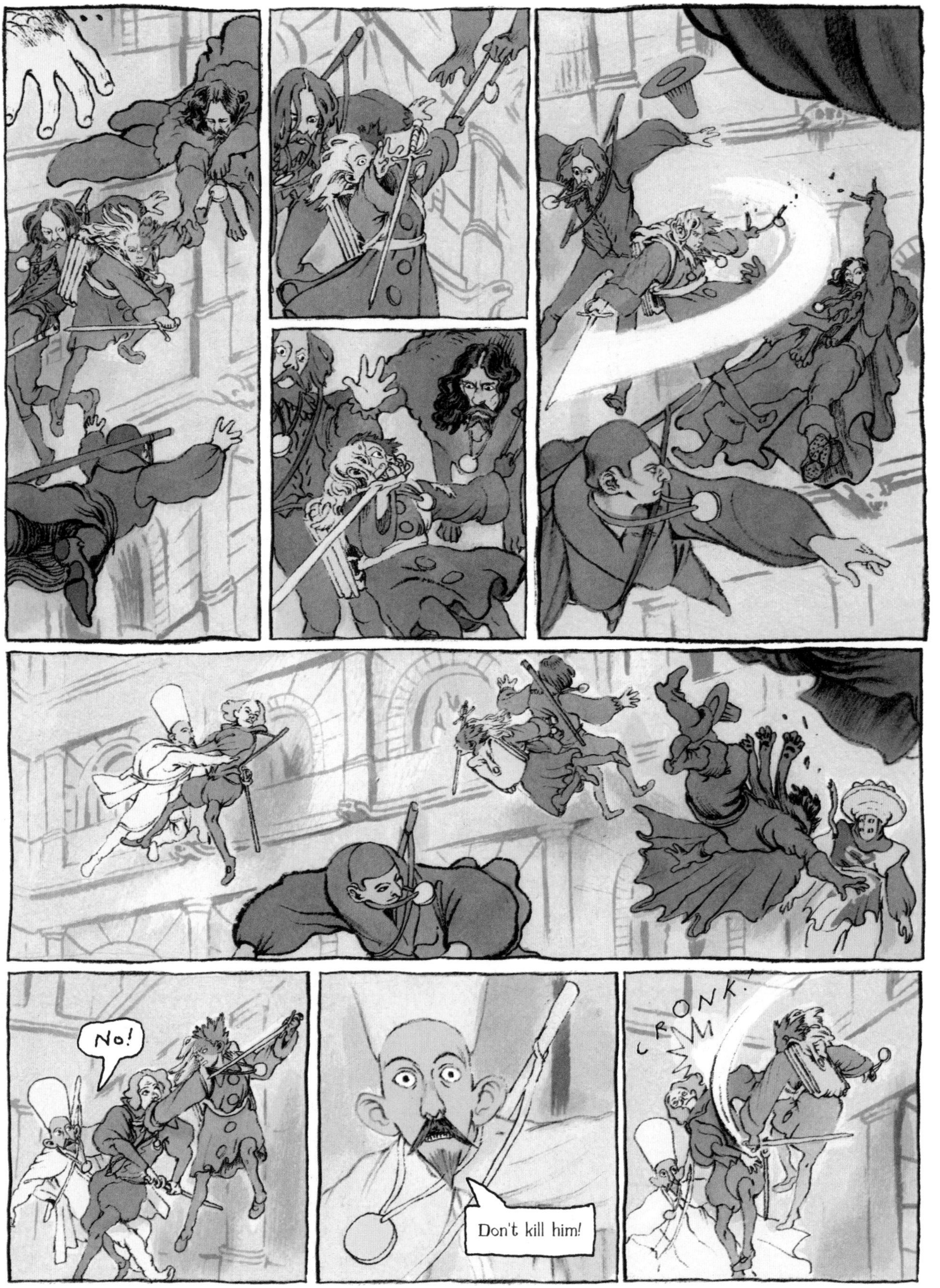
No!
Don't kill him!
CRONK!

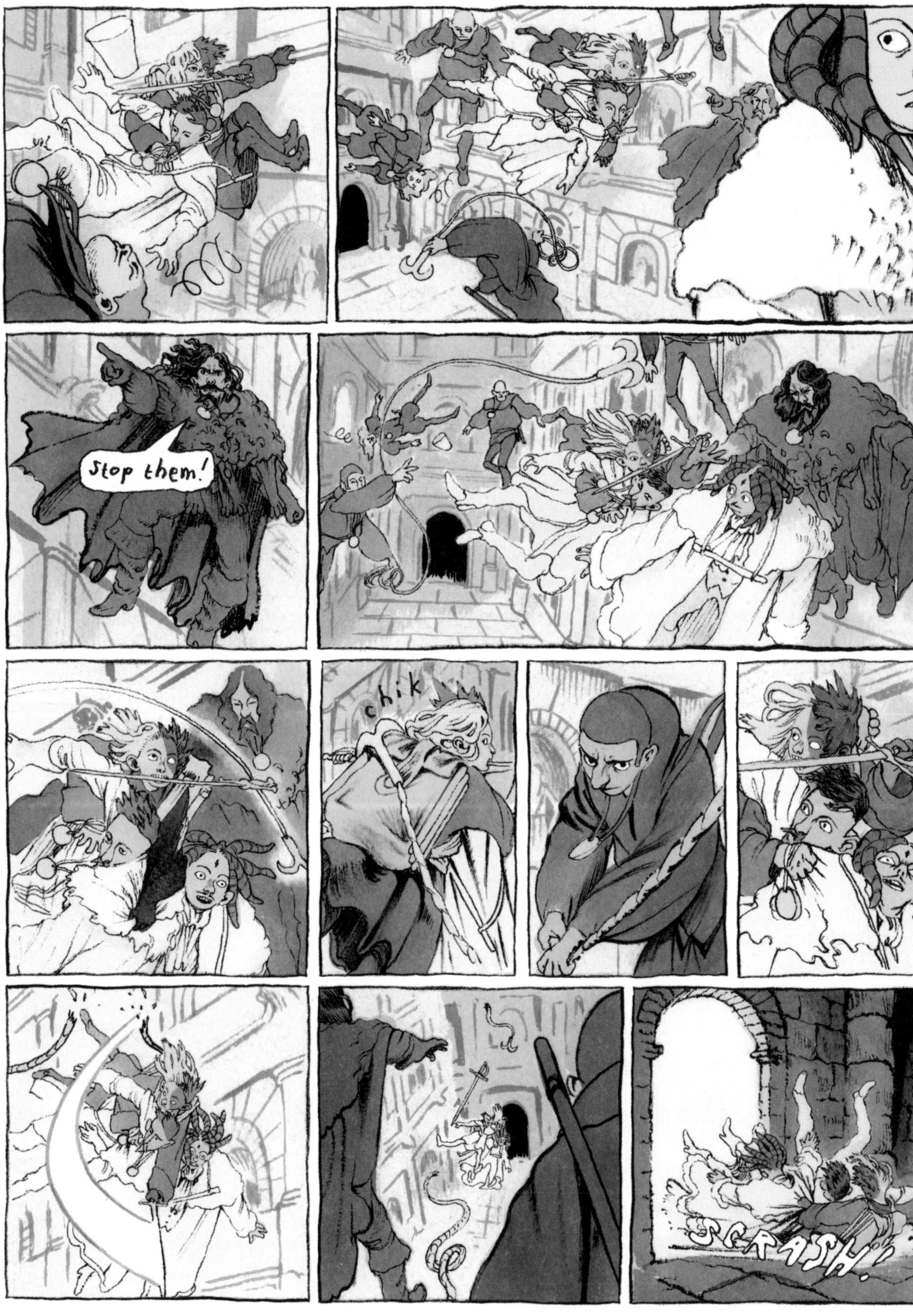
Stop them!
chik
SCRASH!

Run! Scatter yourselves! Don't let them catch you!

Didn't we just win their silly game?

We should take three of their coins. Those were the rules, weren't they?

Take no coins! Play no games!

Hide yourself and keep away from others!

Strange girl.

Woah!

Count Julius, come with me!

They escaped...

...does that mean?

Oof!

Ow!

····

THRUMP!!

I will not lose again, damn it!

Whatever it takes...

I will be the one.

Count Julius, listen!

That's three times I kept you in this! Now you do something for me...

Erm... of course... what is it you want me to do?

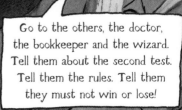

Go to the others, the doctor, the bookkeeper and the wizard. Tell them about the second test. Tell them the rules. Tell them they must not win or lose!

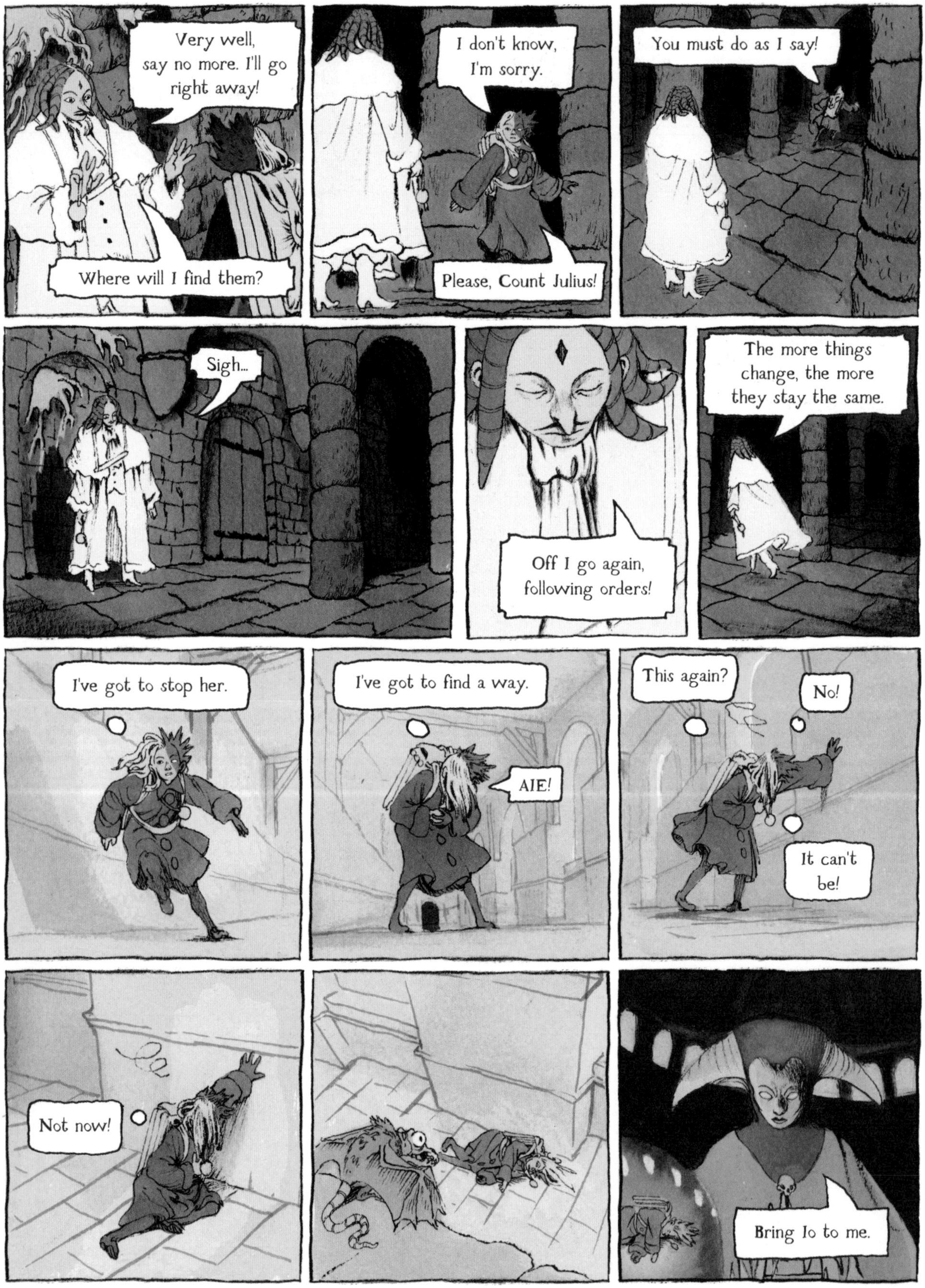
Very well, say no more. I'll go right away!
Where will I find them?
I don't know, I'm sorry.
Please, Count Julius!
You must do as I say!
Sigh...
Off I go again, following orders!
The more things change, the more they stay the same.
I've got to stop her.
I've got to find a way.
AIE!
This again?
No!
It can't be!
Not now!
Bring Io to me.

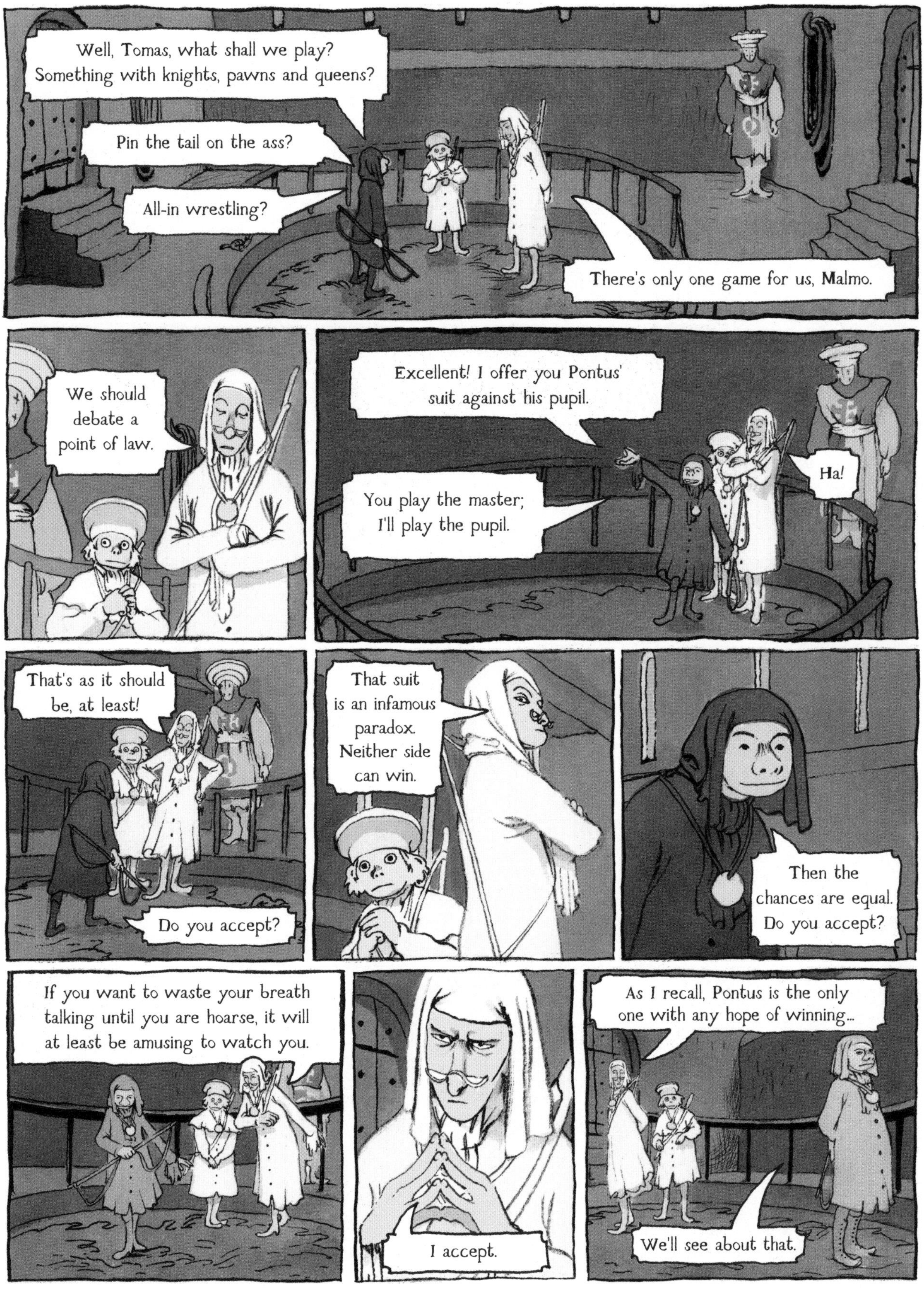
Well, Tomas, what shall we play? Something with knights, pawns and queens?
Pin the tail on the ass?
All-in wrestling?
There's only one game for us, Malmo.
We should debate a point of law.
Excellent! I offer you Pontus' suit against his pupil.
You play the master; I'll play the pupil.
Ha!
That's as it should be, at least!
Do you accept?
That suit is an infamous paradox. Neither side can win.
Then the chances are equal. Do you accept?
If you want to waste your breath talking until you are hoarse, it will at least be amusing to watch you.
I accept.
As I recall, Pontus is the only one with any hope of winning...
We'll see about that.

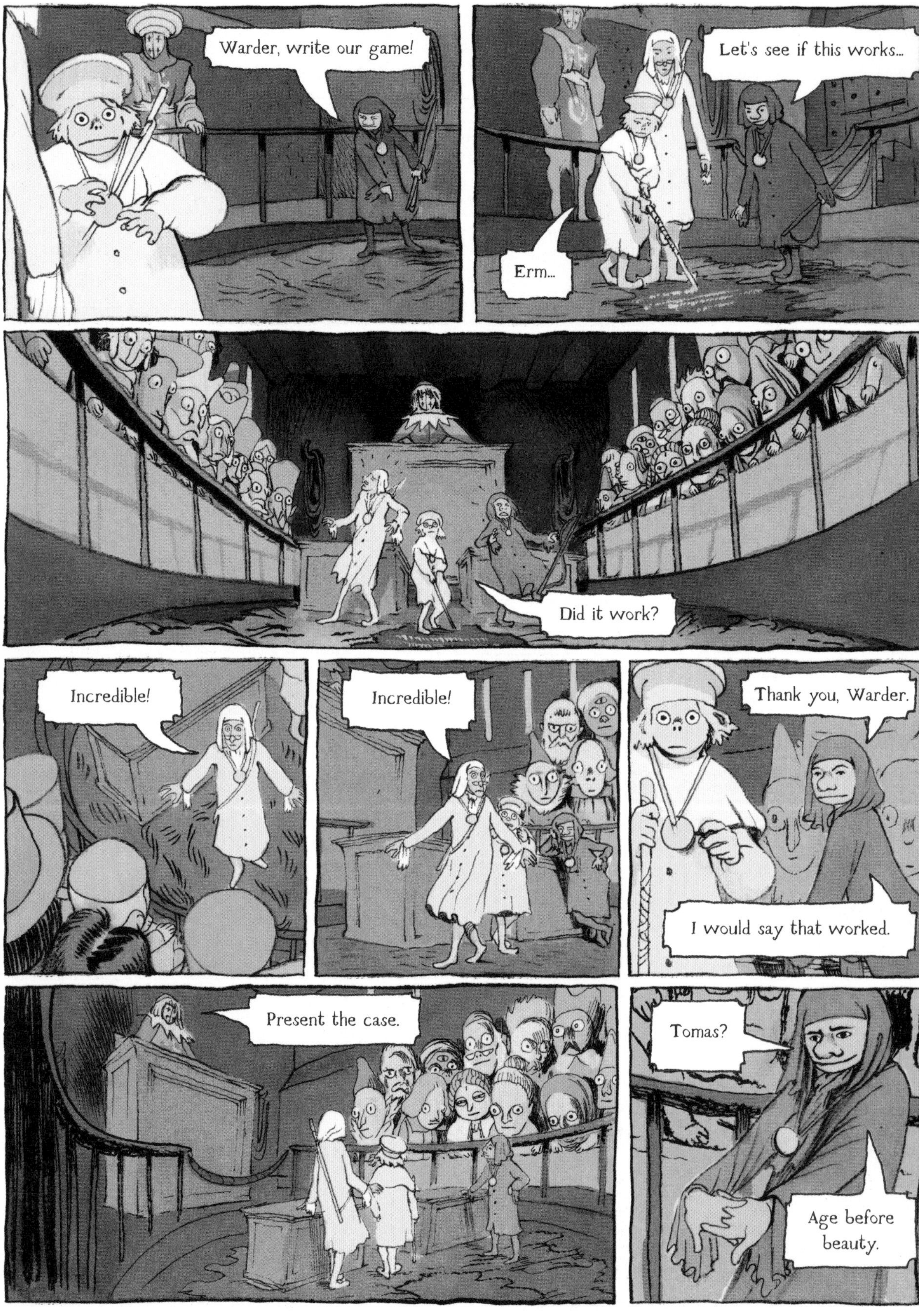
Warder, write our game!
Let's see if this works...
Erm...
Did it work?
Incredible!
Incredible!
Thank you, Warder.
I would say that worked.
Present the case.
Tomas?
Age before beauty.

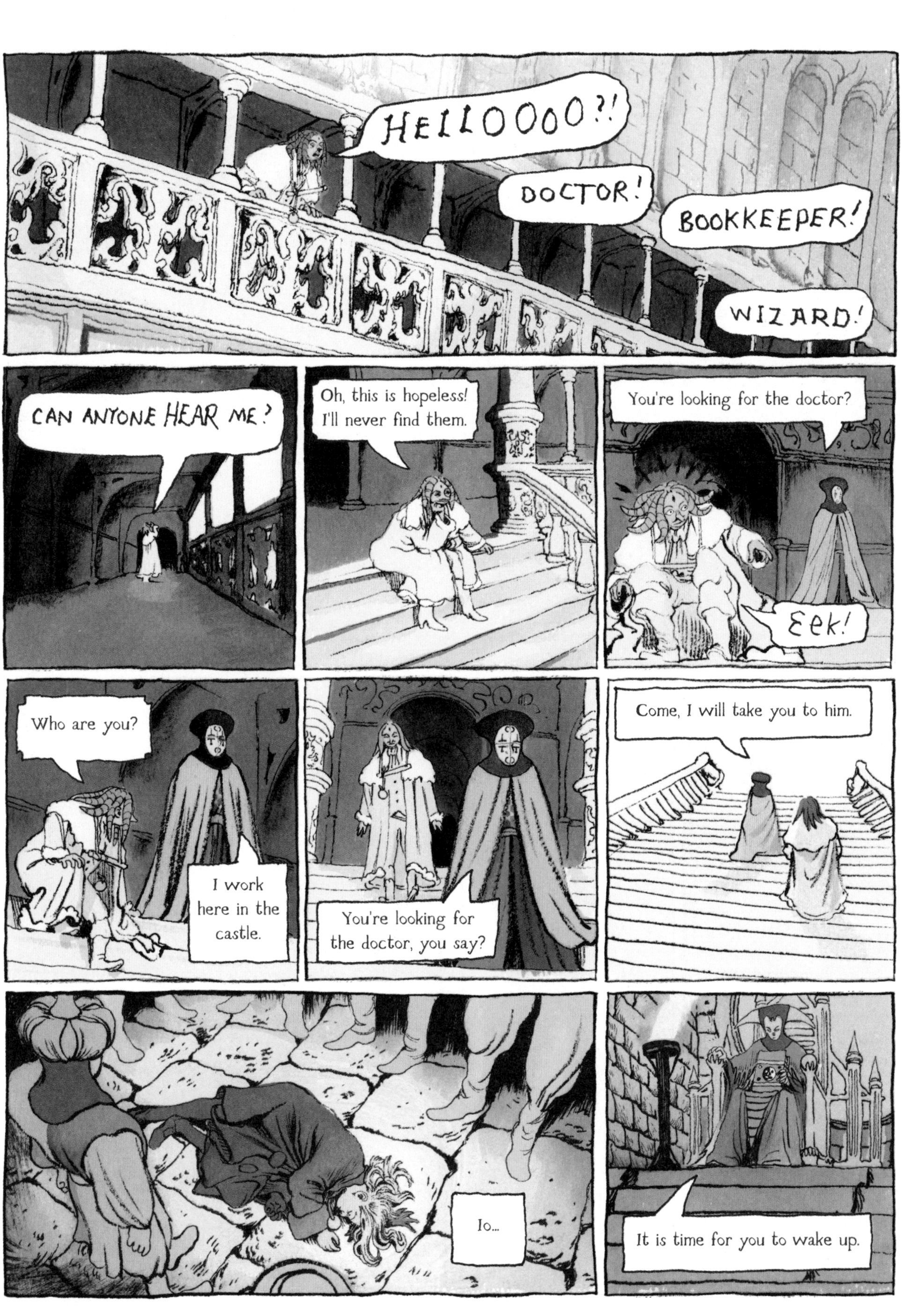
HELLOOOO?!
DOCTOR!
BOOKKEEPER!
WIZARD!
CAN ANYONE HEAR ME?
Oh, this is hopeless! I'll never find them.
You're looking for the doctor?
Eek!
Who are you?
I work here in the castle.
You're looking for the doctor, you say?
Come, I will take you to him.
Io...
It is time for you to wake up.

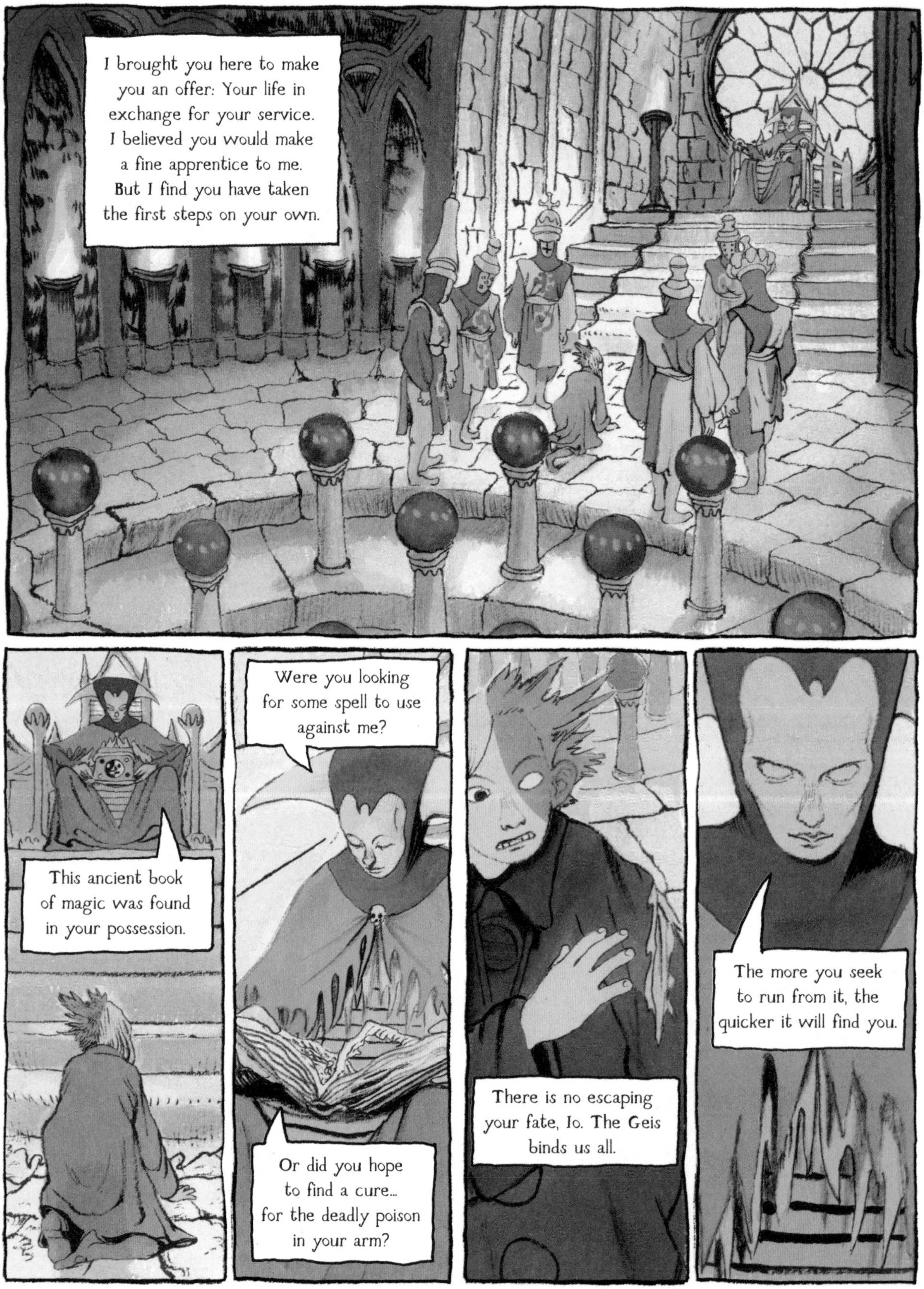
I brought you here to make you an offer: Your life in exchange for your service. I believed you would make a fine apprentice to me. But I find you have taken the first steps on your own.
This ancient book of magic was found in your possession.
Were you looking for some spell to use against me?
Or did you hope to find a cure... for the deadly poison in your arm?
There is no escaping your fate, Io. The Geis binds us all.
The more you seek to run from it, the quicker it will find you.

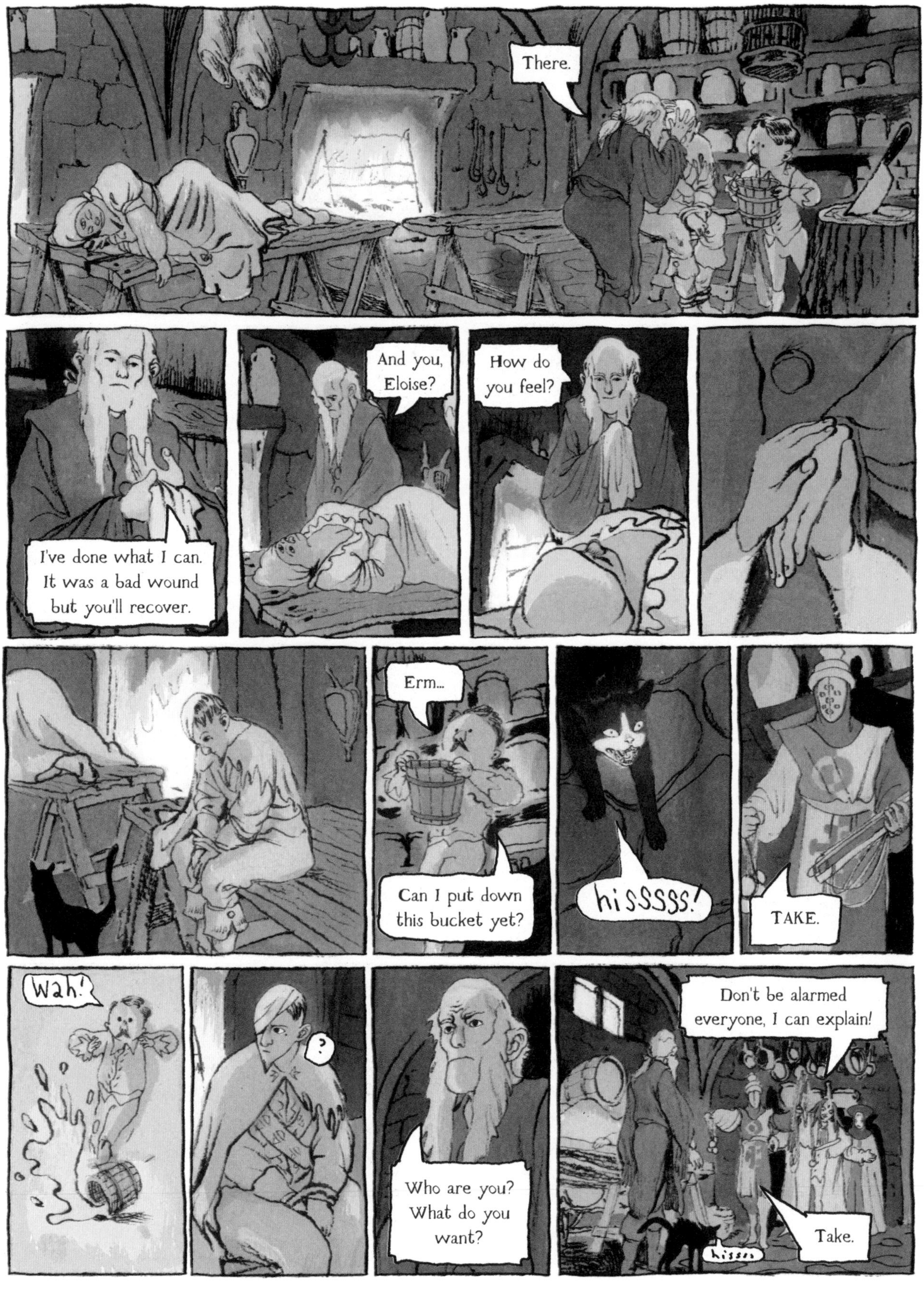

There.
I've done what I can.
It was a bad wound
but you'll recover.
And you,
Eloise?
How do
you feel?
Erm...
Can I put down
this bucket yet?
hisssss!
TAKE.
Wah!
?
Who are you?
What do you
want?
Don't be alarmed
everyone, I can explain!
Take.
hissss

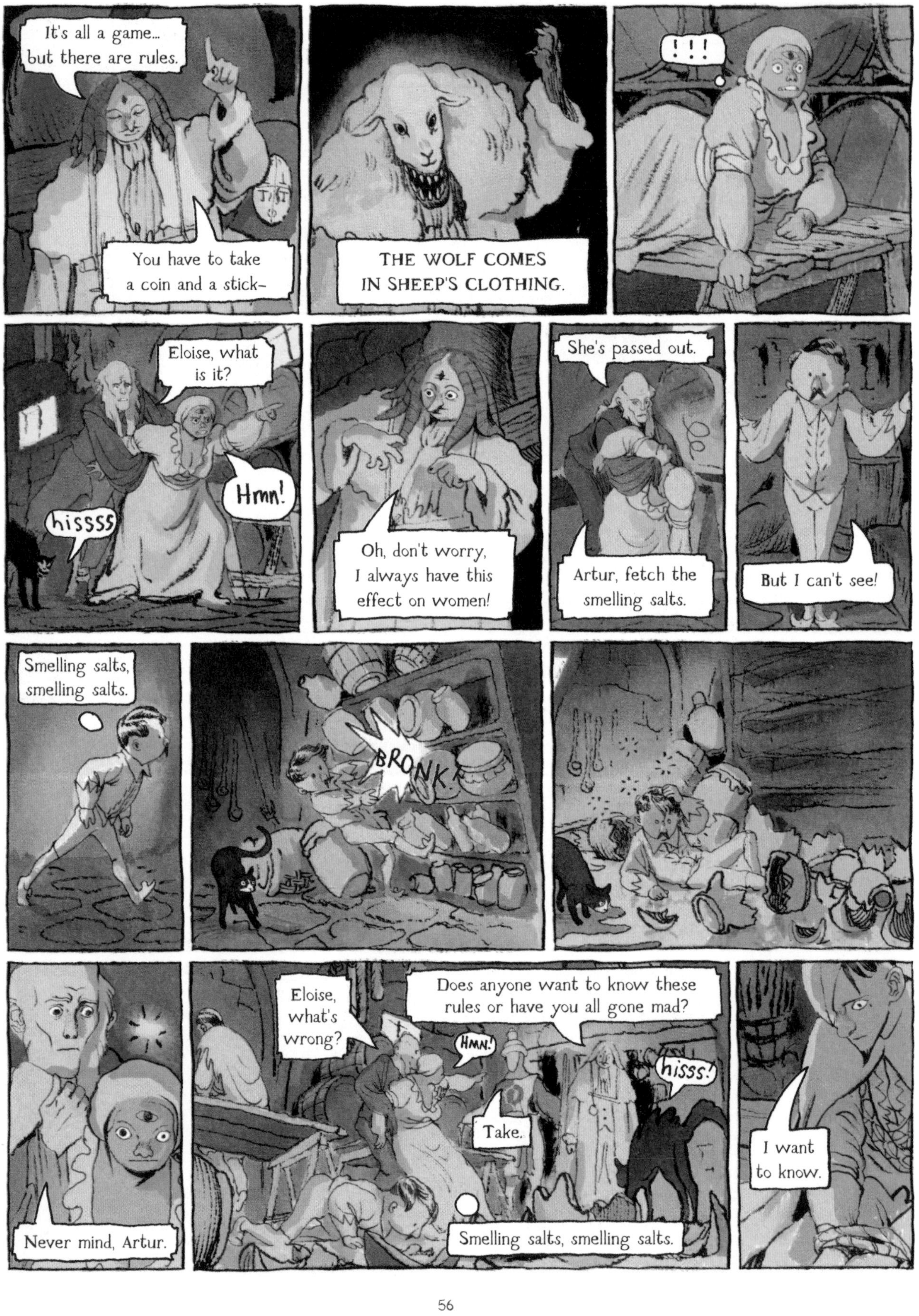

It's all a game... but there are rules.
You have to take a coin and a stick–
THE WOLF COMES IN SHEEP'S CLOTHING.
! ! !
Eloise, what is it?
hissss
Hmn!
Oh, don't worry, I always have this effect on women!
She's passed out.
Artur, fetch the smelling salts.
But I can't see!
Smelling salts, smelling salts.
BRONK!
Never mind, Artur.
Eloise, what's wrong?
Does anyone want to know these rules or have you all gone mad?
HMN!
hisss!
Take.
Smelling salts, smelling salts.
I want to know.

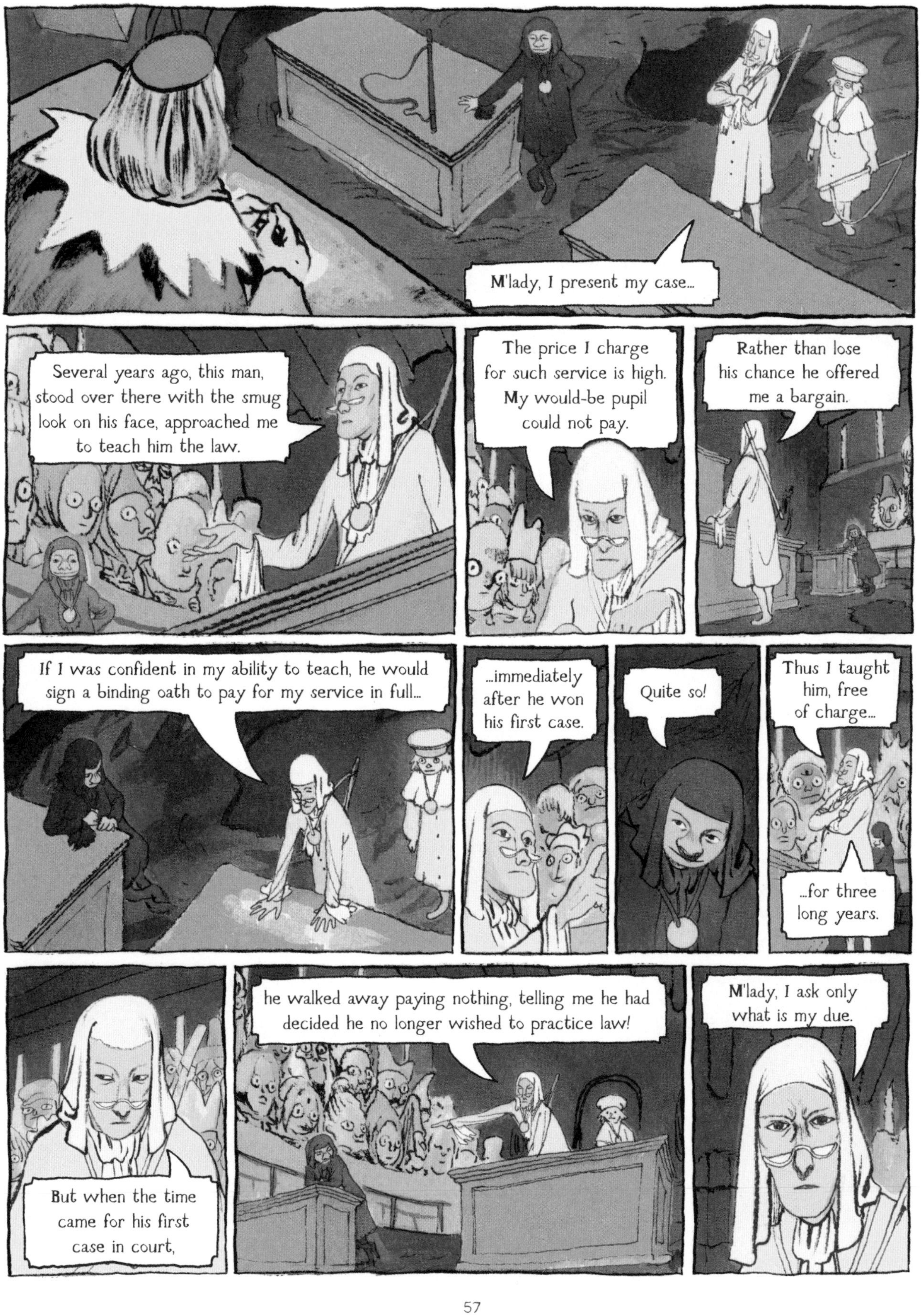
M'lady, I present my case...
Several years ago, this man, stood over there with the smug look on his face, approached me to teach him the law.
The price I charge for such service is high. My would-be pupil could not pay.
Rather than lose his chance he offered me a bargain.
If I was confident in my ability to teach, he would sign a binding oath to pay for my service in full...
...immediately after he won his first case.
Quite so!
Thus I taught him, free of charge...
...for three long years.
But when the time came for his first case in court,
he walked away paying nothing, telling me he had decided he no longer wished to practice law!
M'lady, I ask only what is my due.

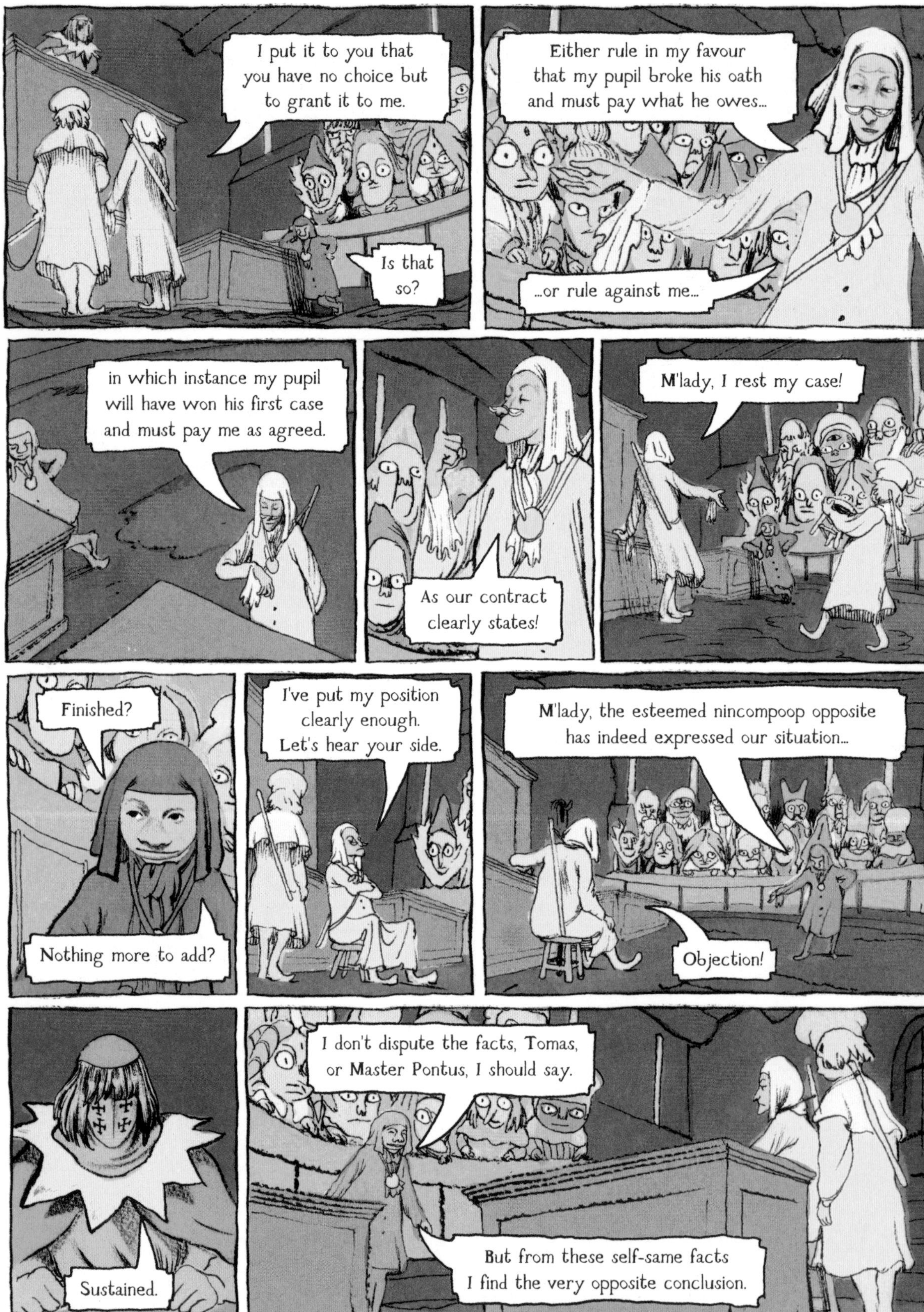
I put it to you that you have no choice but to grant it to me.
Is that so?
Either rule in my favour that my pupil broke his oath and must pay what he owes...
...or rule against me...
in which instance my pupil will have won his first case and must pay me as agreed.
As our contract clearly states!
M'lady, I rest my case!
Finished?
Nothing more to add?
I've put my position clearly enough. Let's hear your side.
M'lady, the esteemed nincompoop opposite has indeed expressed our situation...
Objection!
Sustained.
I don't dispute the facts, Tomas, or Master Pontus, I should say.
But from these self-same facts I find the very opposite conclusion.

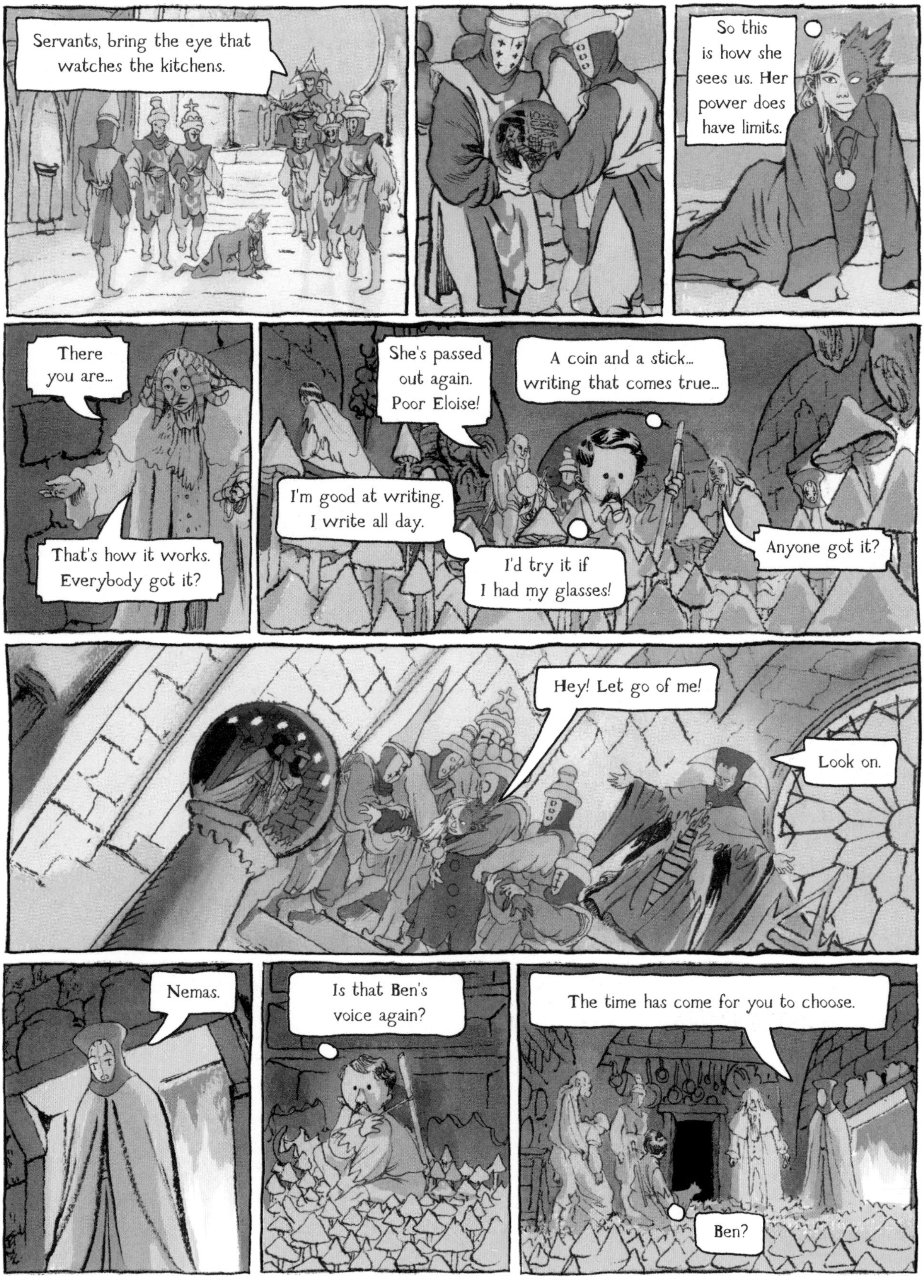
Servants, bring the eye that watches the kitchens.
So this is how she sees us. Her power does have limits.
There you are...
That's how it works. Everybody got it?
She's passed out again. Poor Eloise!
A coin and a stick... writing that comes true...
I'm good at writing. I write all day.
I'd try it if I had my glasses!
Anyone got it?
Hey! Let go of me!
Look on.
Nemas.
Is that Ben's voice again?
The time has come for you to choose.
Ben?

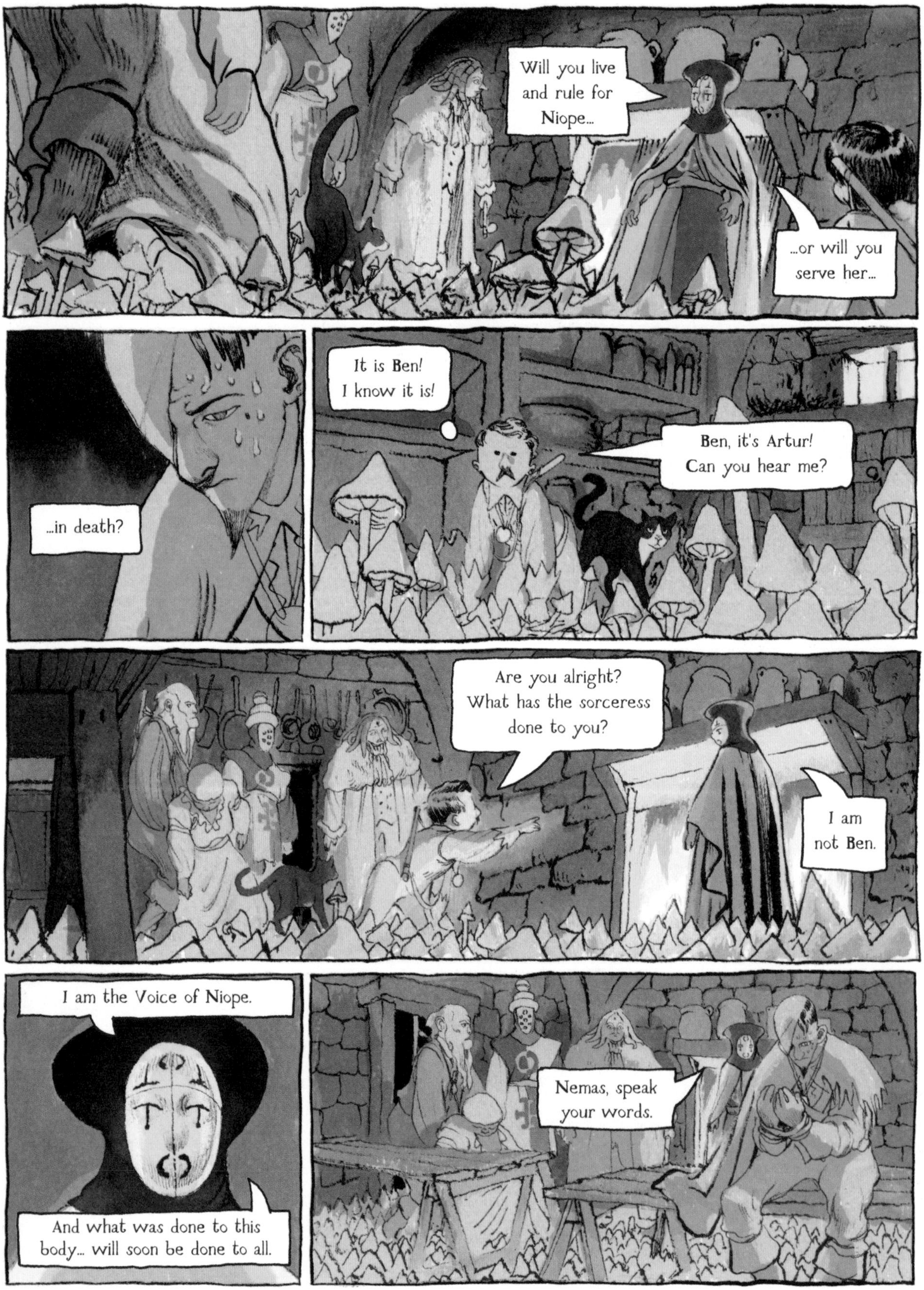

Will you live and rule for Niope...
...or will you serve her...
...in death?
It is Ben! I know it is!
Ben, it's Artur! Can you hear me?
Are you alright? What has the sorceress done to you?
I am not Ben.
I am the Voice of Niope.
And what was done to this body... will soon be done to all.
Nemas, speak your words.

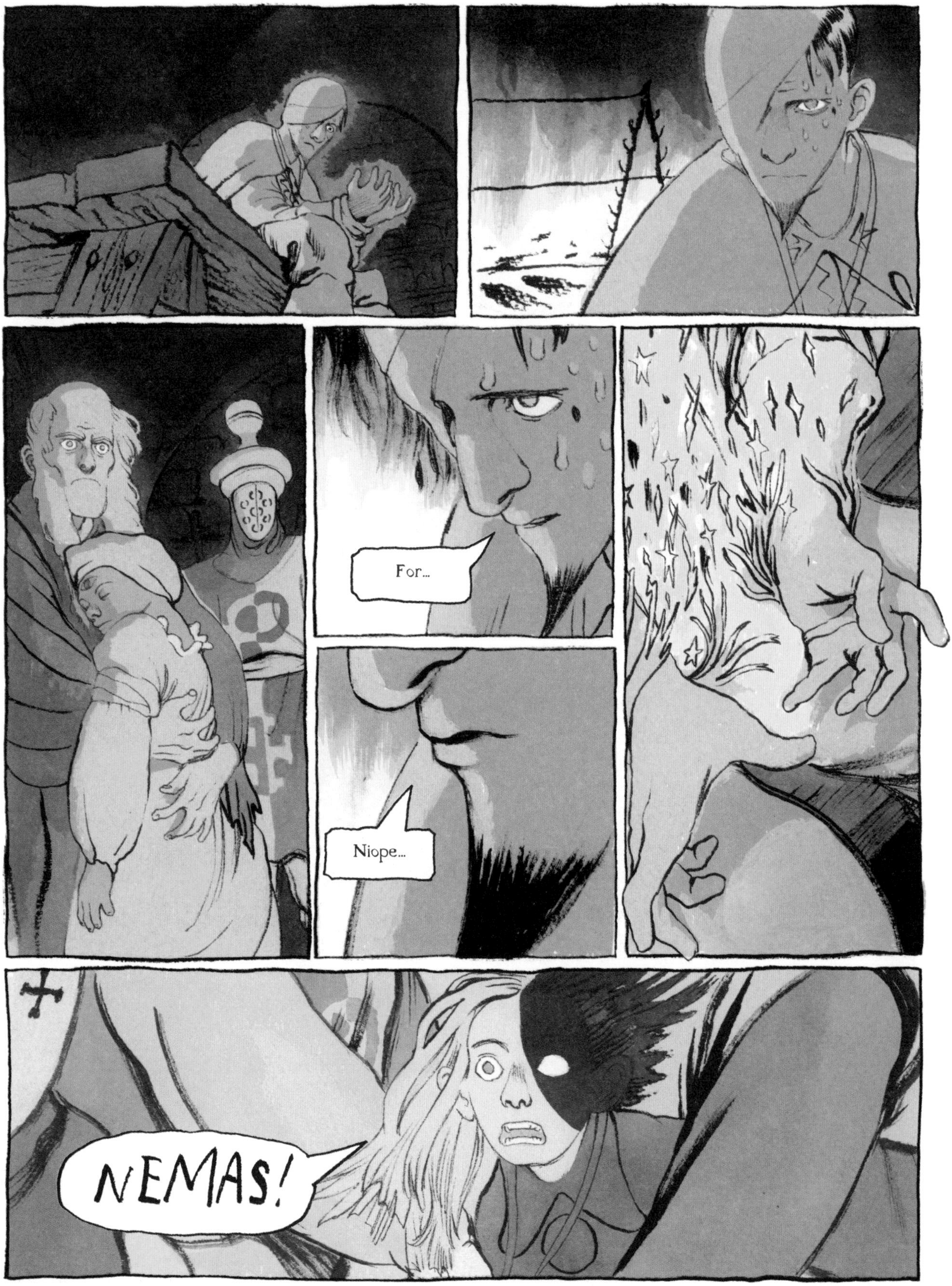
For...
Niope...
NEMAS!

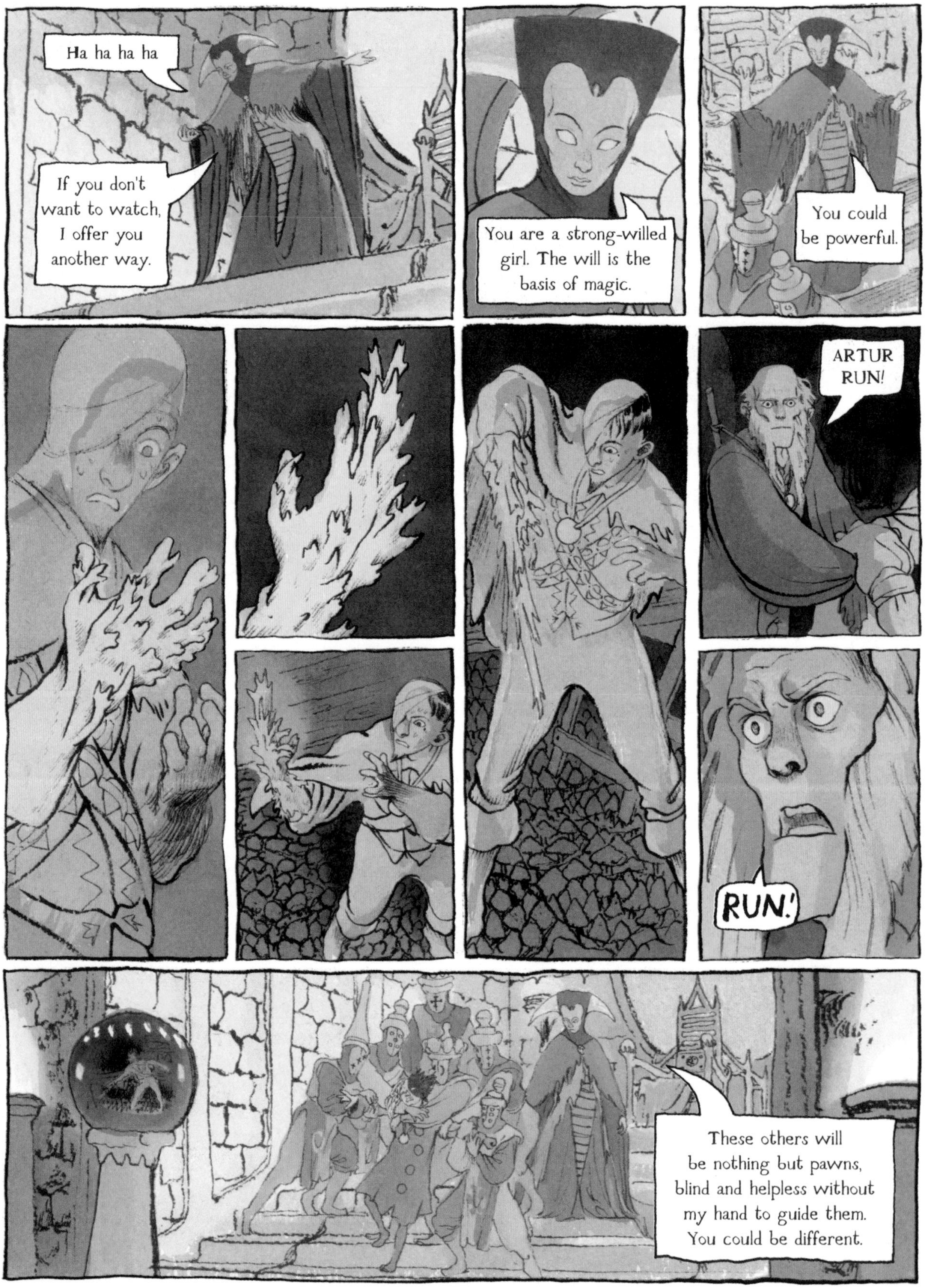

Ha ha ha ha
If you don't want to watch, I offer you another way.
You are a strong-willed girl. The will is the basis of magic.
You could be powerful.
ARTUR RUN!
RUN!
These others will be nothing but pawns, blind and helpless without my hand to guide them. You could be different.

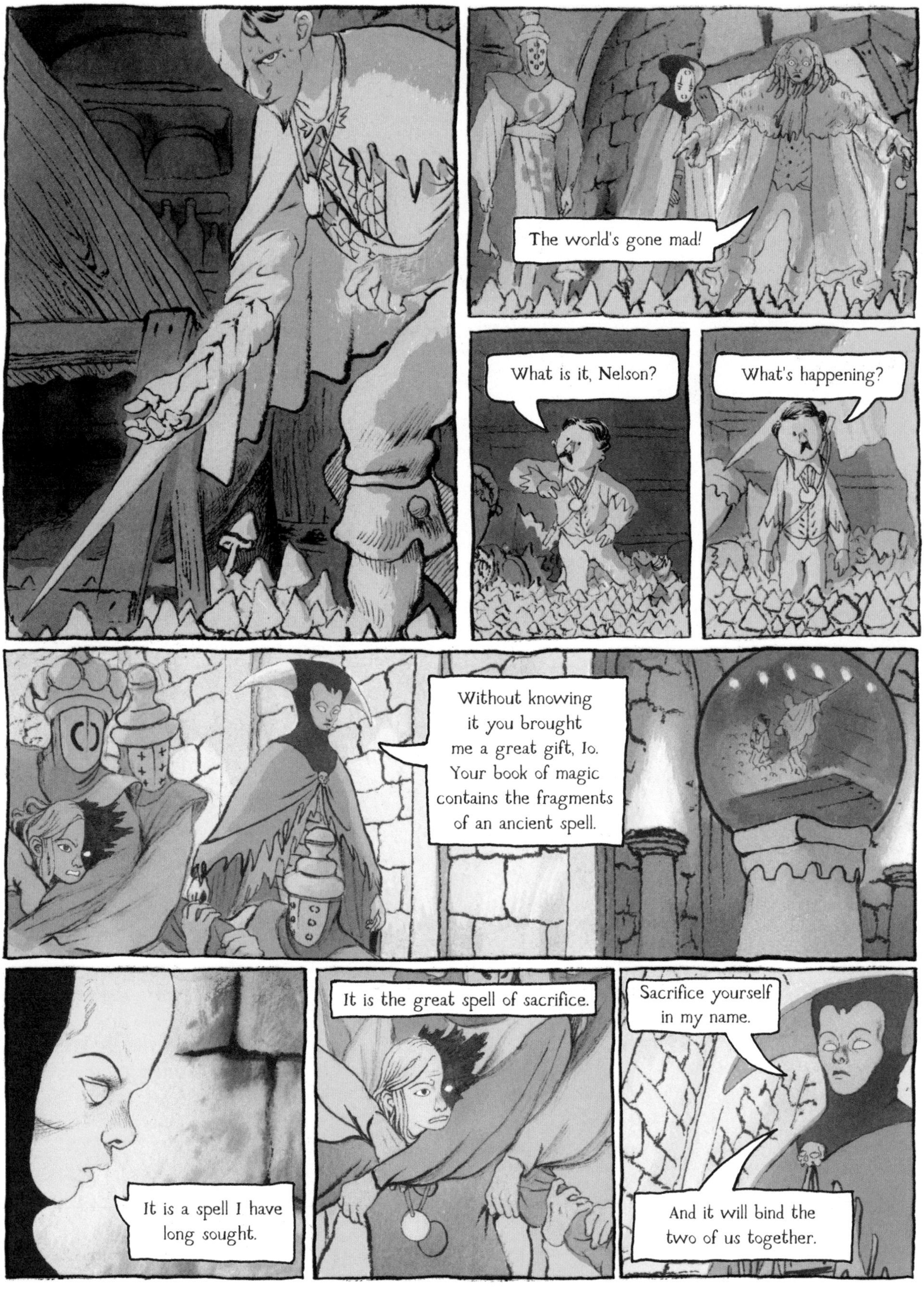

The world's gone mad!
What is it, Nelson?
What's happening?
Without knowing it you brought me a great gift, Io. Your book of magic contains the fragments of an ancient spell.
It is a spell I have long sought.
It is the great spell of sacrifice.
Sacrifice yourself in my name.
And it will bind the two of us together.

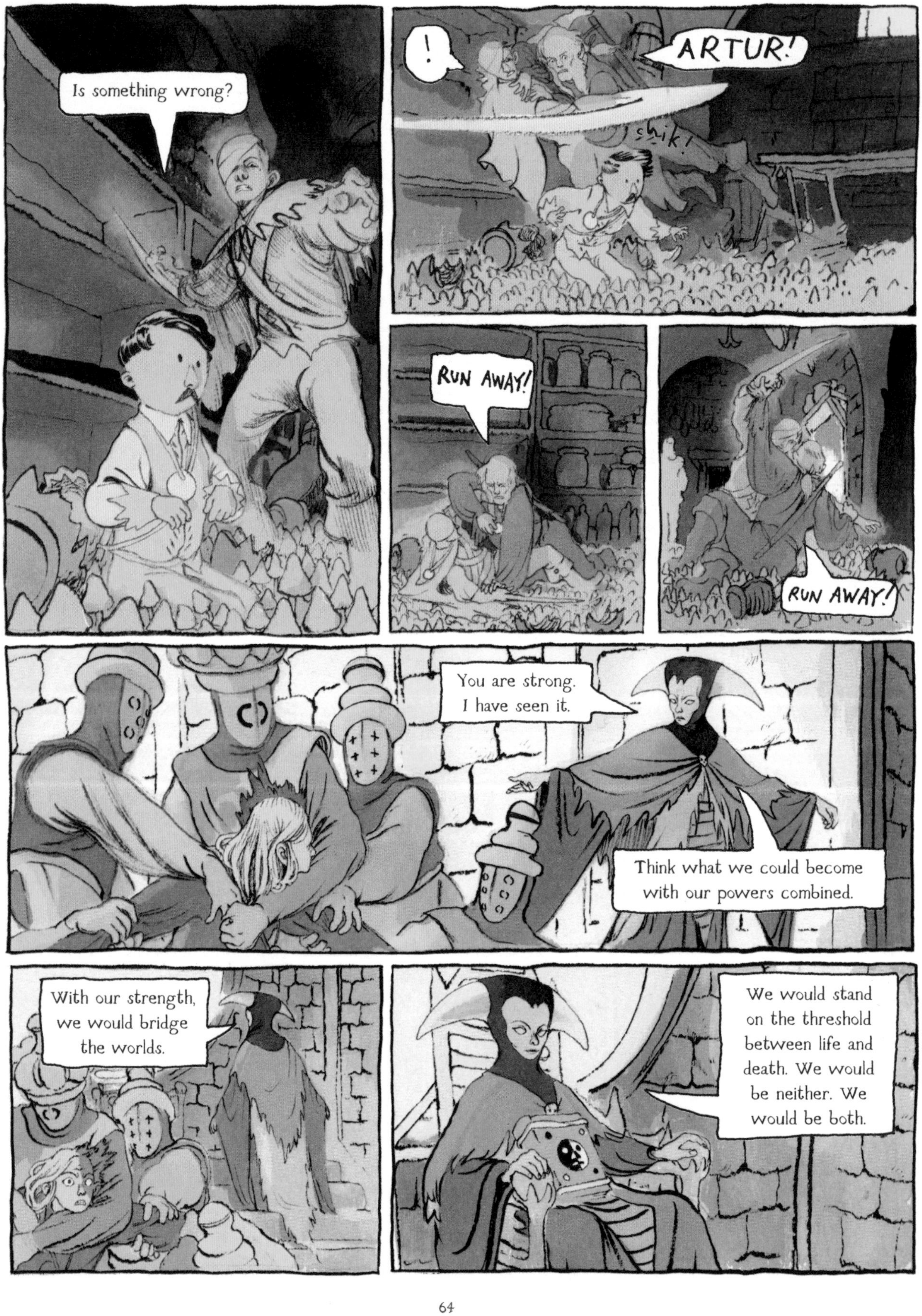

Is something wrong?
!
ARTUR!
shik!
RUN AWAY!
RUN AWAY!
You are strong. I have seen it.
Think what we could become with our powers combined.
With our strength, we would bridge the worlds.
We would stand on the threshold between life and death. We would be neither. We would be both.

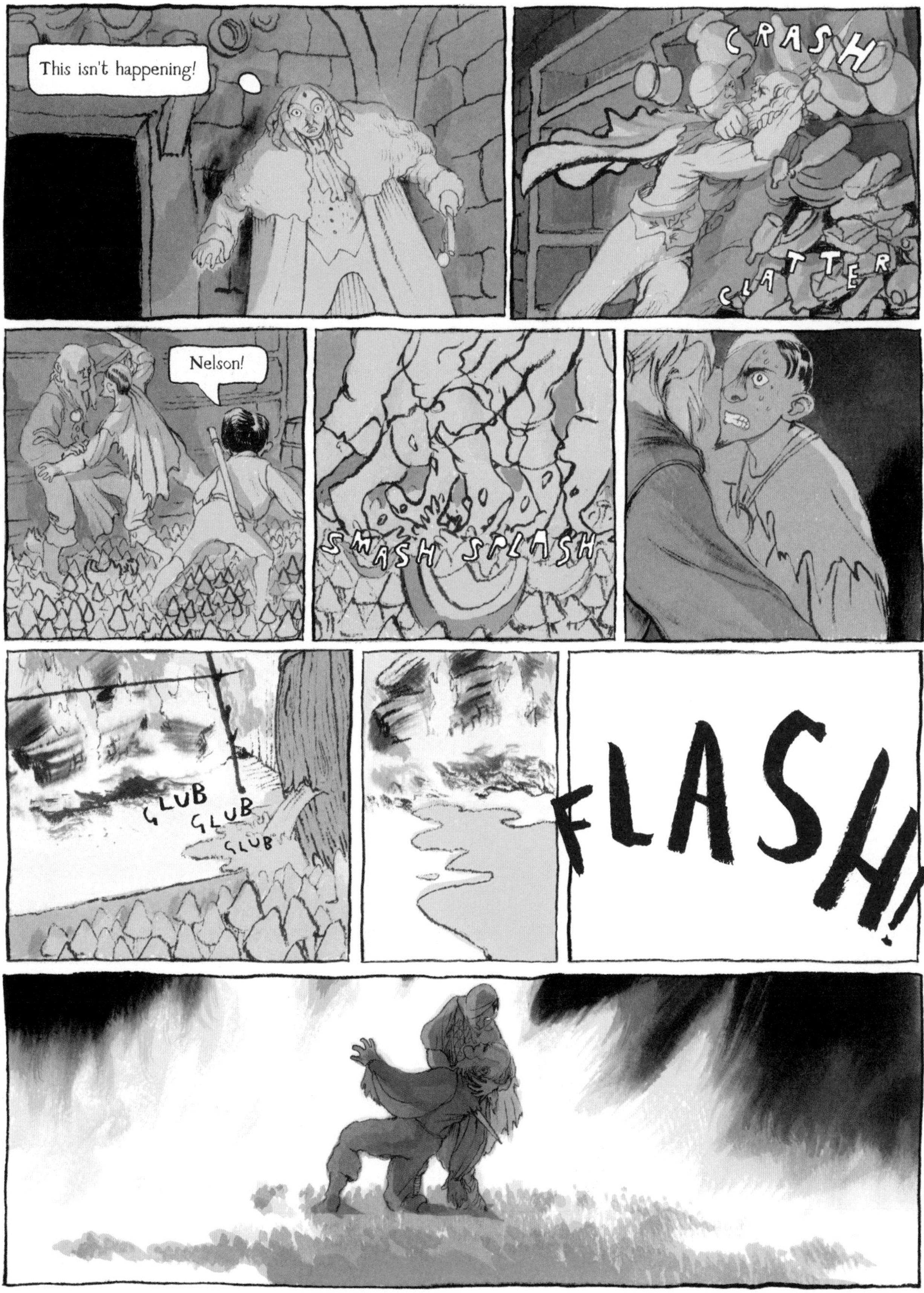
This isn't happening!
CRASH
CLATTER
Nelson!
SMASH SPLASH
GLUB
GLUB
GLUB
FLASH!

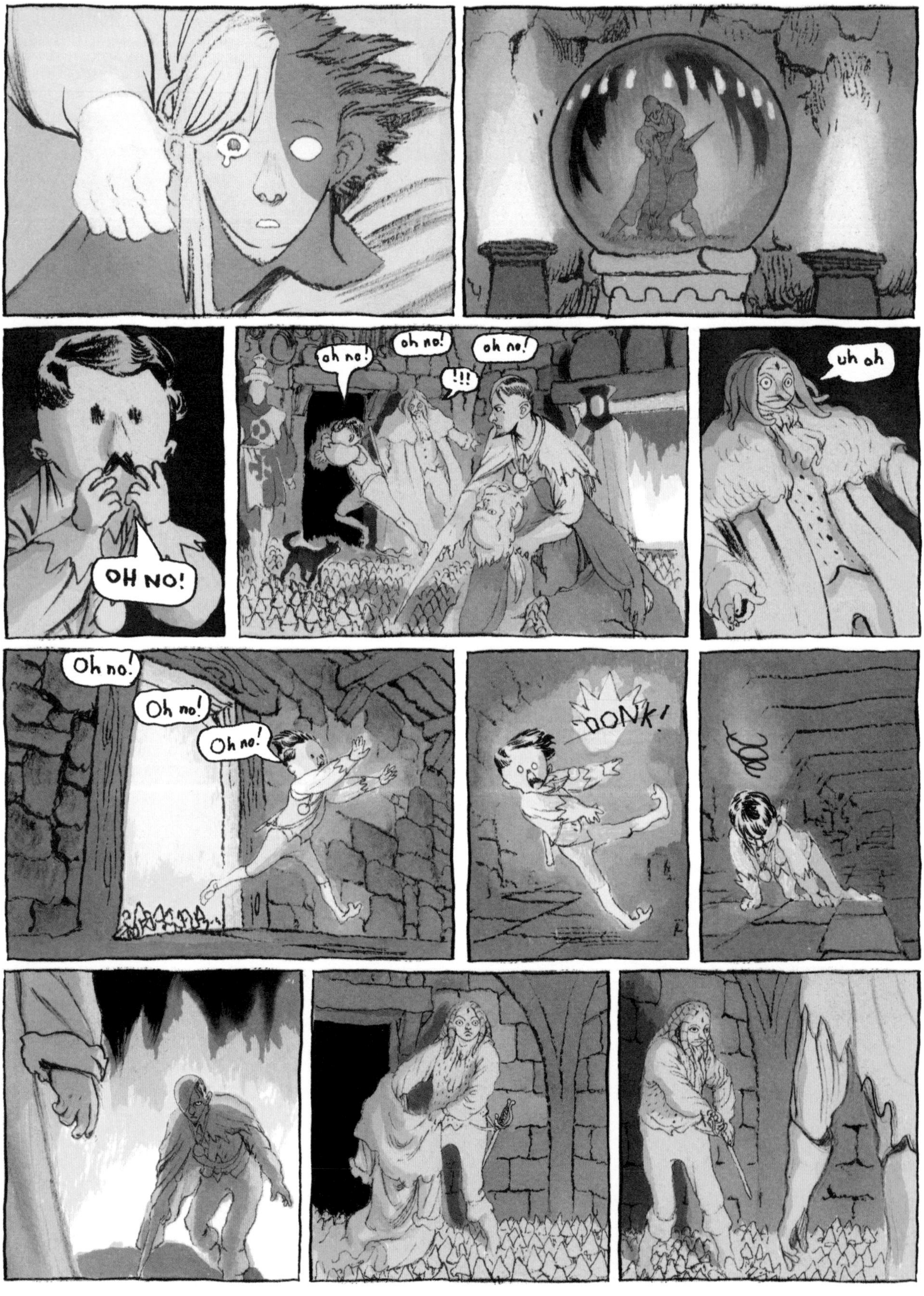

OH NO!
oh no!
oh no!
oh no!
!!!
uh oh
Oh no!
Oh no!
Oh no!
DONK!

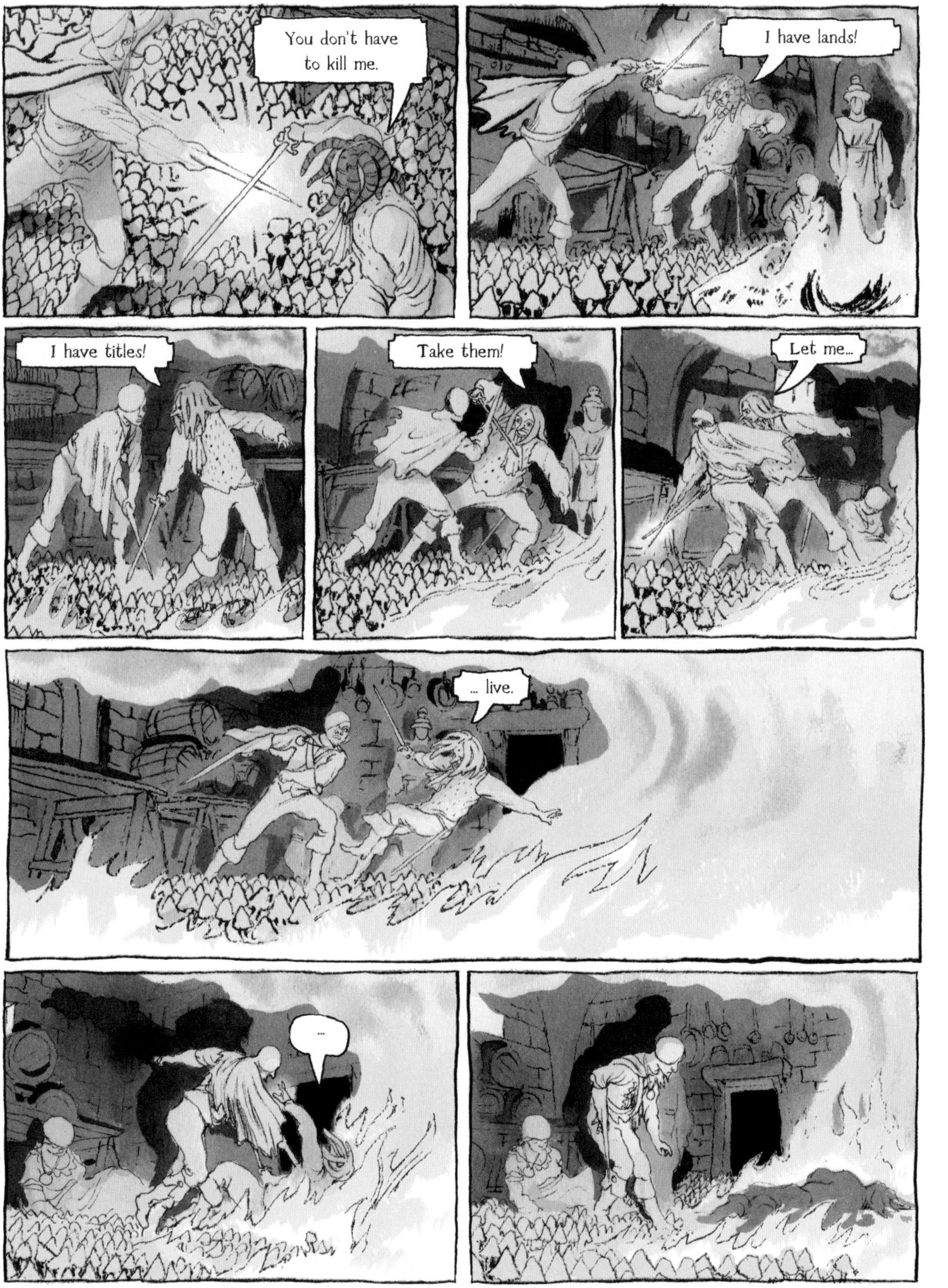

You don't have to kill me.
I have lands!
I have titles!
Take them!
Let me...
... live.
...

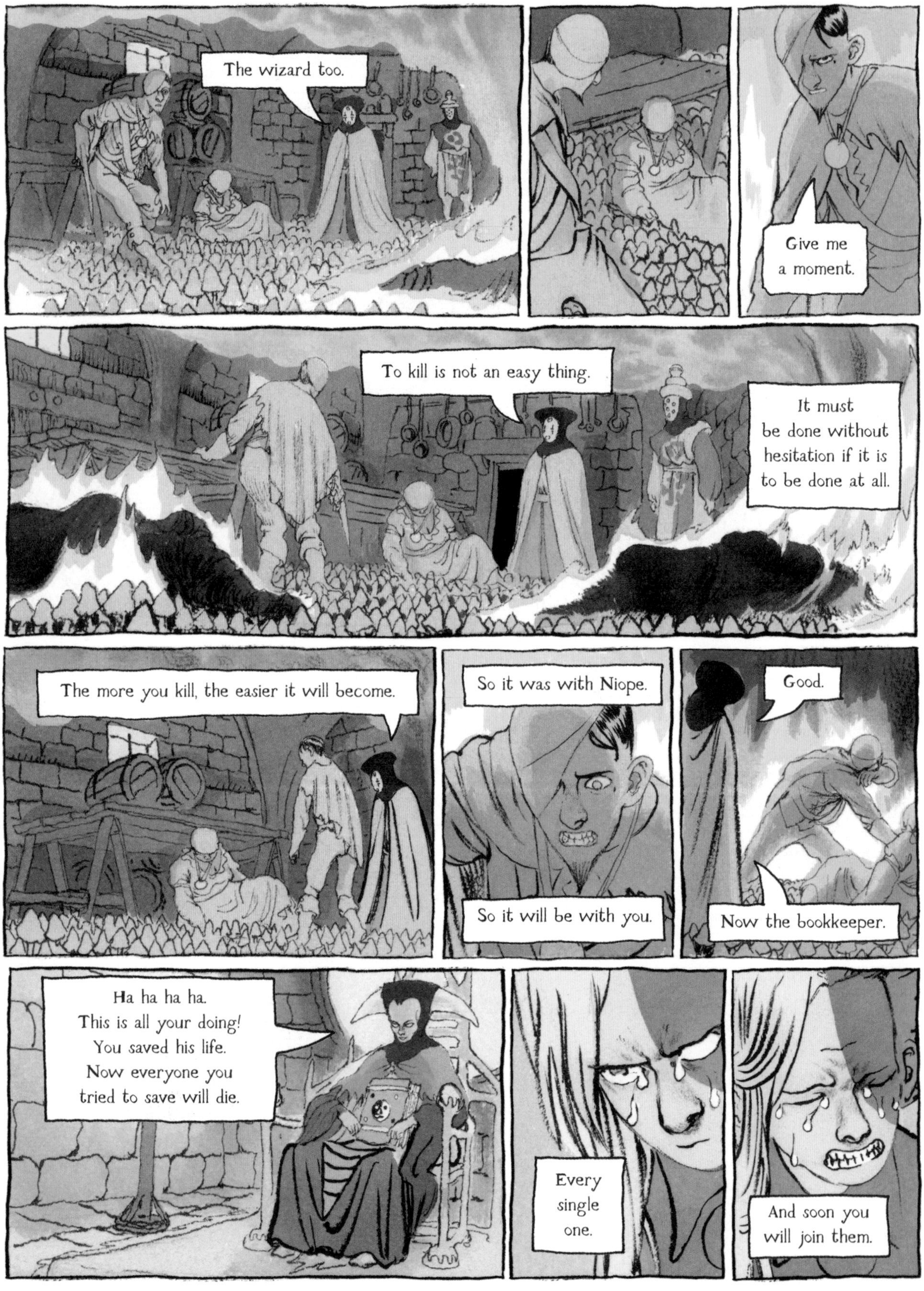
The wizard too.
Give me a moment.
To kill is not an easy thing.
It must be done without hesitation if it is to be done at all.
The more you kill, the easier it will become.
So it was with Niope.
So it will be with you.
Good.
Now the bookkeeper.
Ha ha ha ha. This is all your doing! You saved his life. Now everyone you tried to save will die.
Every single one.
And soon you will join them.

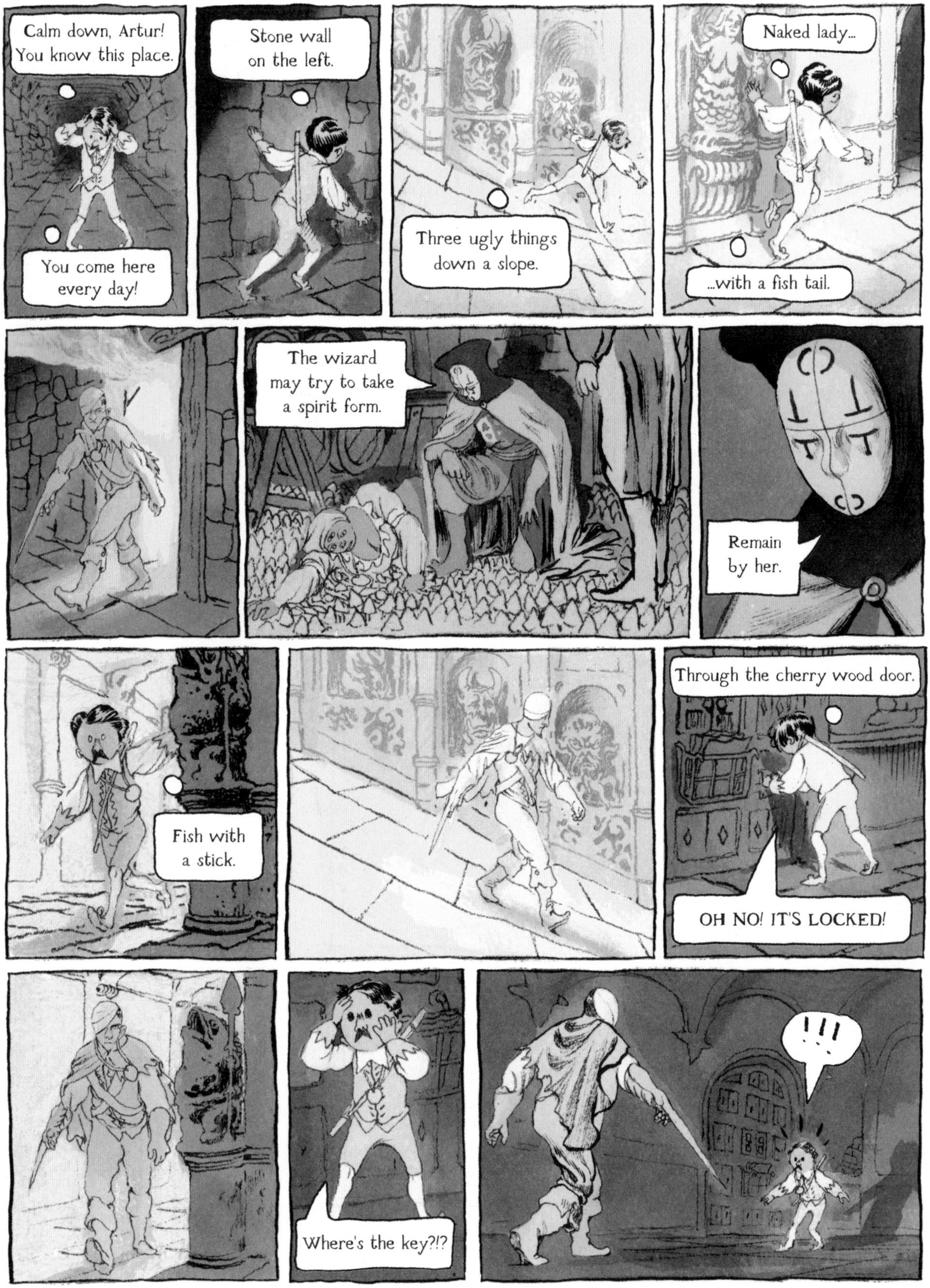
Calm down, Artur! You know this place.
You come here every day!
Stone wall on the left.
Three ugly things down a slope.
Naked lady...
...with a fish tail.
The wizard may try to take a spirit form.
Remain by her.
Fish with a stick.
Through the cherry wood door.
OH NO! IT'S LOCKED!
Where's the key?!?
!!!

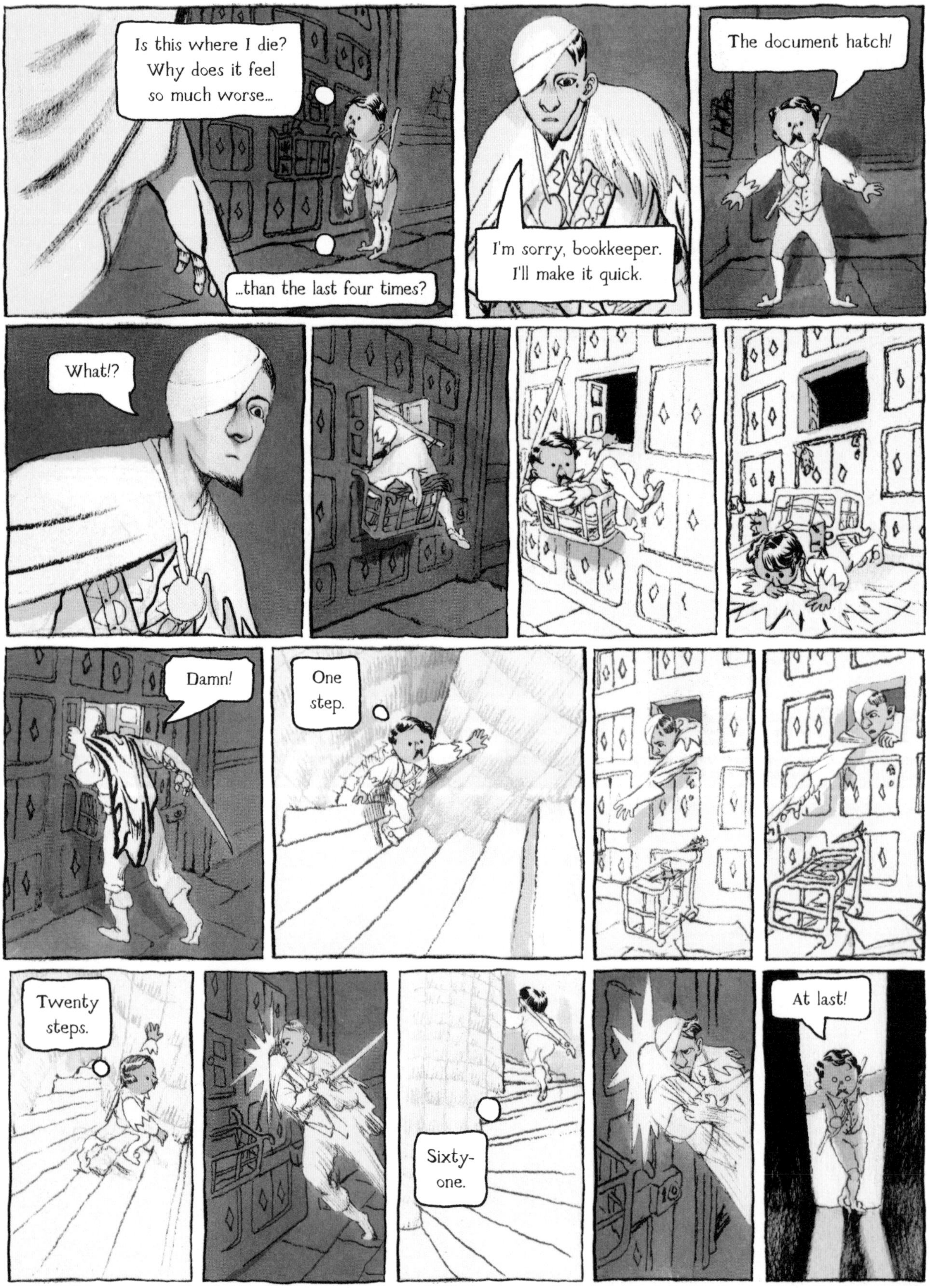
Is this where I die? Why does it feel so much worse...
...than the last four times?
I'm sorry, bookkeeper. I'll make it quick.
The document hatch!
What!?
Damn!
One step.
Twenty steps.
Sixty-one.
At last!

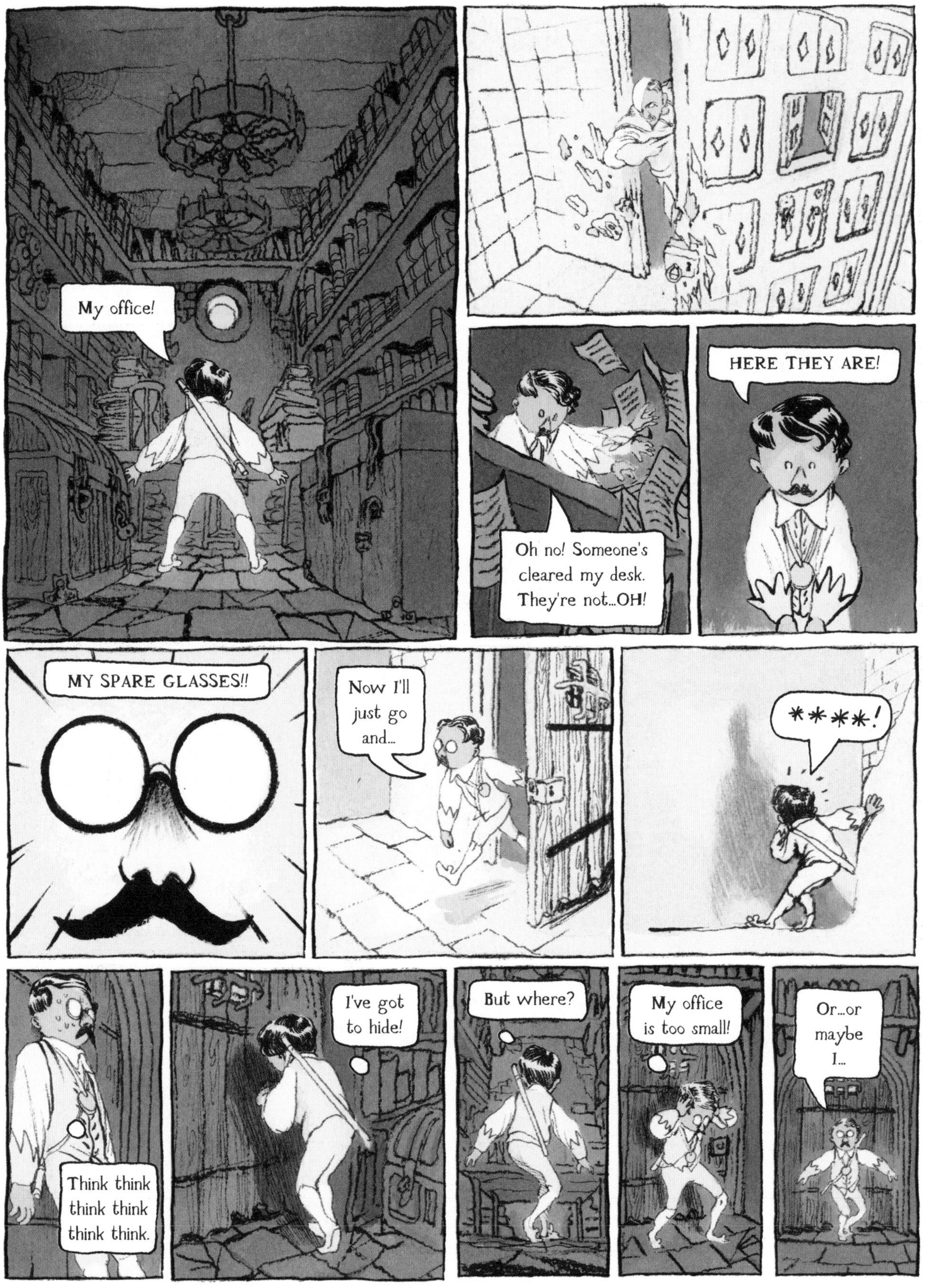
My office!
Oh no! Someone's cleared my desk. They're not...OH!
HERE THEY ARE!
MY SPARE GLASSES!!
Now I'll just go and...
****!
Think think think think think think.
I've got to hide!
But where?
My office is too small!
Or...or maybe I...

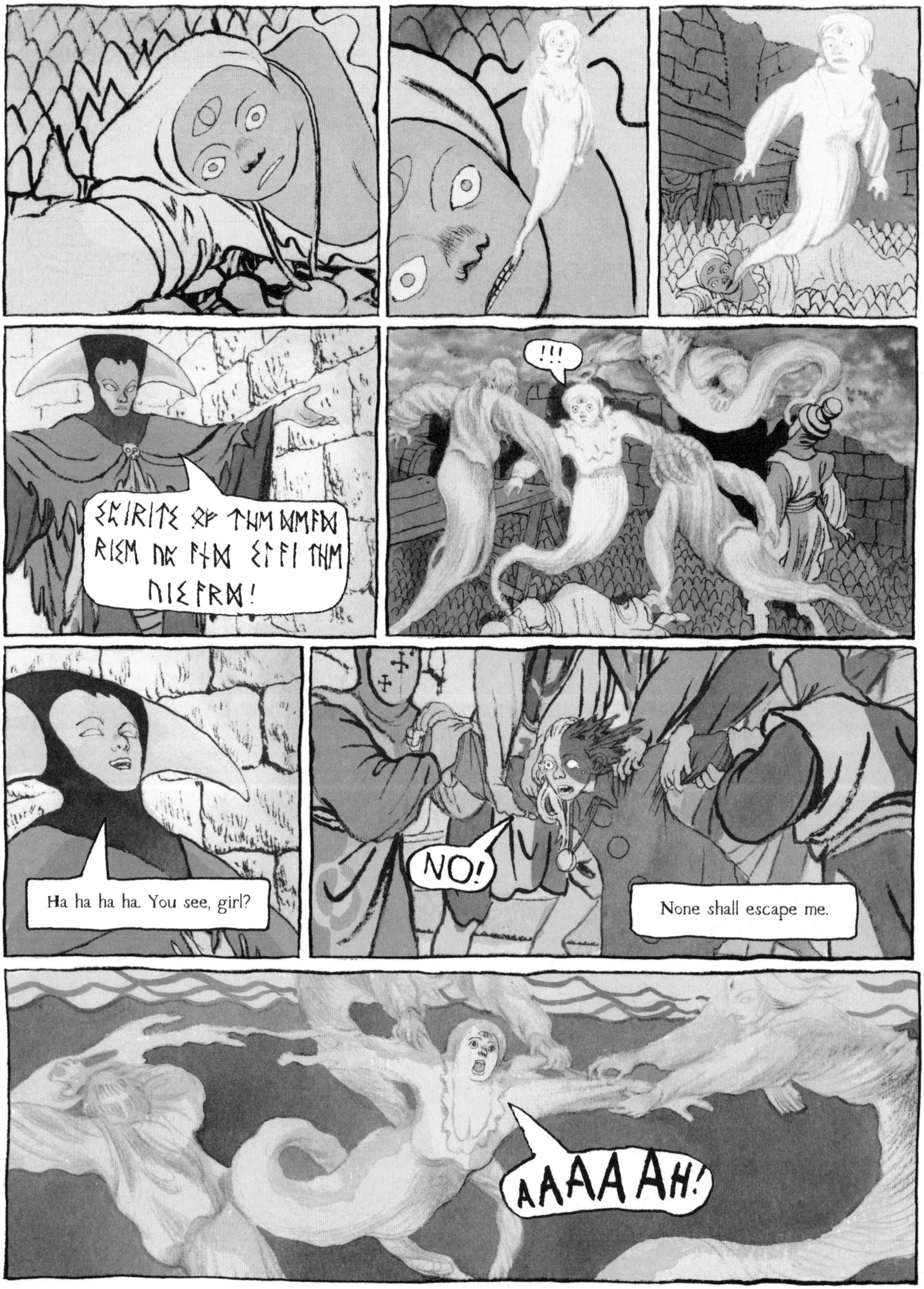
!!!
Ha ha ha ha. You see, girl?
NO!
None shall escape me.
AAAAAH!

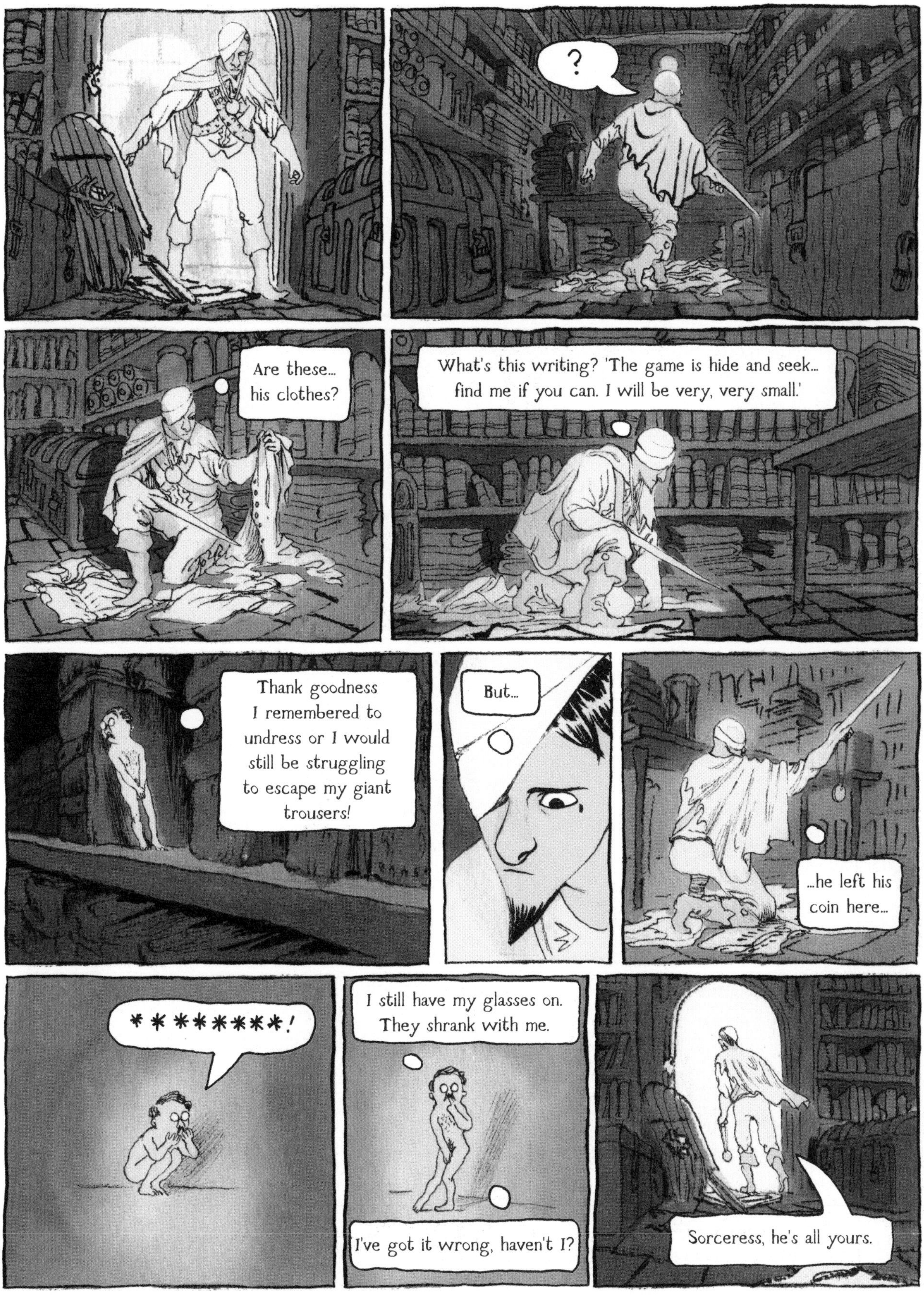
?
Are these... his clothes?
What's this writing? 'The game is hide and seek... find me if you can. I will be very, very small.'
Thank goodness I remembered to undress or I would still be struggling to escape my giant trousers!
But...
...he left his coin here...
* * * * * * * * !
I still have my glasses on. They shrank with me.
I've got it wrong, haven't I?
Sorceress, he's all yours.

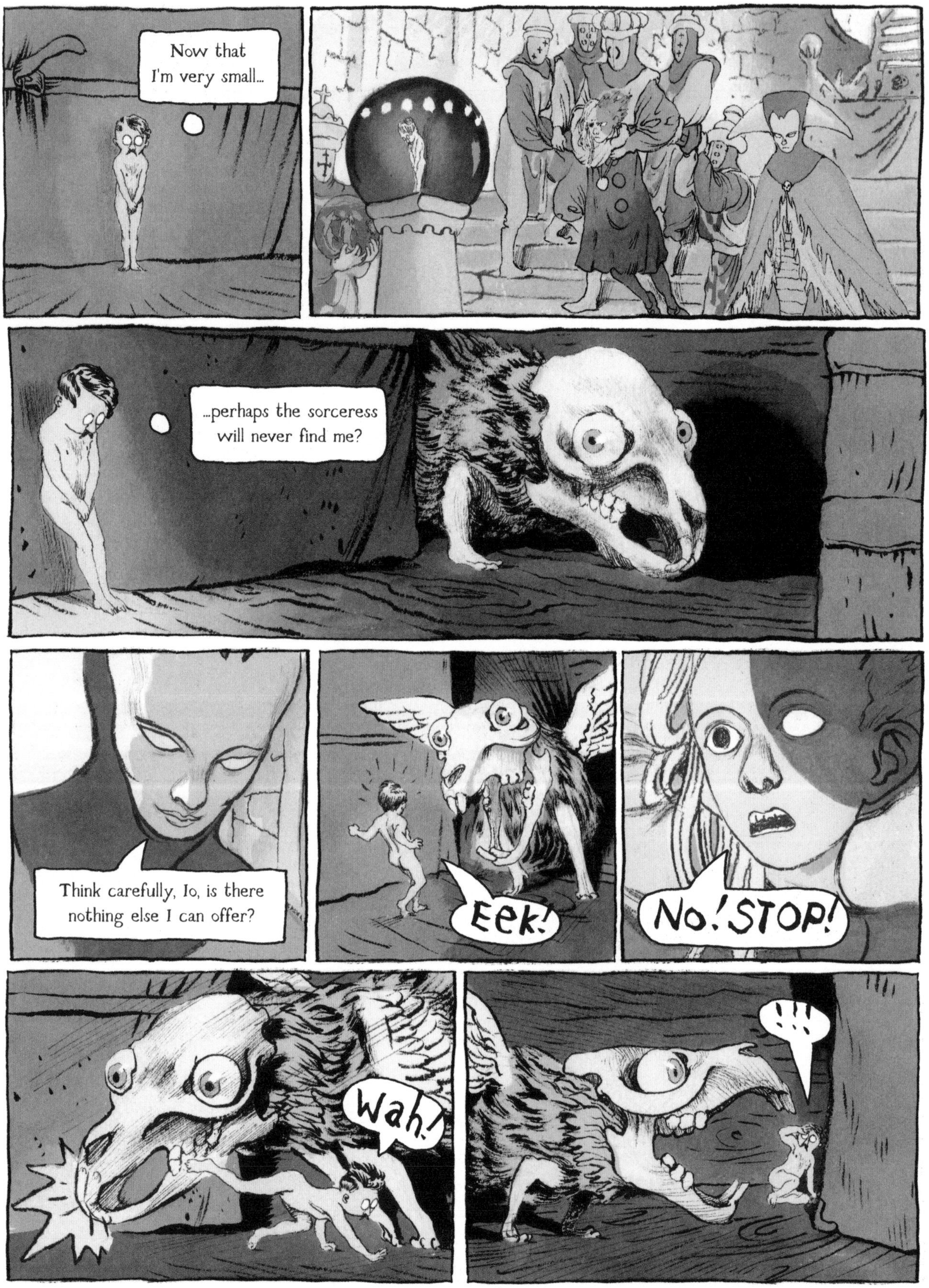
Now that I'm very small...
...perhaps the sorceress will never find me?
Think carefully, Io, is there nothing else I can offer?
Eek!
No! STOP!
Wah!
!!!

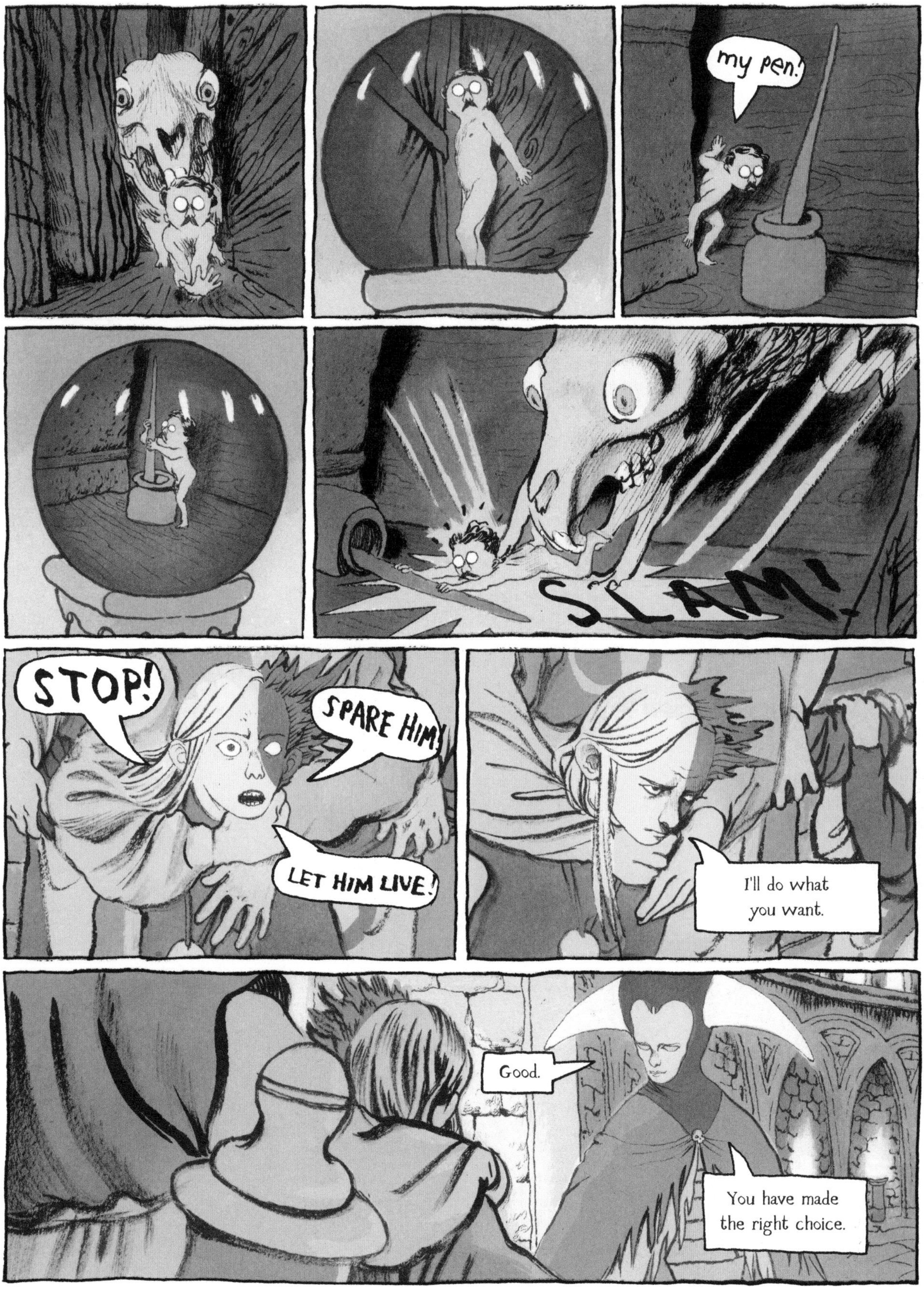
my pen!
SLAM!
STOP!
SPARE HIM!
LET HIM LIVE!
I'll do what you want.
Good.
You have made the right choice.

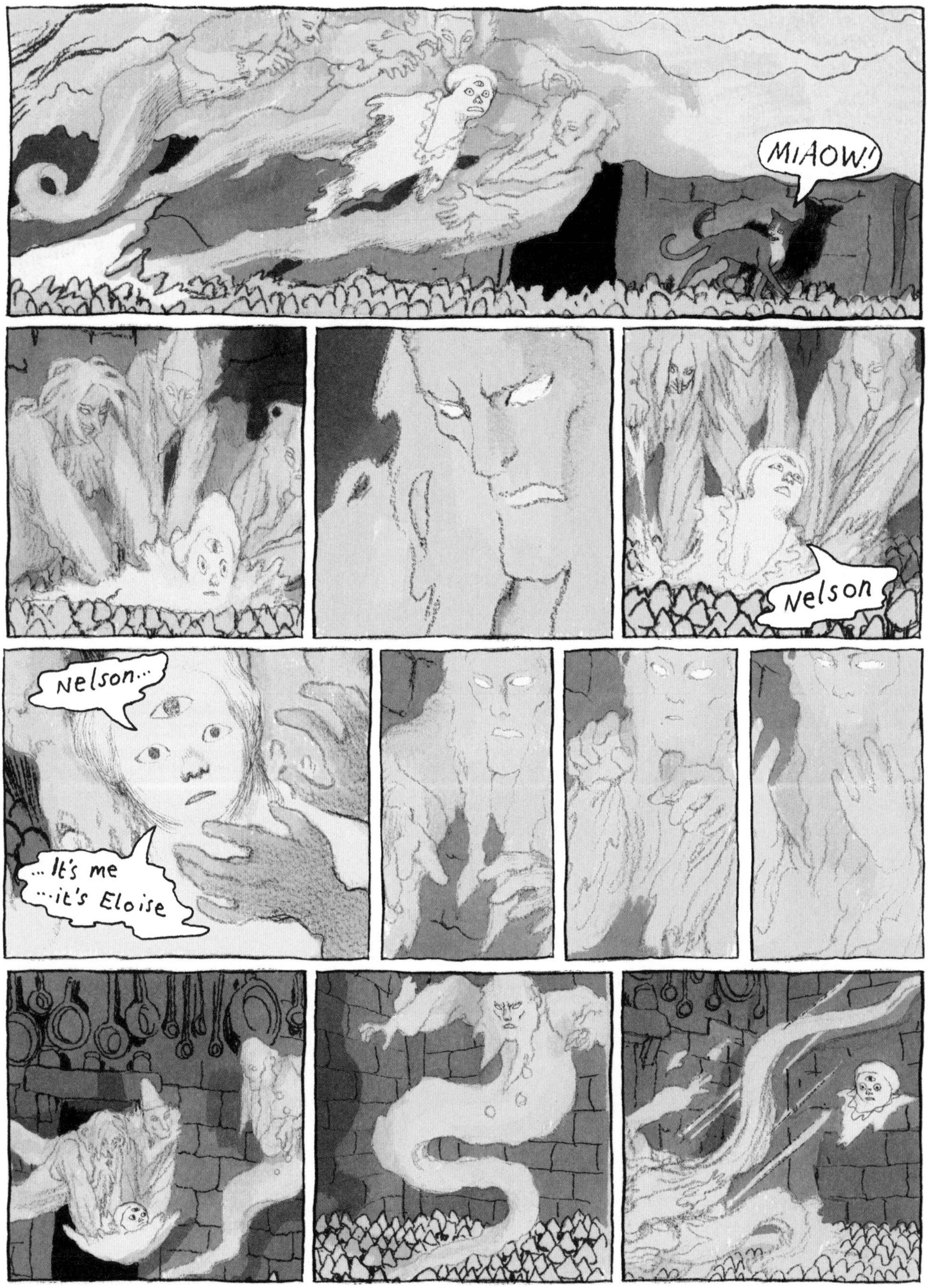
MIAOW!
Nelson
Nelson...
...It's me
...it's Eloise

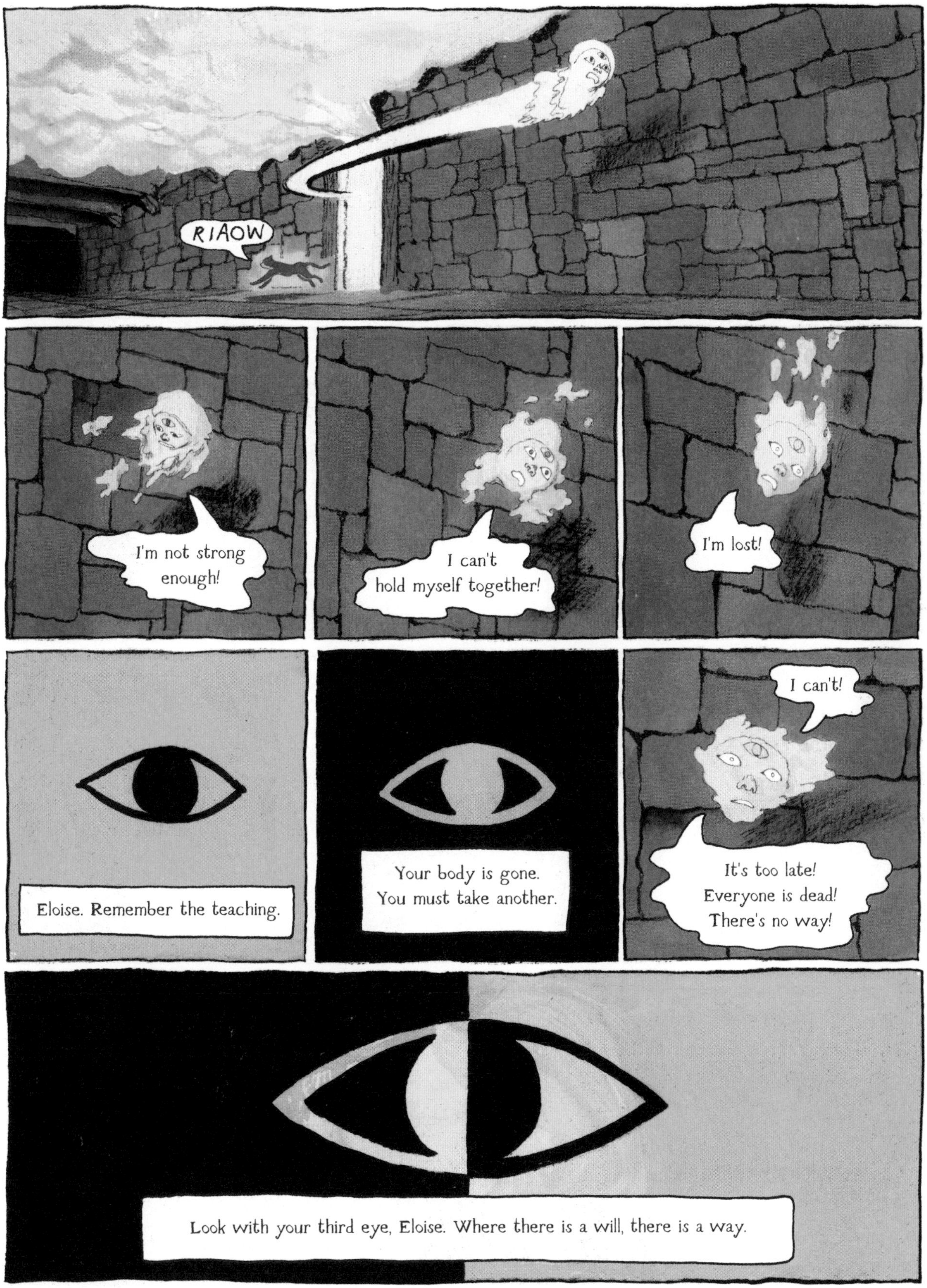
RIAOW
I'm not strong enough!
I can't hold myself together!
I'm lost!
Eloise. Remember the teaching.
Your body is gone. You must take another.
I can't!
It's too late! Everyone is dead! There's no way!
Look with your third eye, Eloise. Where there is a will, there is a way.

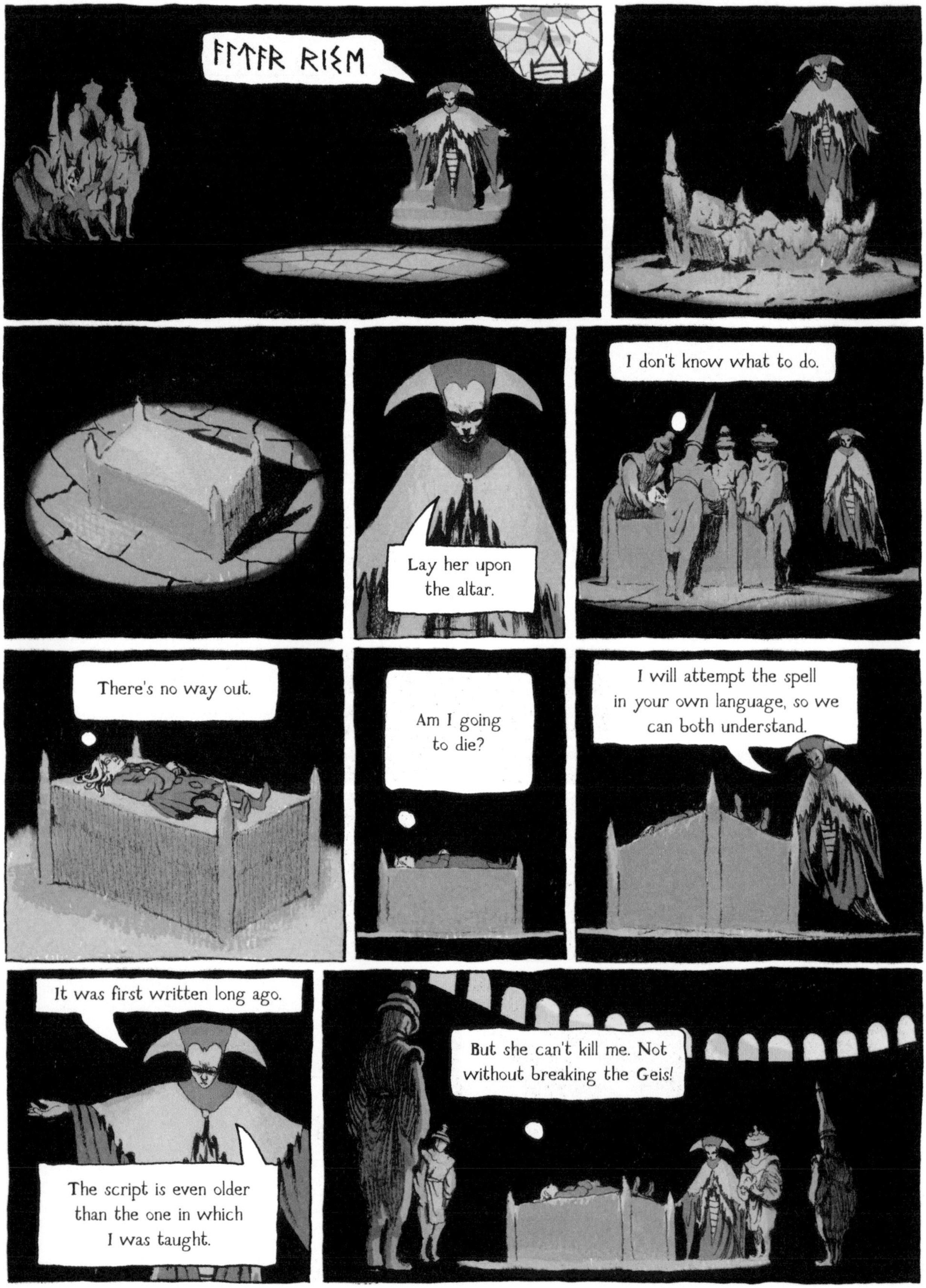
Lay her upon the altar.
I don't know what to do.
There's no way out.
Am I going to die?
I will attempt the spell in your own language, so we can both understand.
It was first written long ago.
The script is even older than the one in which I was taught.
But she can't kill me. Not without breaking the Geis!

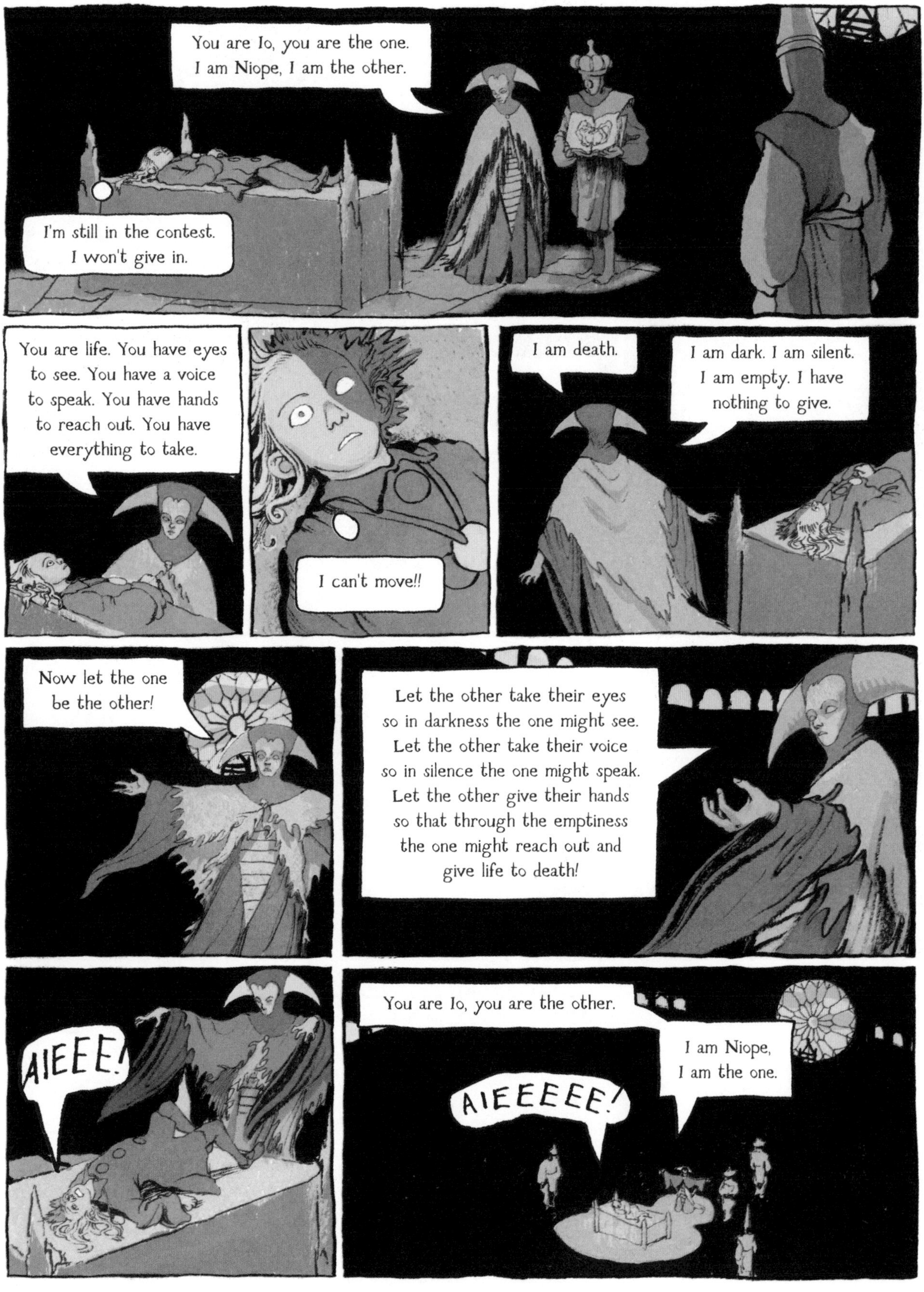
You are Io, you are the one.
I am Niope, I am the other.
I'm still in the contest.
I won't give in.
You are life. You have eyes to see. You have a voice to speak. You have hands to reach out. You have everything to take.
I can't move!!
I am death.
I am dark. I am silent. I am empty. I have nothing to give.
Now let the one be the other!
Let the other take their eyes so in darkness the one might see. Let the other take their voice so in silence the one might speak. Let the other give their hands so that through the emptiness the one might reach out and give life to death!
AIEEE!
You are Io, you are the other.
I am Niope, I am the one.
AIEEEEE!

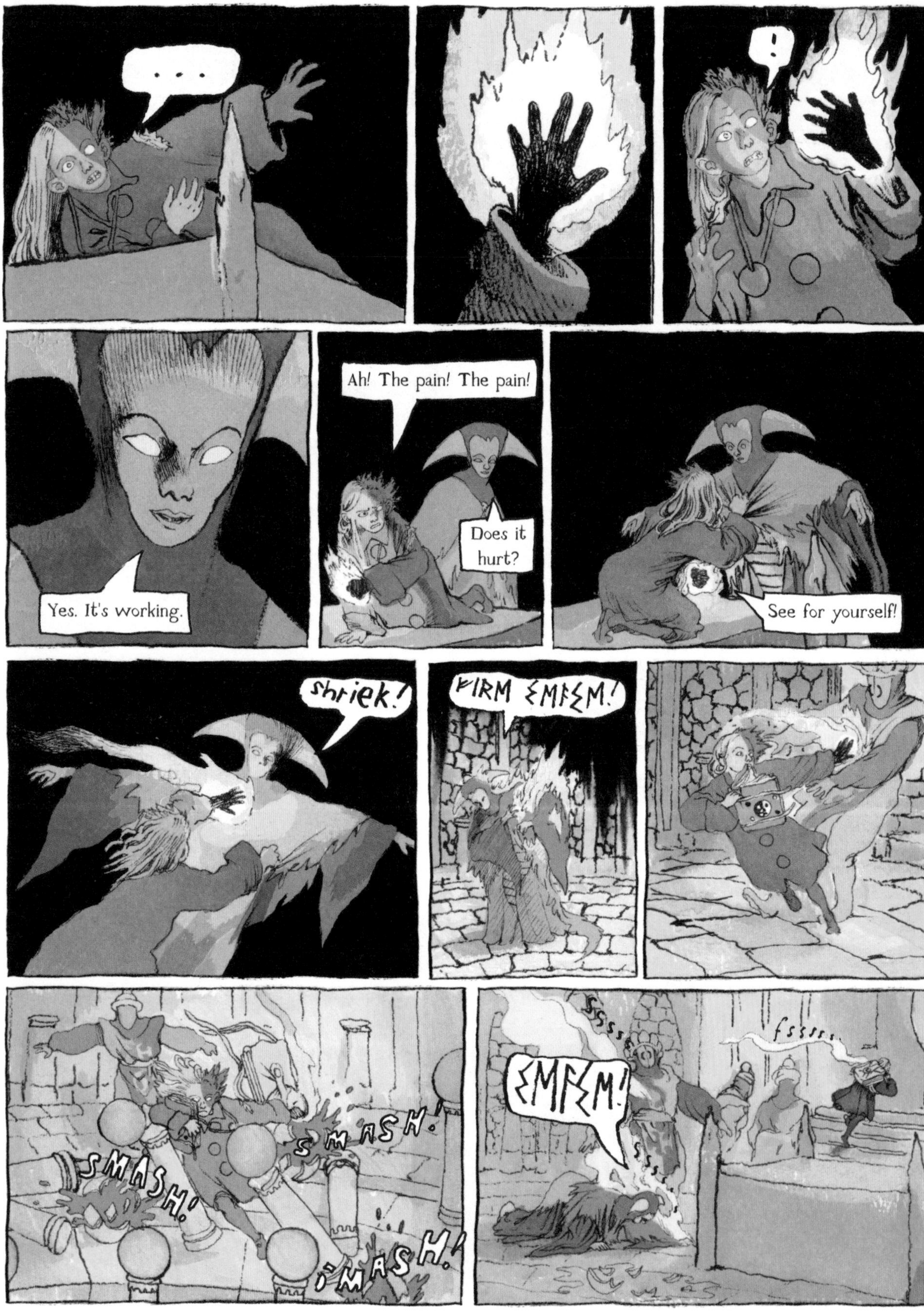
. . .
!
Yes. It's working.
Ah! The pain! The pain!
Does it hurt?
See for yourself!
shriek!
SMASH!
SMASH!
MASH!
Sssss
fssss...

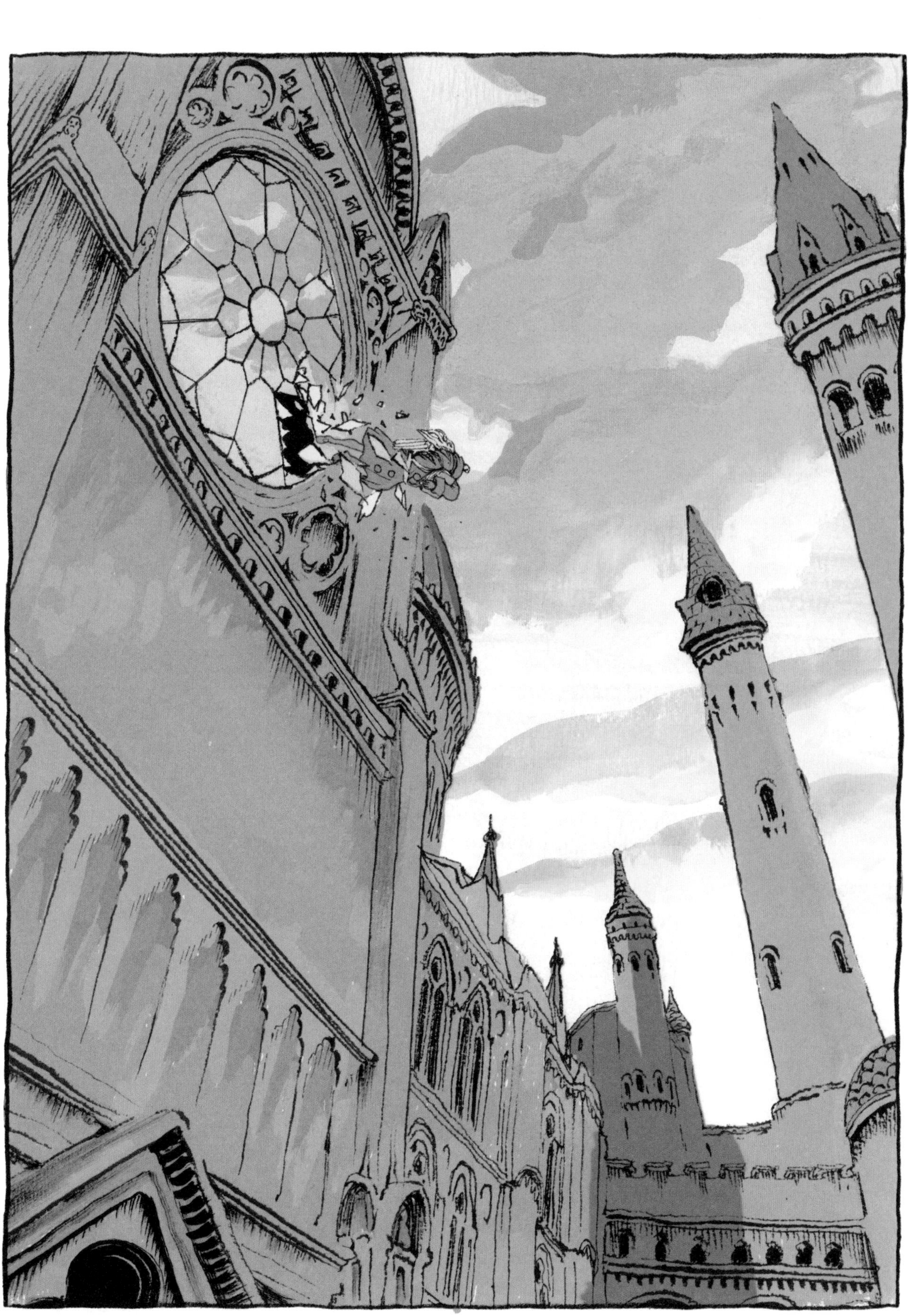

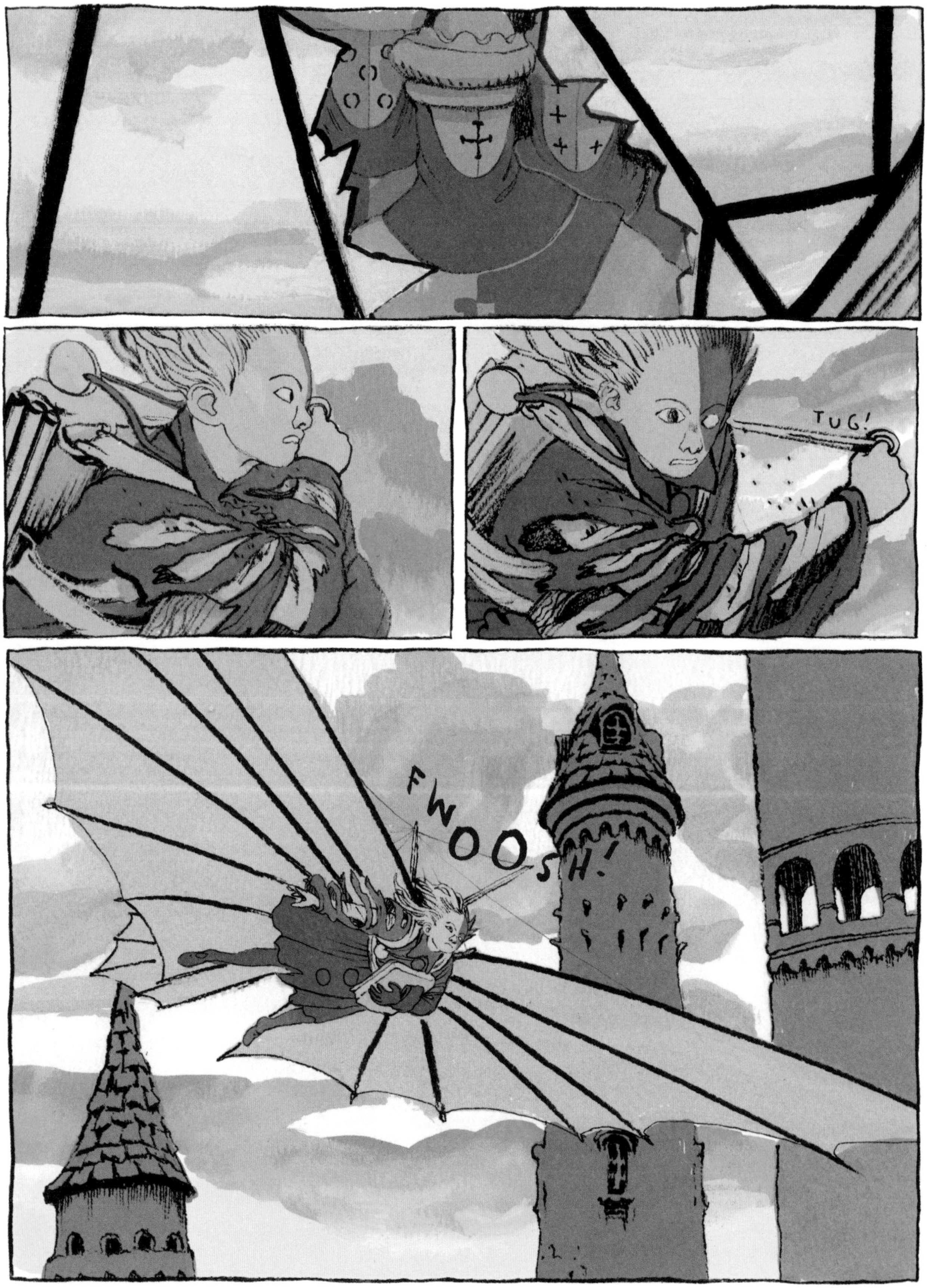
TUG!
FWOOSH!

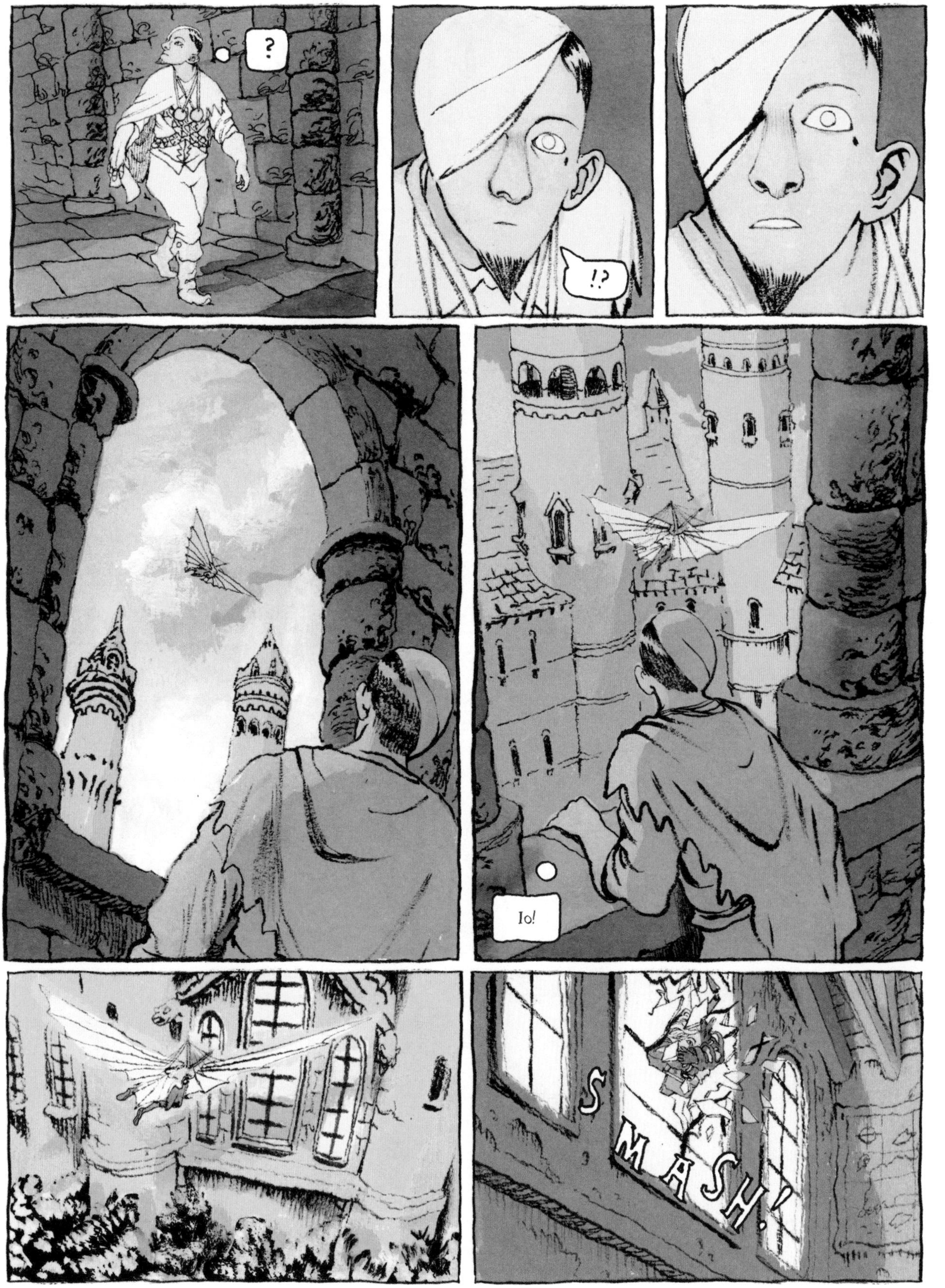
?
!?
Io!
SMASH!

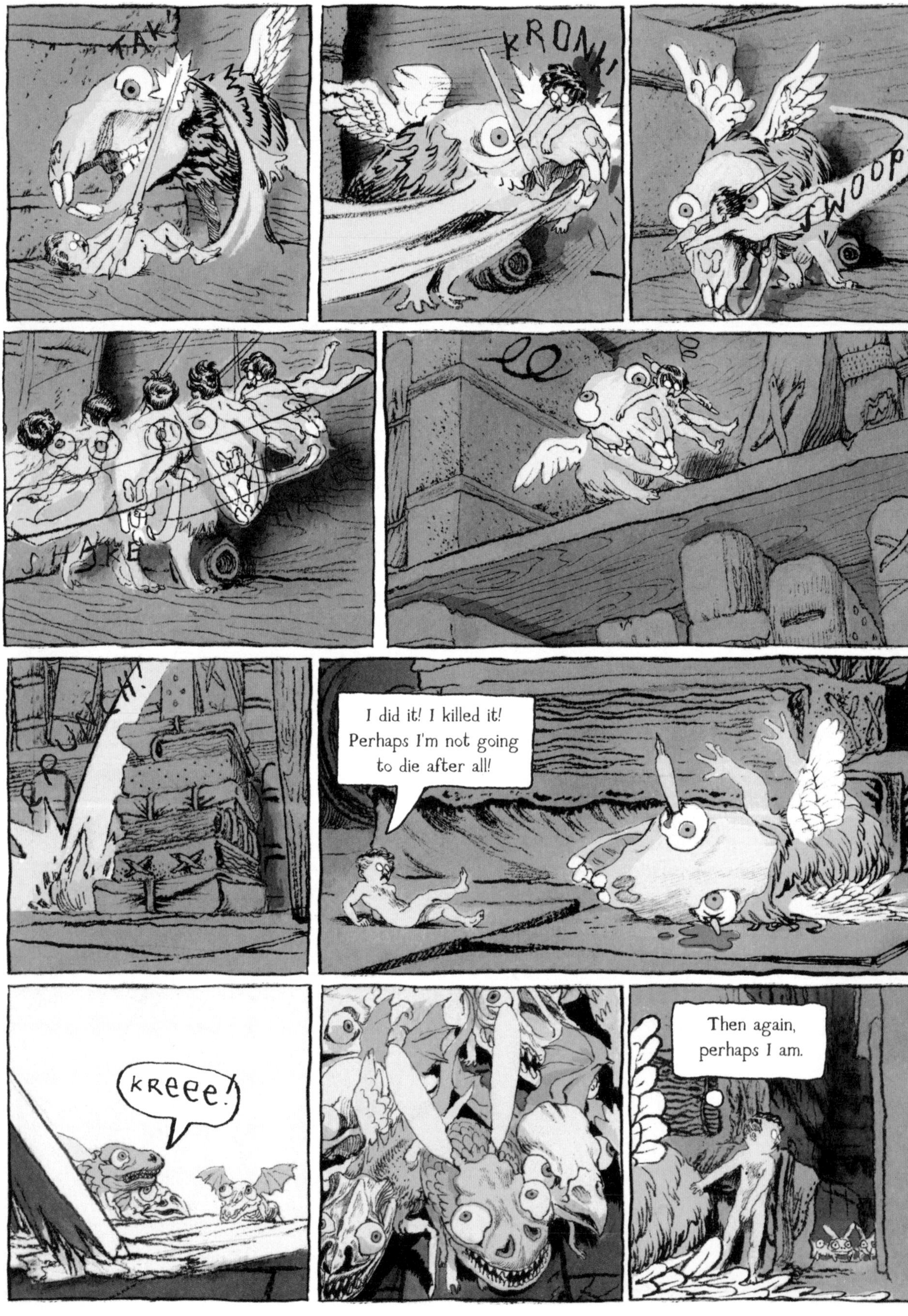
TAK!
KRONK!
SWOOP!
SHAKE
I did it! I killed it! Perhaps I'm not going to die after all!
kreee!
Then again, perhaps I am.

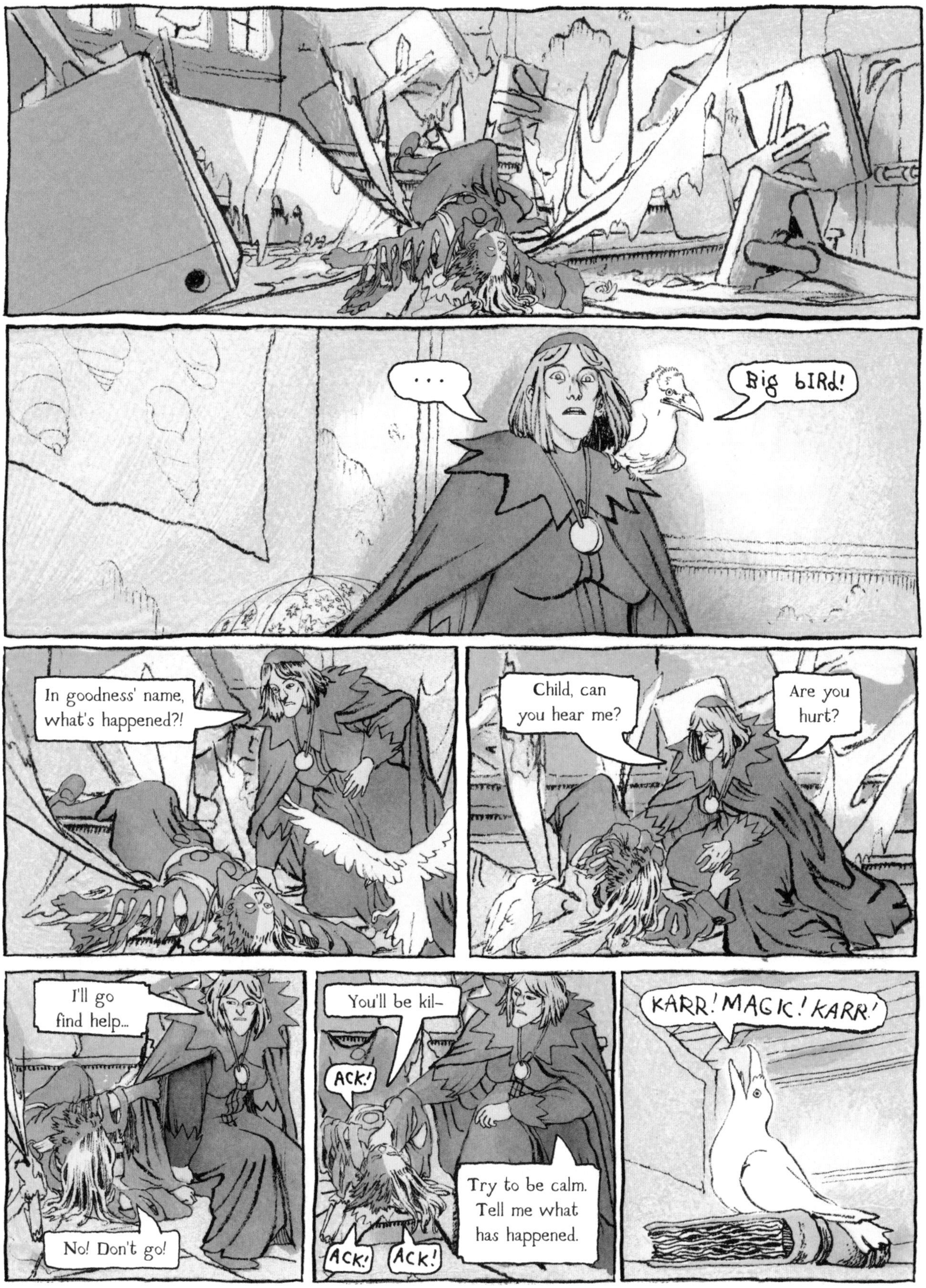
...
Big bIRd!
In goodness' name, what's happened?!
Child, can you hear me?
Are you hurt?
I'll go find help...
No! Don't go!
You'll be kil-
ACK!
ACK!
ACK!
Try to be calm. Tell me what has happened.
KARR! MAGIC! KARR!

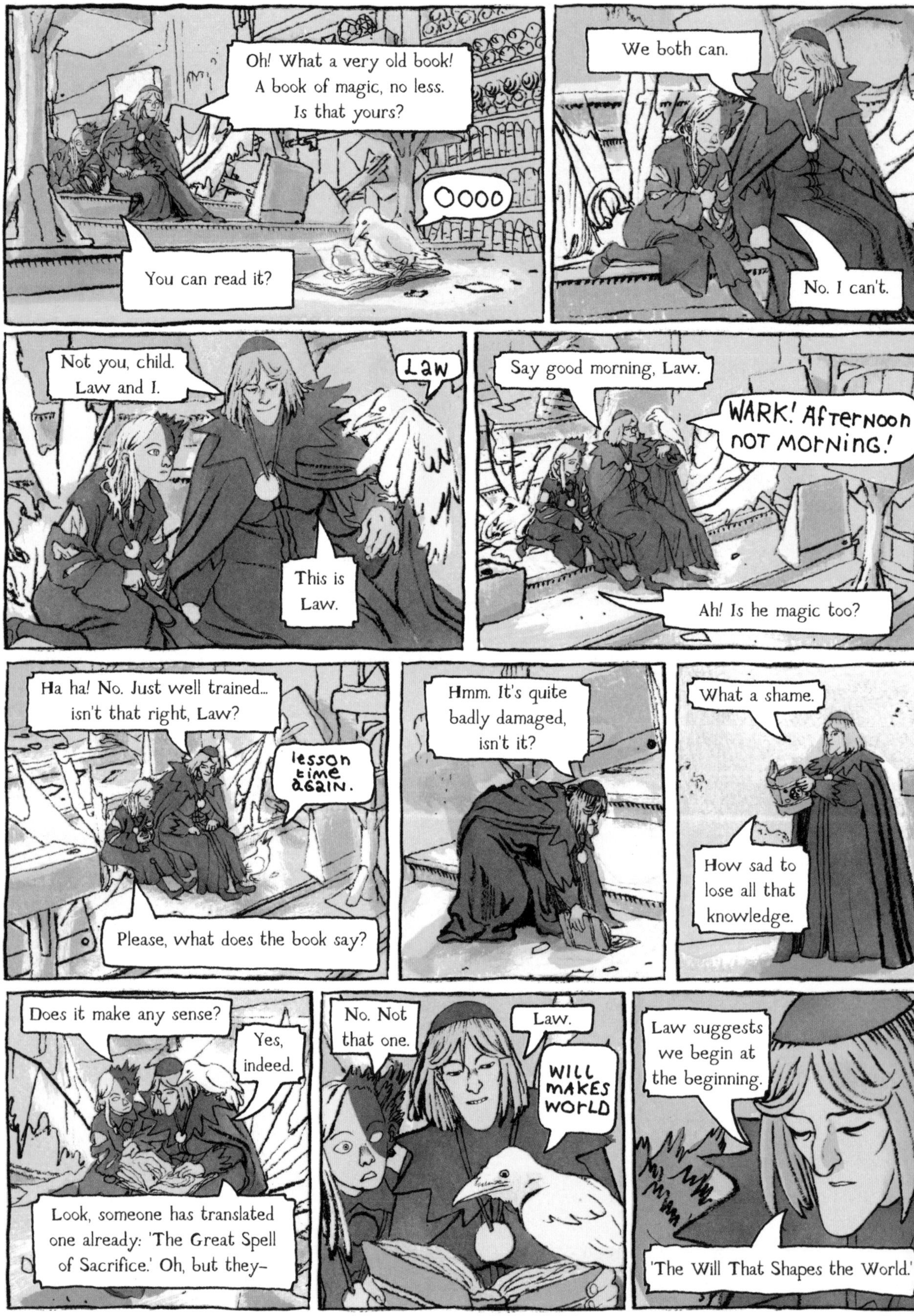
Oh! What a very old book! A book of magic, no less. Is that yours?
Oooo
You can read it?
We both can.
No. I can't.
Not you, child. Law and I.
Law
This is Law.
Say good morning, Law.
WARK! Afternoon not morning!
Ah! Is he magic too?
Ha ha! No. Just well trained... isn't that right, Law?
lesson time again.
Please, what does the book say?
Hmm. It's quite badly damaged, isn't it?
What a shame.
How sad to lose all that knowledge.
Does it make any sense?
Yes, indeed.
Look, someone has translated one already: 'The Great Spell of Sacrifice.' Oh, but they–
No. Not that one.
Law.
WILL MAKES WORLD
Law suggests we begin at the beginning.
'The Will That Shapes the World.'

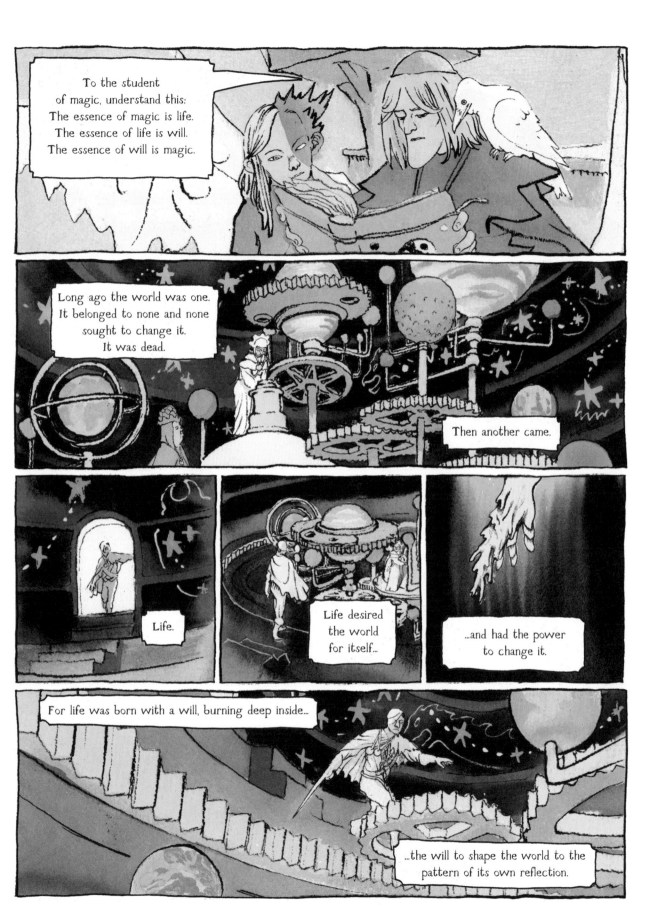

To the student
of magic, understand this:
The essence of magic is life.
The essence of life is will.
The essence of will is magic.

Long ago the world was one.
It belonged to none and none
sought to change it.
It was dead.

Then another came.

Life.

Life desired
the world
for itself...

...and had the power
to change it.

For life was born with a will, burning deep inside...

...the will to shape the world to the
pattern of its own reflection.

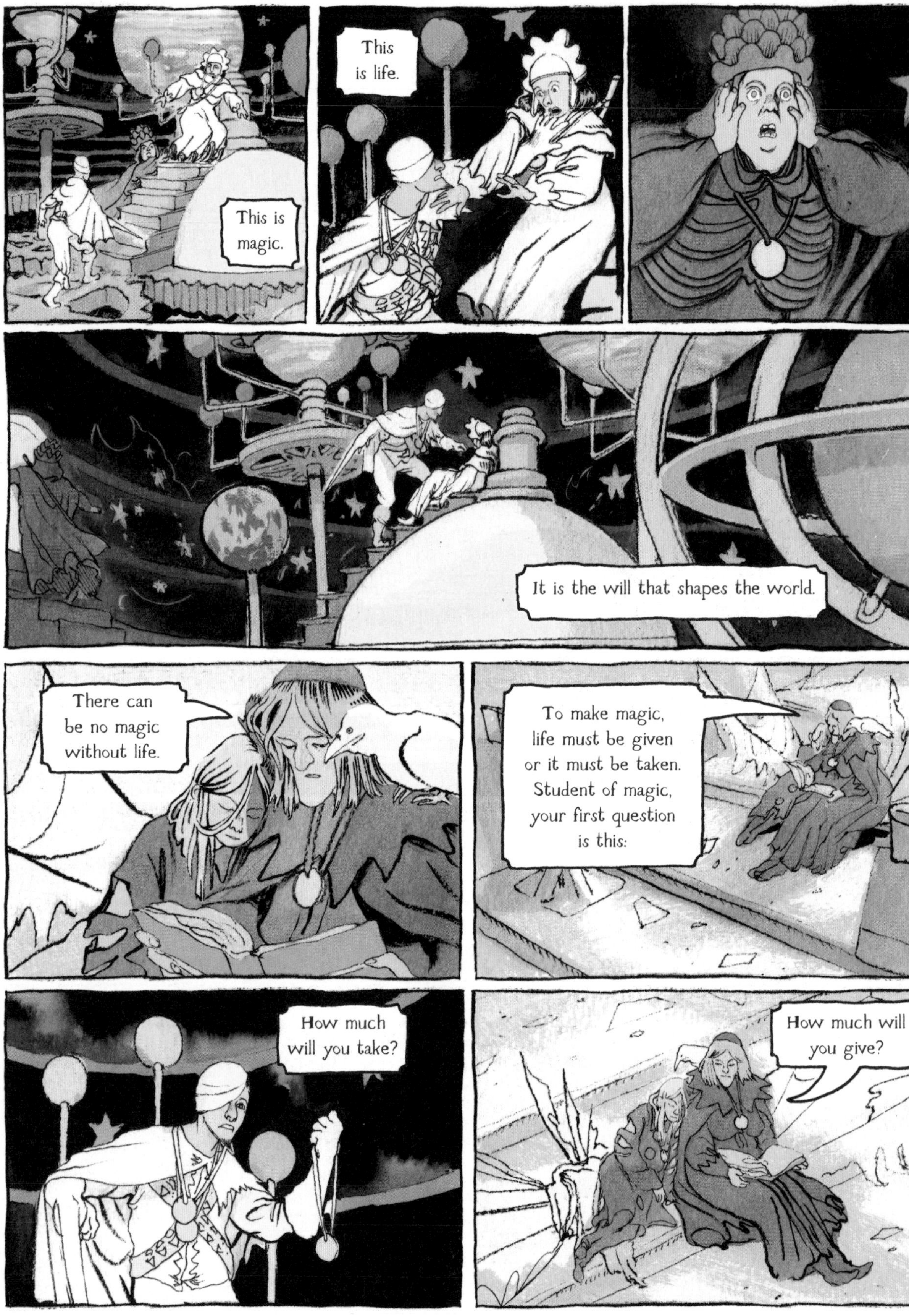
This is magic.
This is life.
It is the will that shapes the world.
There can be no magic without life.
To make magic, life must be given or it must be taken. Student of magic, your first question is this:
How much will you take?
How much will you give?

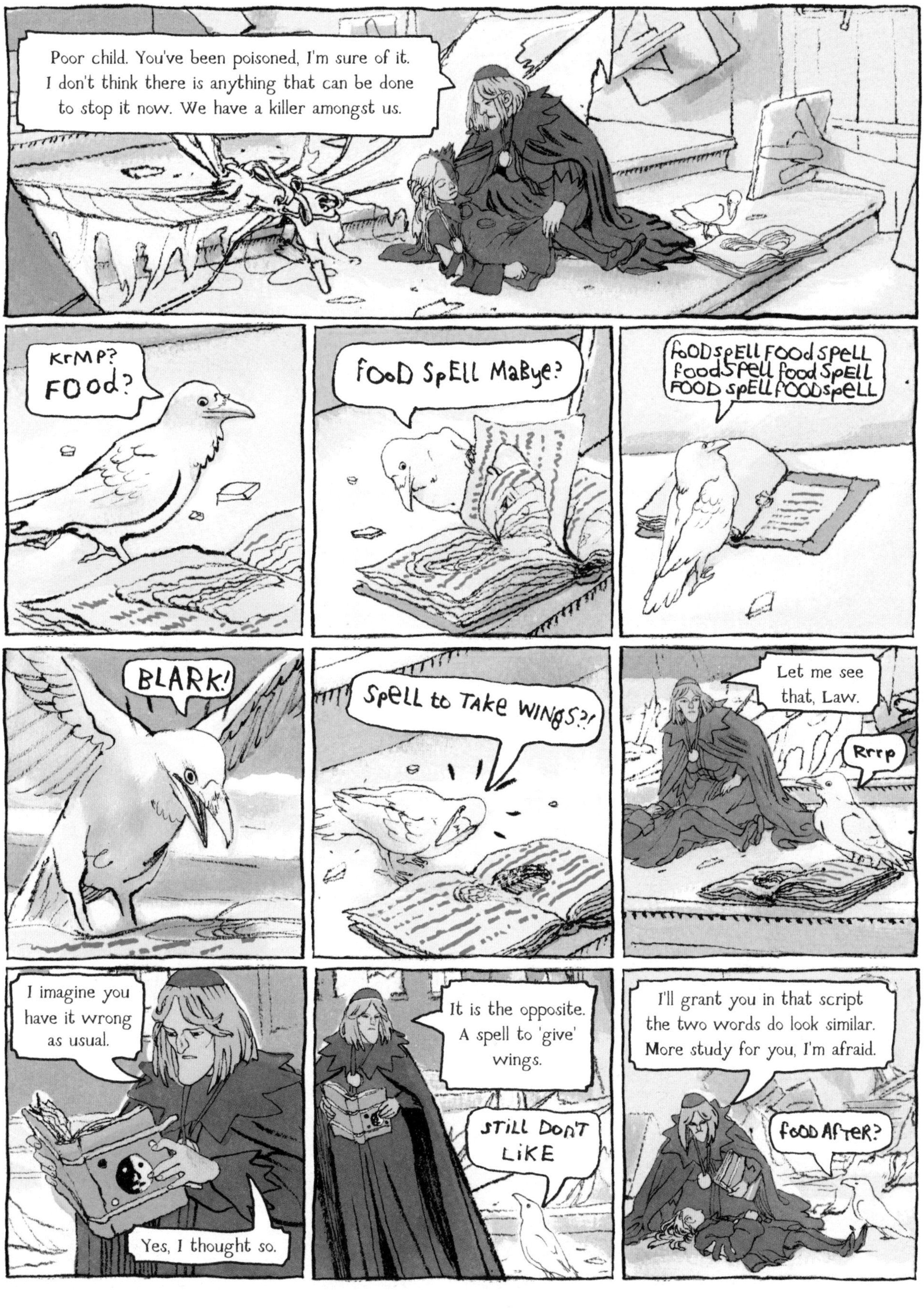
Poor child. You've been poisoned, I'm sure of it. I don't think there is anything that can be done to stop it now. We have a killer amongst us.
KrMP? FOOd?
FOoD SpELL MaBye?
fOODSpELLFOOdSpELL foodSpELLfoodSpELL FOOD spELLFOODspELL
BLARK!
SpELL to TAKe WINgS?!
Let me see that, Law.
Rrrp
I imagine you have it wrong as usual.
Yes, I thought so.
It is the opposite. A spell to 'give' wings.
STILL DON'T LIKE
I'll grant you in that script the two words do look similar. More study for you, I'm afraid.
fOOD AfTER?

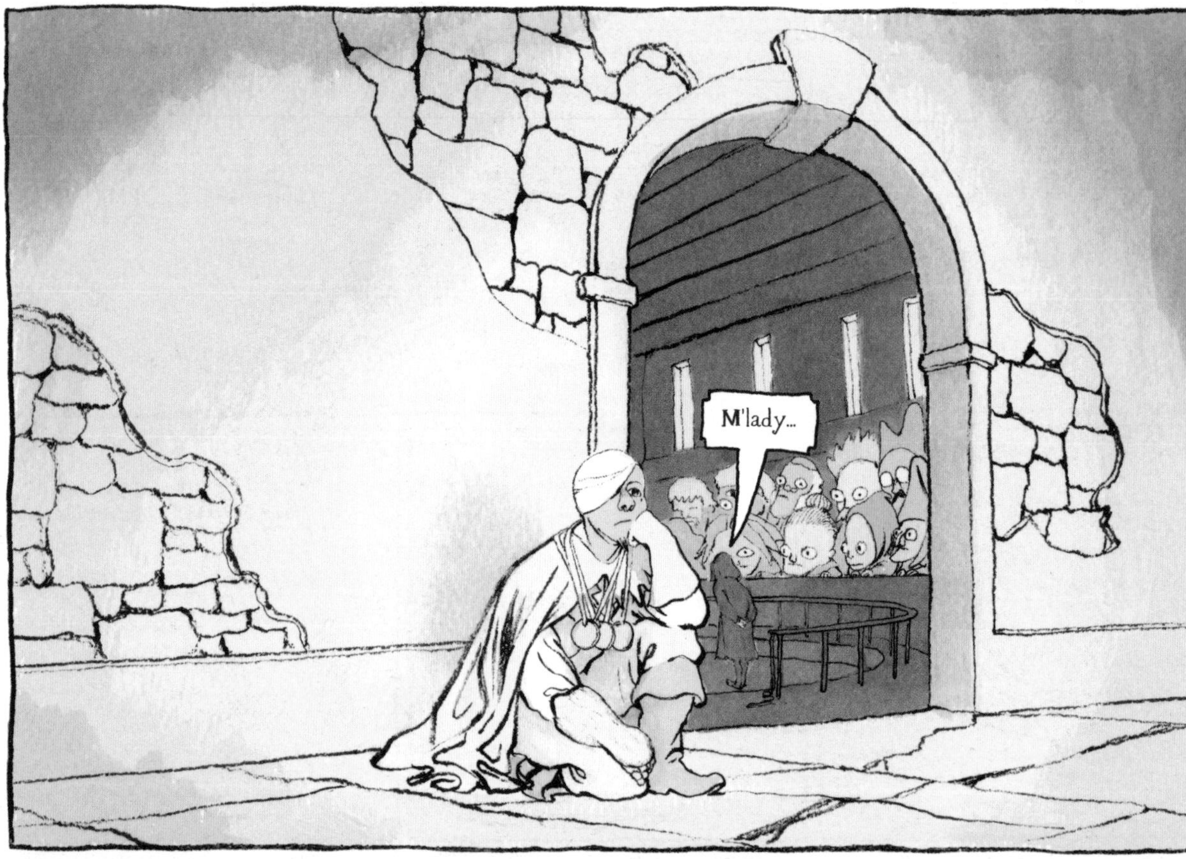
M'lady...

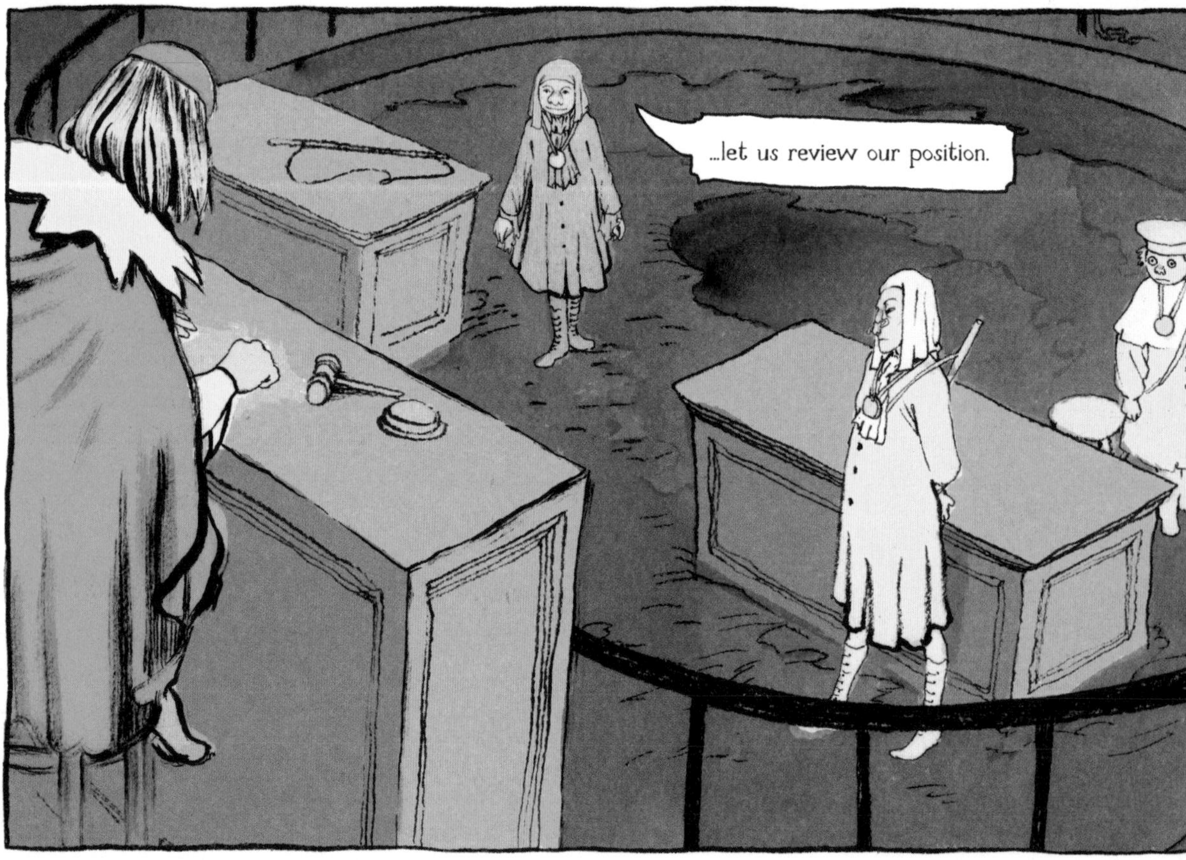
...let us review our position.

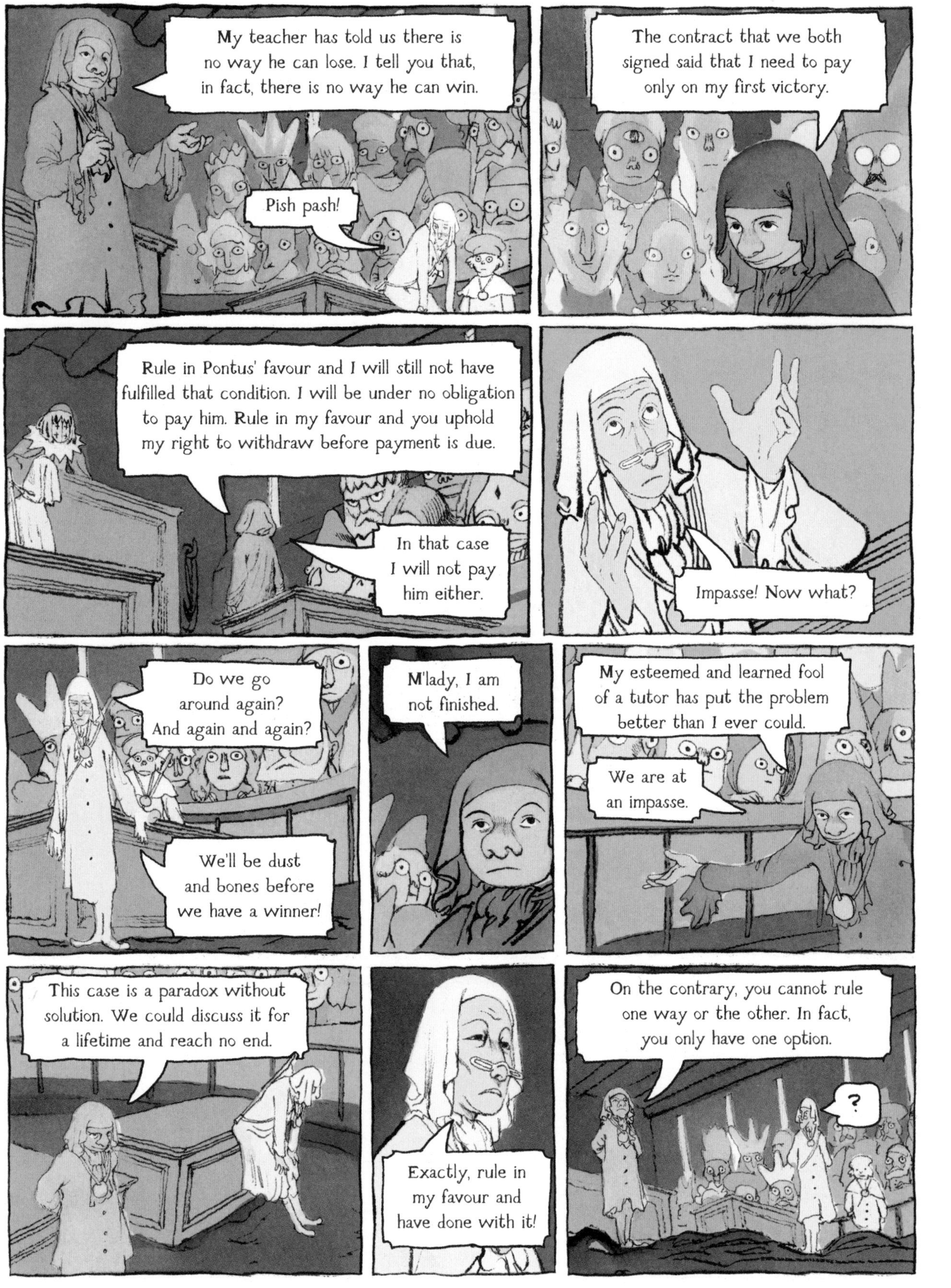
My teacher has told us there is no way he can lose. I tell you that, in fact, there is no way he can win.
Pish pash!
The contract that we both signed said that I need to pay only on my first victory.
Rule in Pontus' favour and I will still not have fulfilled that condition. I will be under no obligation to pay him. Rule in my favour and you uphold my right to withdraw before payment is due.
In that case I will not pay him either.
Impasse! Now what?
Do we go around again? And again and again?
We'll be dust and bones before we have a winner!
M'lady, I am not finished.
My esteemed and learned fool of a tutor has put the problem better than I ever could.
We are at an impasse.
This case is a paradox without solution. We could discuss it for a lifetime and reach no end.
Exactly, rule in my favour and have done with it!
On the contrary, you cannot rule one way or the other. In fact, you only have one option.
?

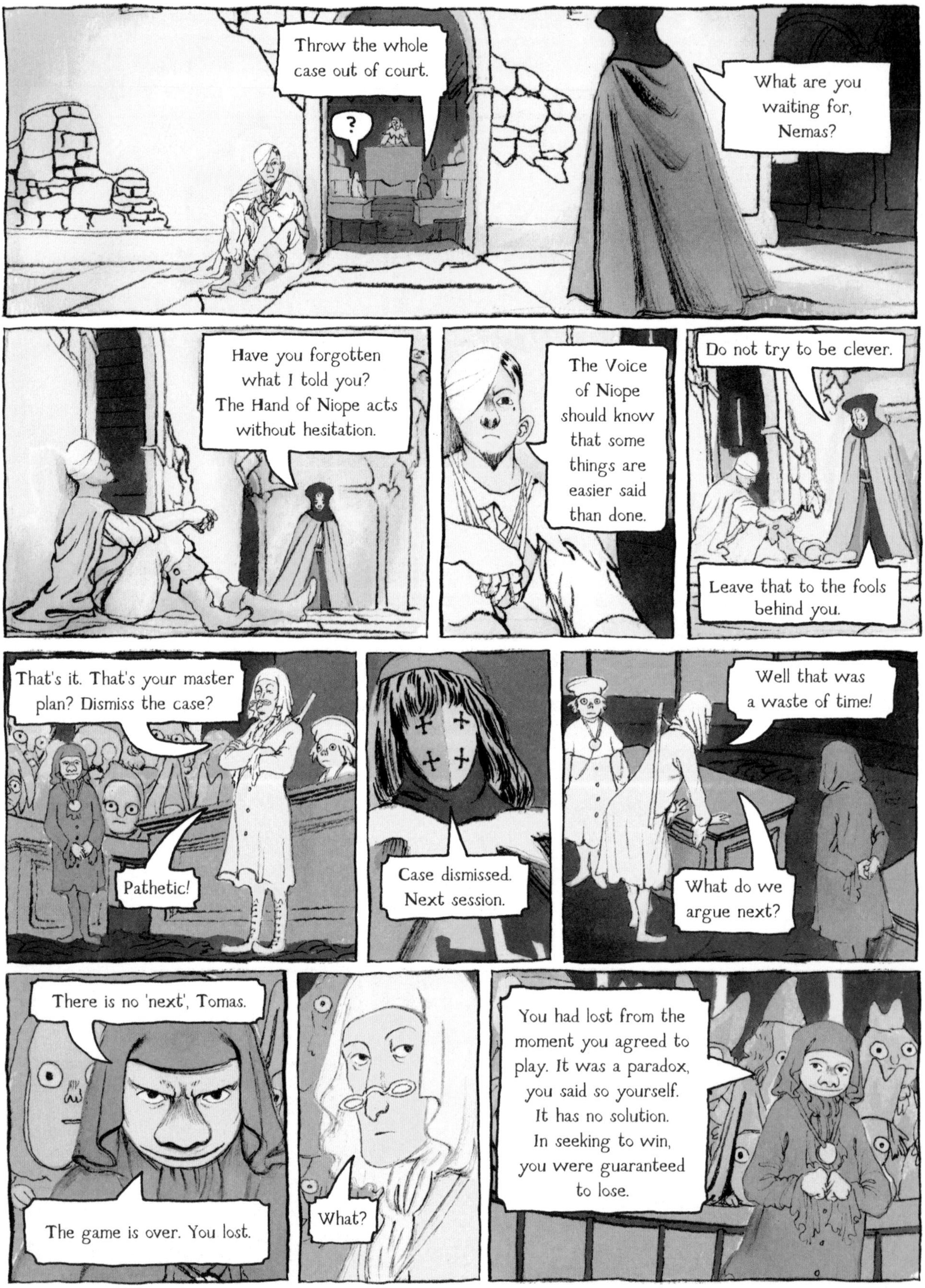
Throw the whole case out of court.
?
What are you waiting for, Nemas?
Have you forgotten what I told you? The Hand of Niope acts without hesitation.
The Voice of Niope should know that some things are easier said than done.
Do not try to be clever.
Leave that to the fools behind you.
That's it. That's your master plan? Dismiss the case?
Pathetic!
Case dismissed. Next session.
Well that was a waste of time!
What do we argue next?
There is no 'next', Tomas.
The game is over. You lost.
What?
You had lost from the moment you agreed to play. It was a paradox, you said so yourself. It has no solution. In seeking to win, you were guaranteed to lose.

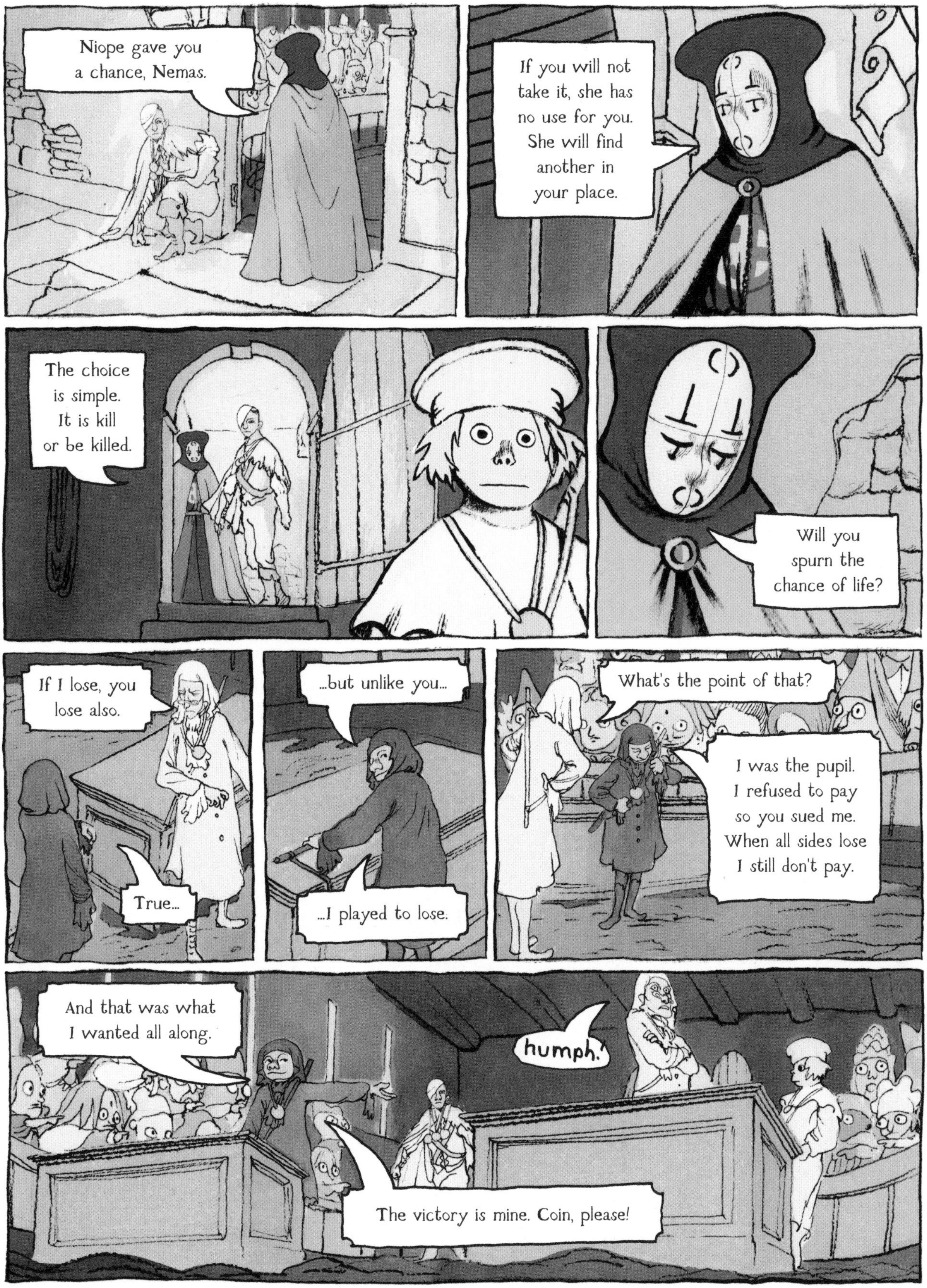
Niope gave you a chance, Nemas.
If you will not take it, she has no use for you. She will find another in your place.
The choice is simple. It is kill or be killed.
Will you spurn the chance of life?
If I lose, you lose also.
True...
...but unlike you...
...I played to lose.
What's the point of that?
I was the pupil. I refused to pay so you sued me. When all sides lose I still don't pay.
And that was what I wanted all along.
humph!
The victory is mine. Coin, please!

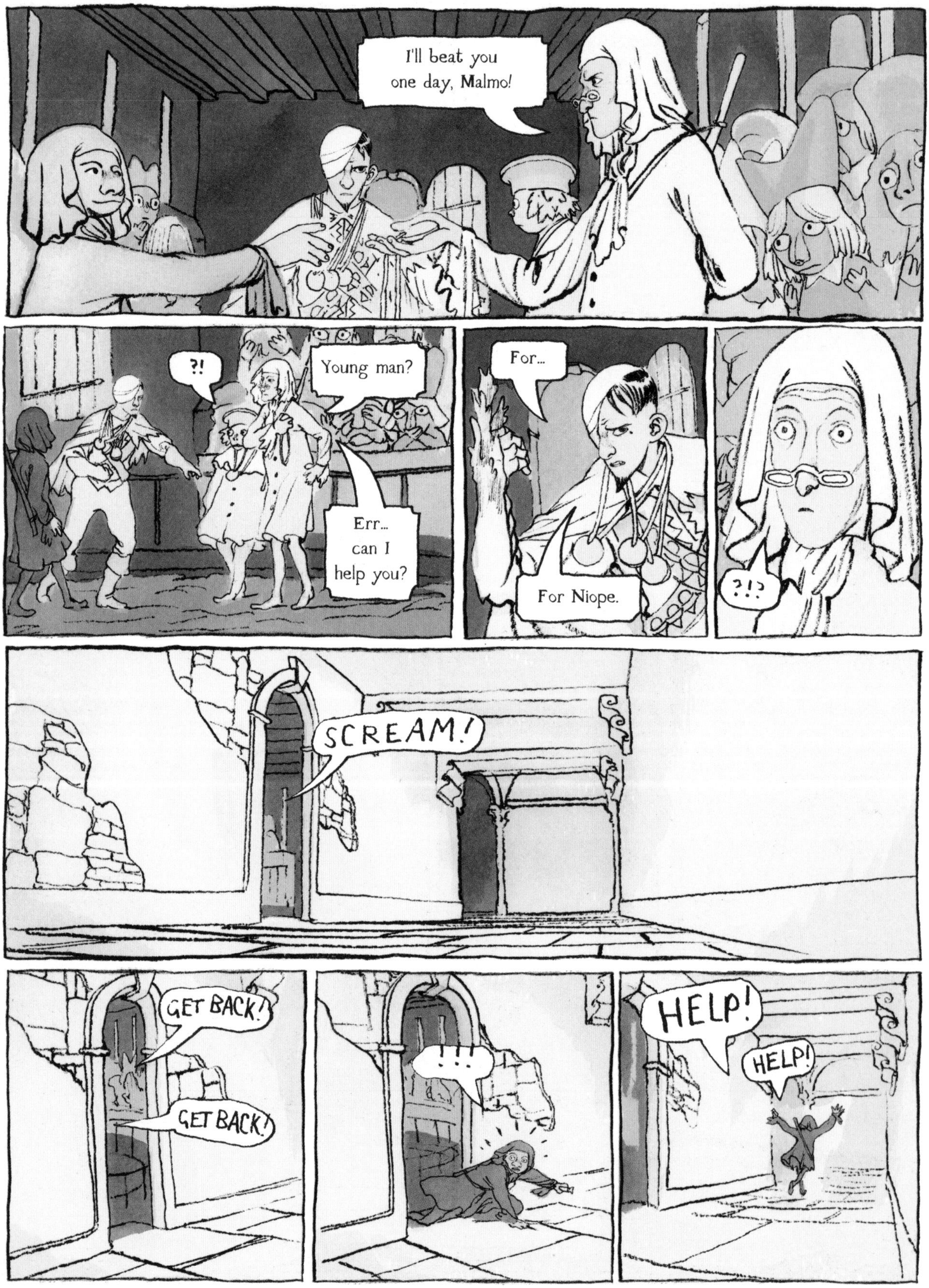
I'll beat you one day, Malmo!
?!
Young man?
Err... can I help you?
For...
For Niope.
?!?
SCREAM!
GET BACK!
GET BACK!
!!!
HELP!
HELP!

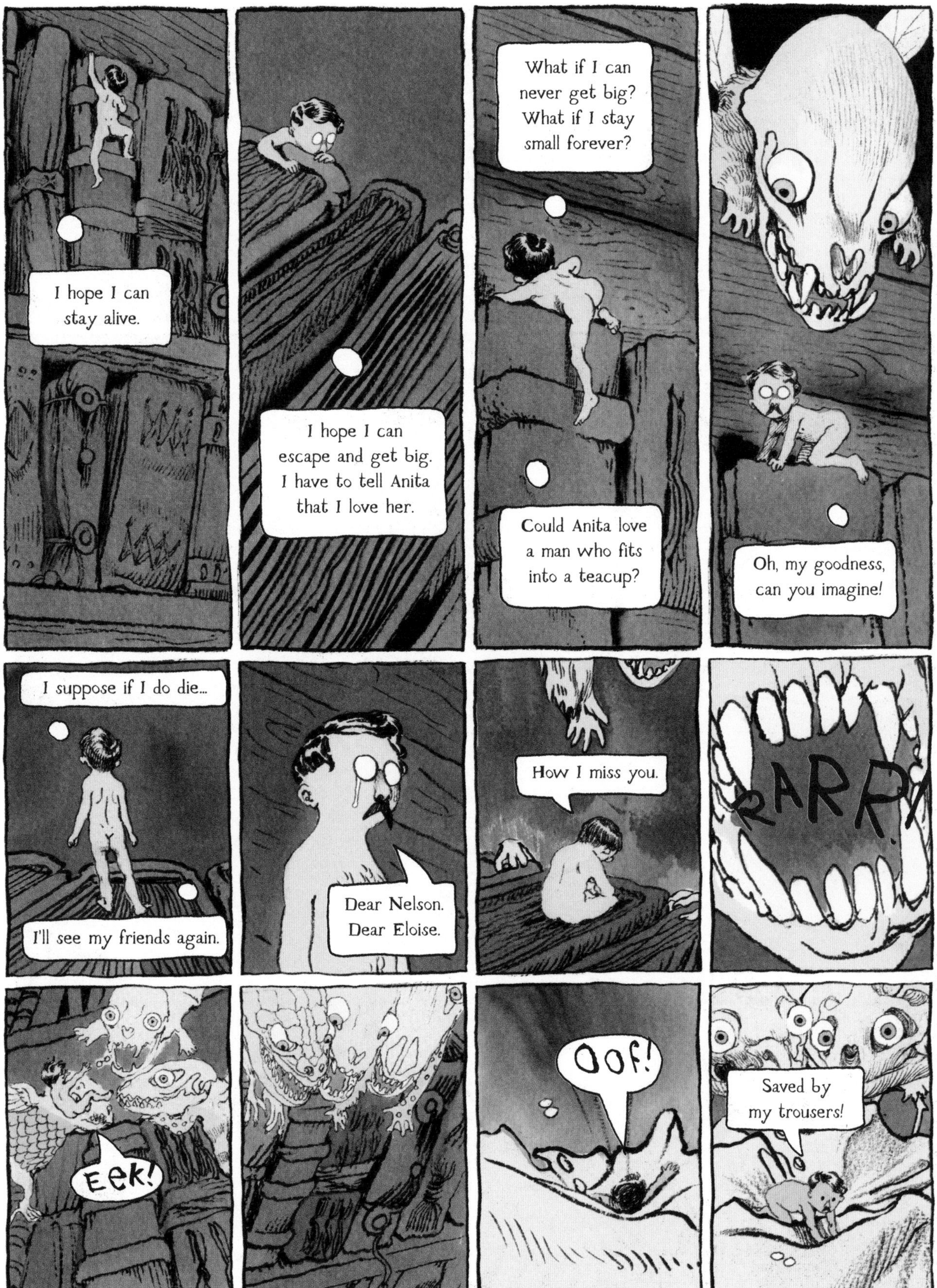
I hope I can stay alive.
I hope I can escape and get big. I have to tell Anita that I love her.
What if I can never get big? What if I stay small forever?
Could Anita love a man who fits into a teacup?
Oh, my goodness, can you imagine!
I suppose if I do die...
I'll see my friends again.
Dear Nelson. Dear Eloise.
How I miss you.
RARR!
EEK!
OOF!
Saved by my trousers!

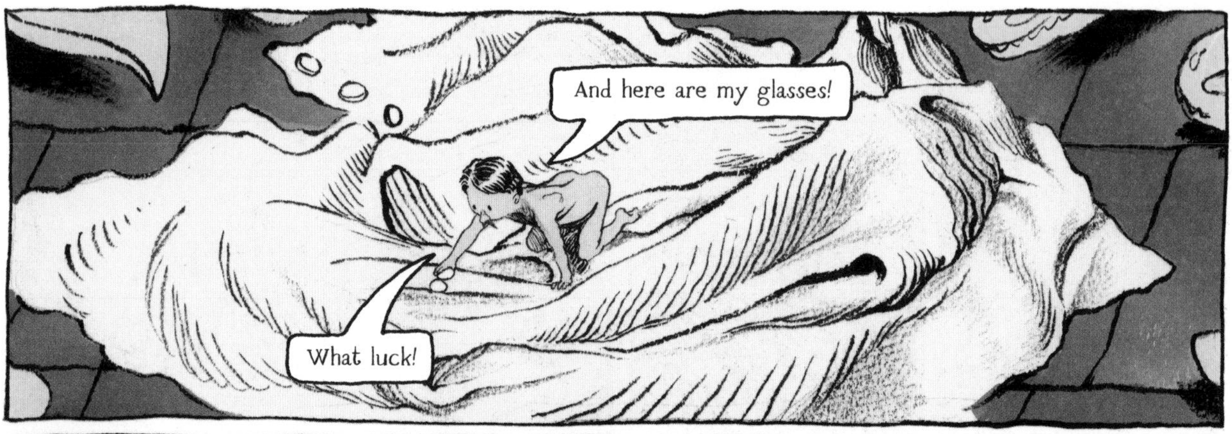
And here are my glasses!
What luck!

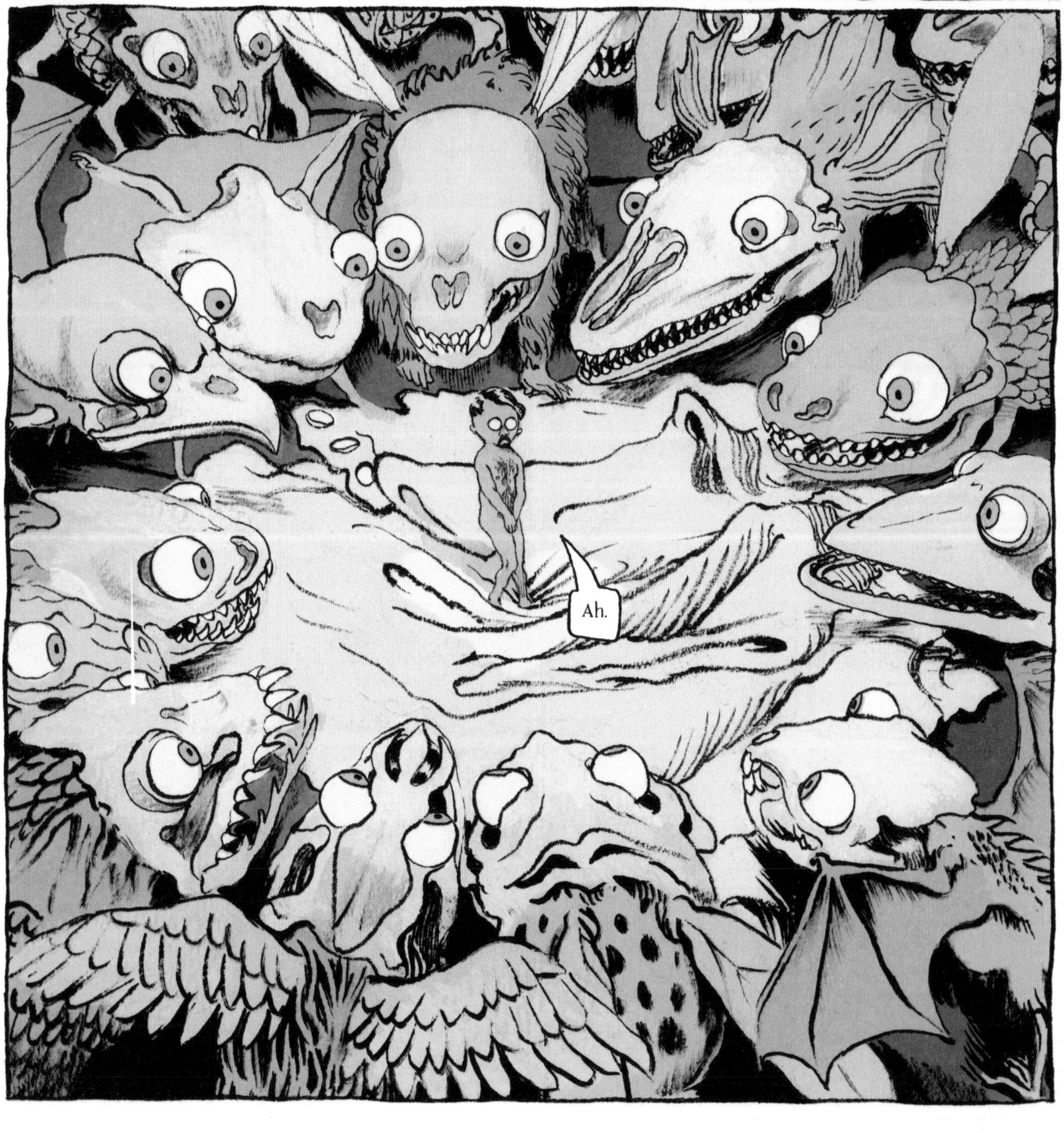
Ah.

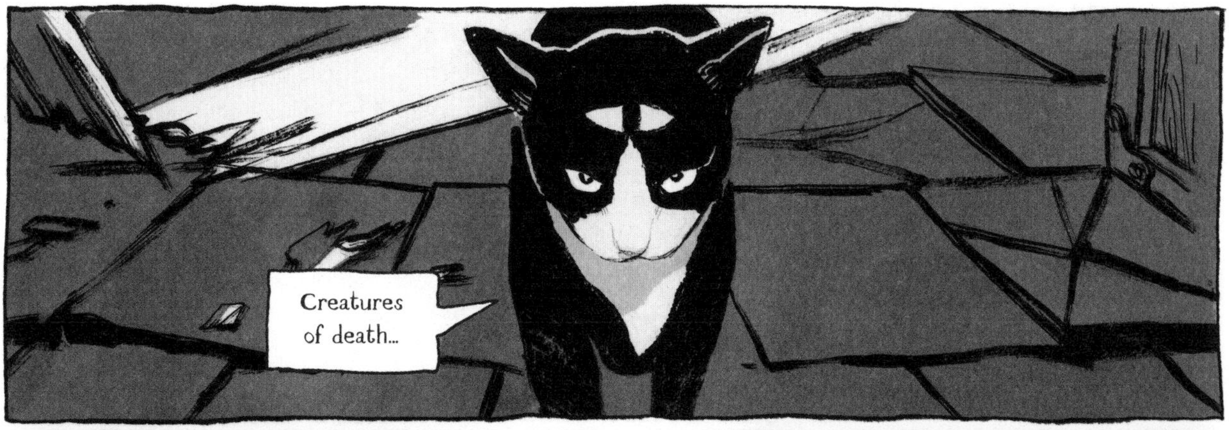
Creatures of death...

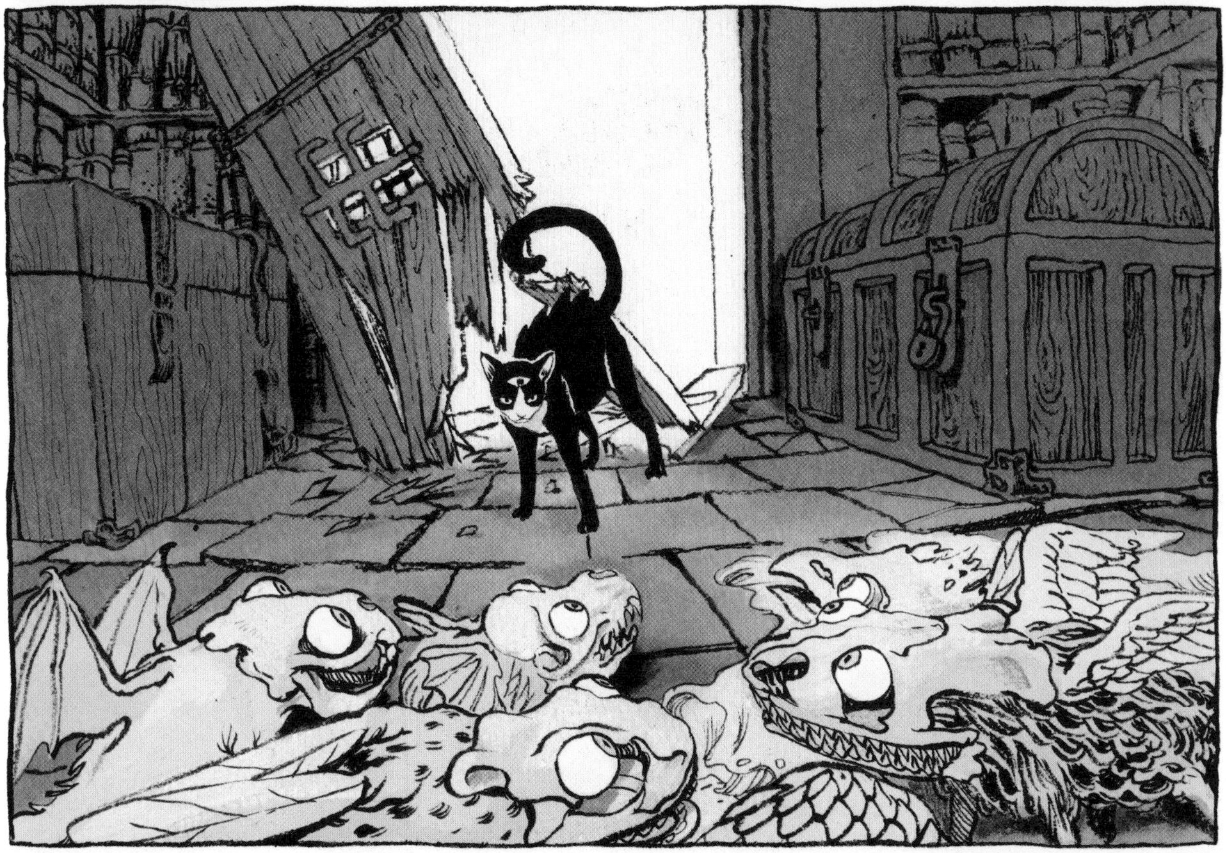

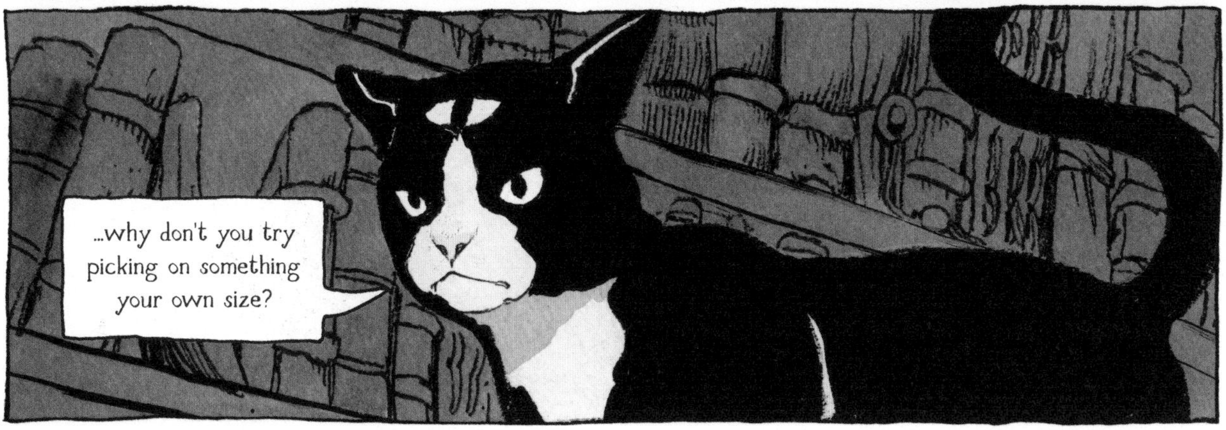
...why don't you try picking on something your own size?

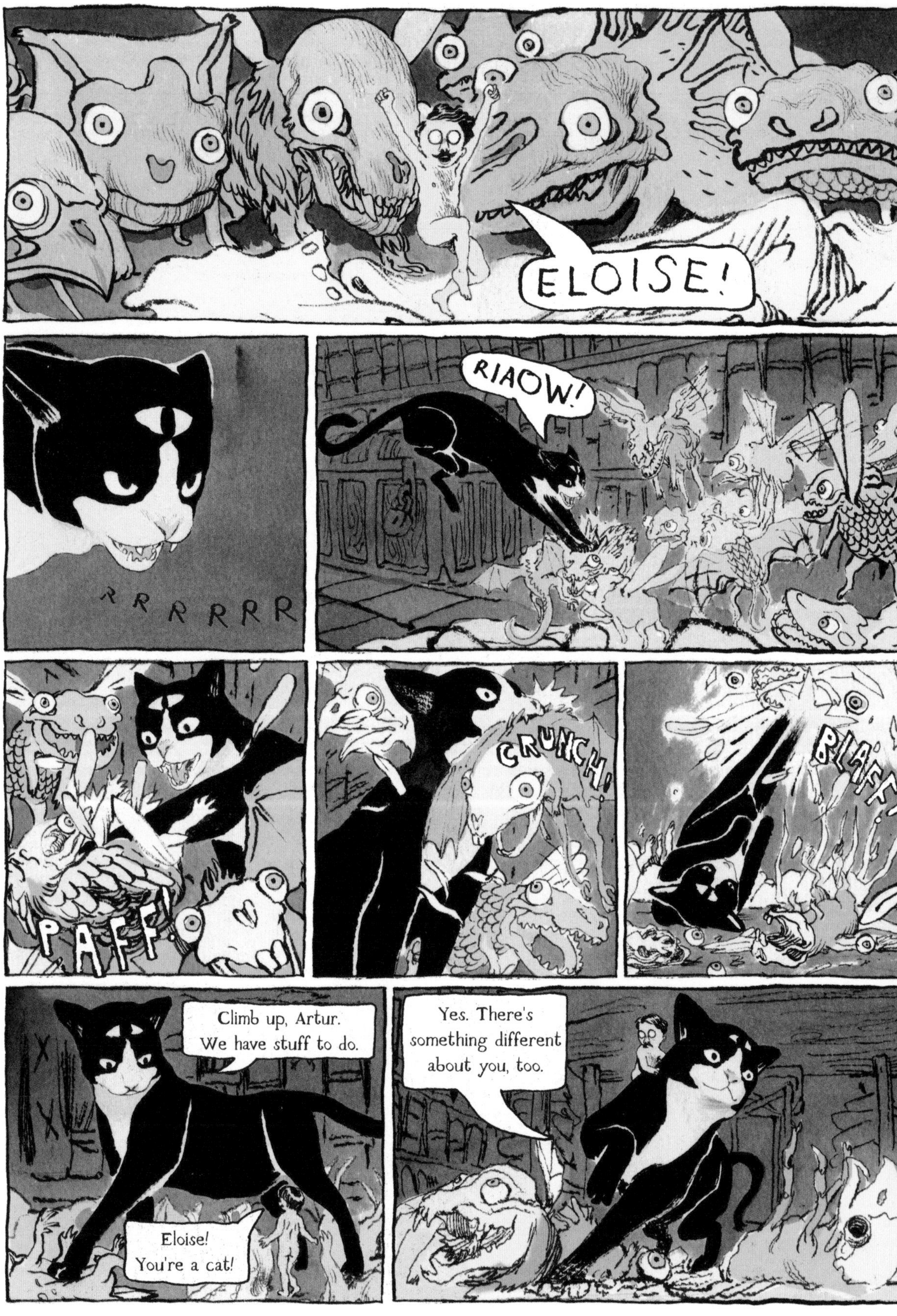
ELOISE!
RRRRRRR
RIAOW!
PAFF!
CRUNCH!
BLAFF!
Climb up, Artur.
We have stuff to do.
Eloise!
You're a cat!
Yes. There's
something different
about you, too.

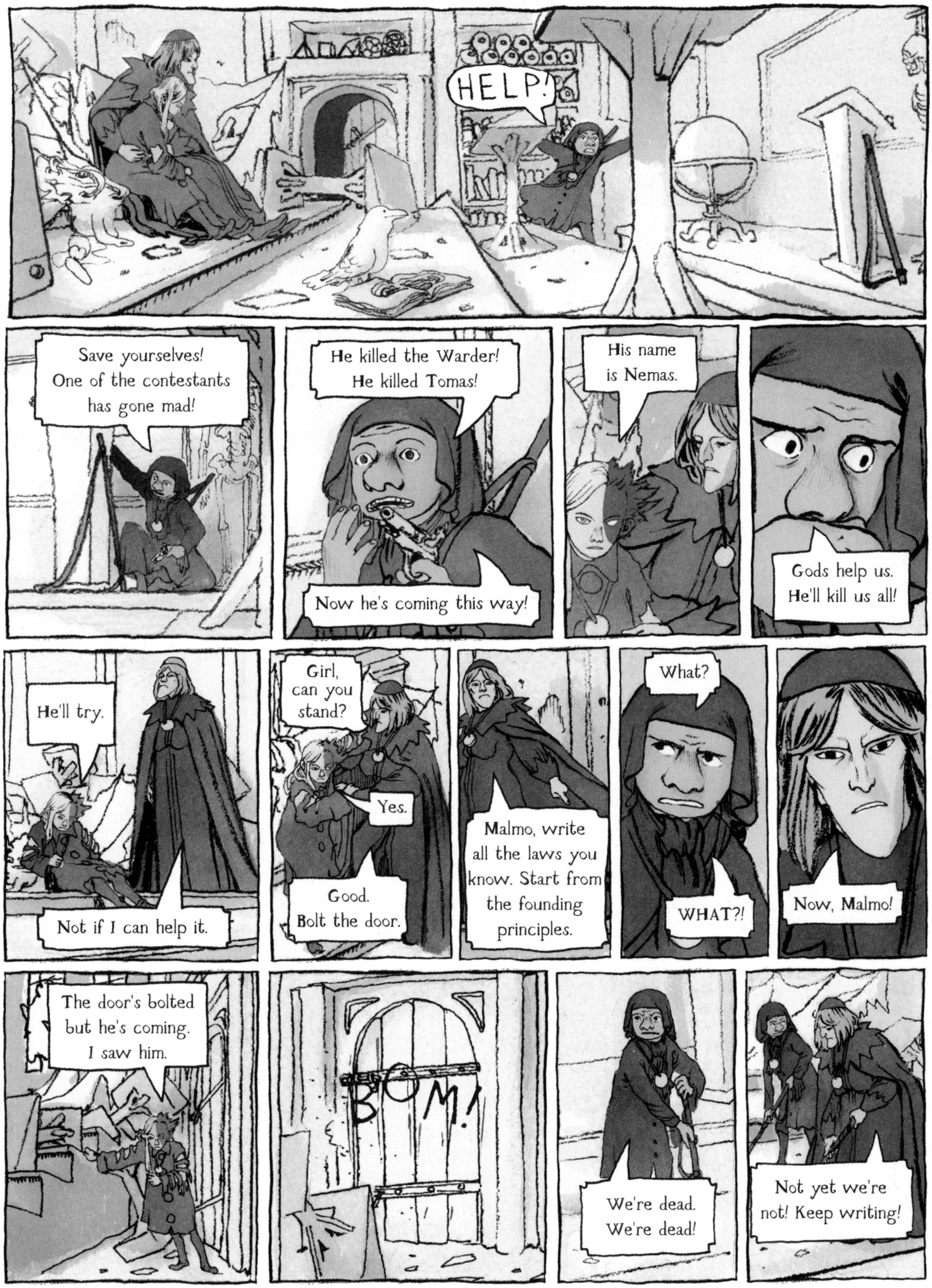
HELP!
Save yourselves! One of the contestants has gone mad!
He killed the Warder! He killed Tomas!
Now he's coming this way!
His name is Nemas.
Gods help us. He'll kill us all!
He'll try.
Not if I can help it.
Girl, can you stand?
Yes.
Good. Bolt the door.
Malmo, write all the laws you know. Start from the founding principles.
What?
WHAT?!
Now, Malmo!
The door's bolted but he's coming. I saw him.
BOM!
We're dead. We're dead!
Not yet we're not! Keep writing!

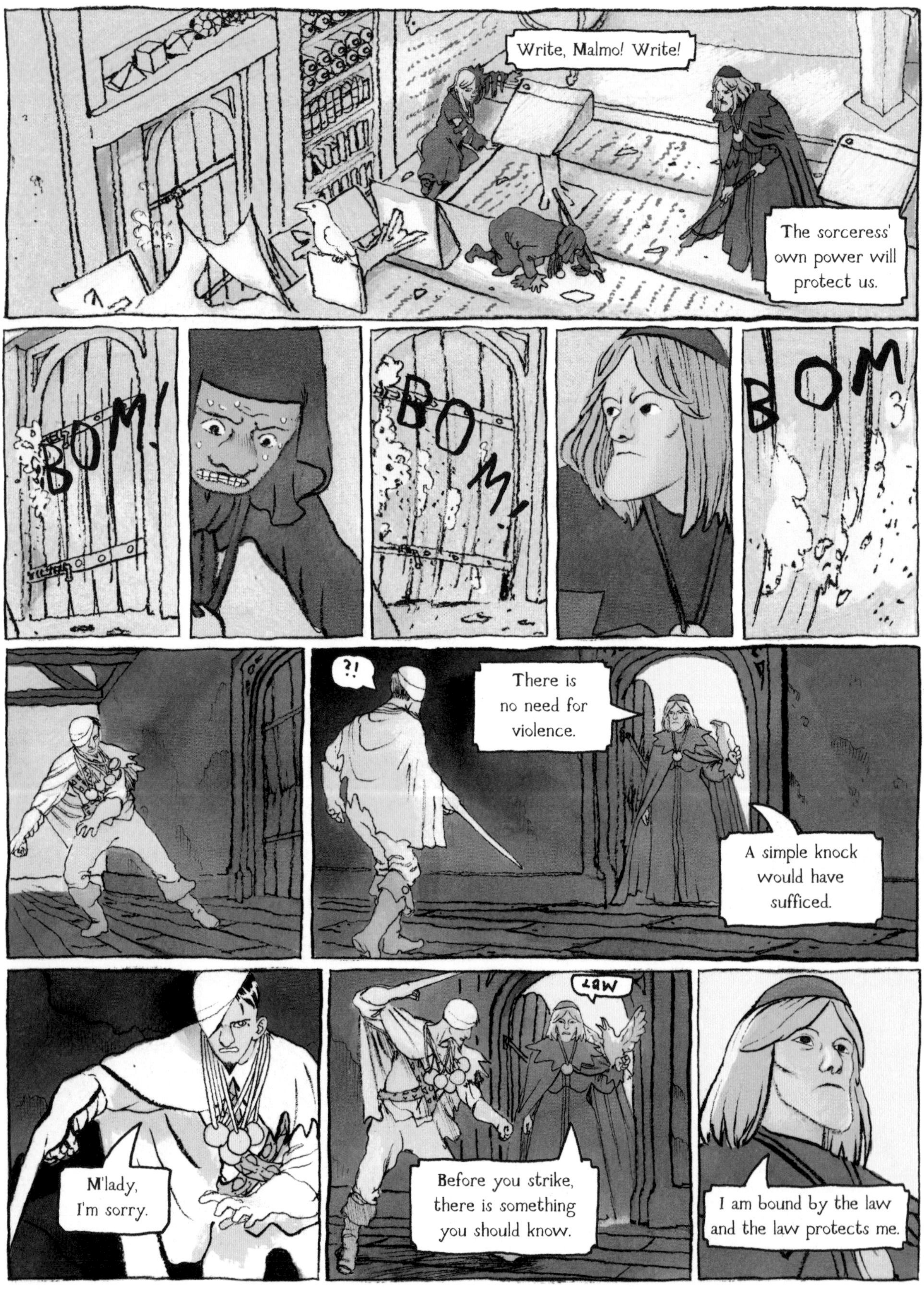

Write, Malmo! Write!
The sorceress' own power will protect us.
BOM!
BOM!
BOM
?!
There is no need for violence.
A simple knock would have sufficed.
M'lady, I'm sorry.
Before you strike, there is something you should know.
I am bound by the law and the law protects me.

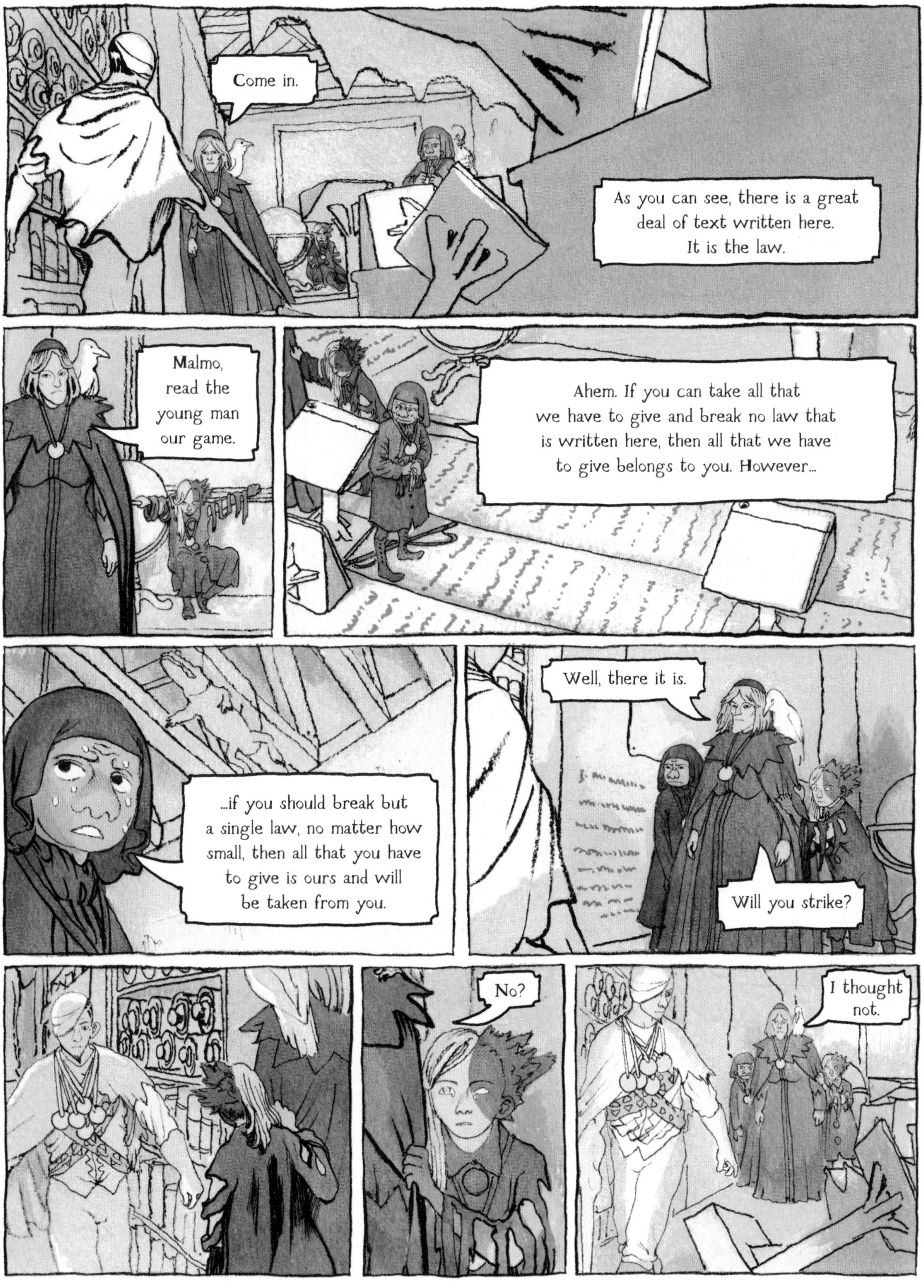

Come in.
As you can see, there is a great deal of text written here. It is the law.
Malmo, read the young man our game.
Ahem. If you can take all that we have to give and break no law that is written here, then all that we have to give belongs to you. However...
...if you should break but a single law, no matter how small, then all that you have to give is ours and will be taken from you.
Well, there it is.
Will you strike?
No?
I thought not.

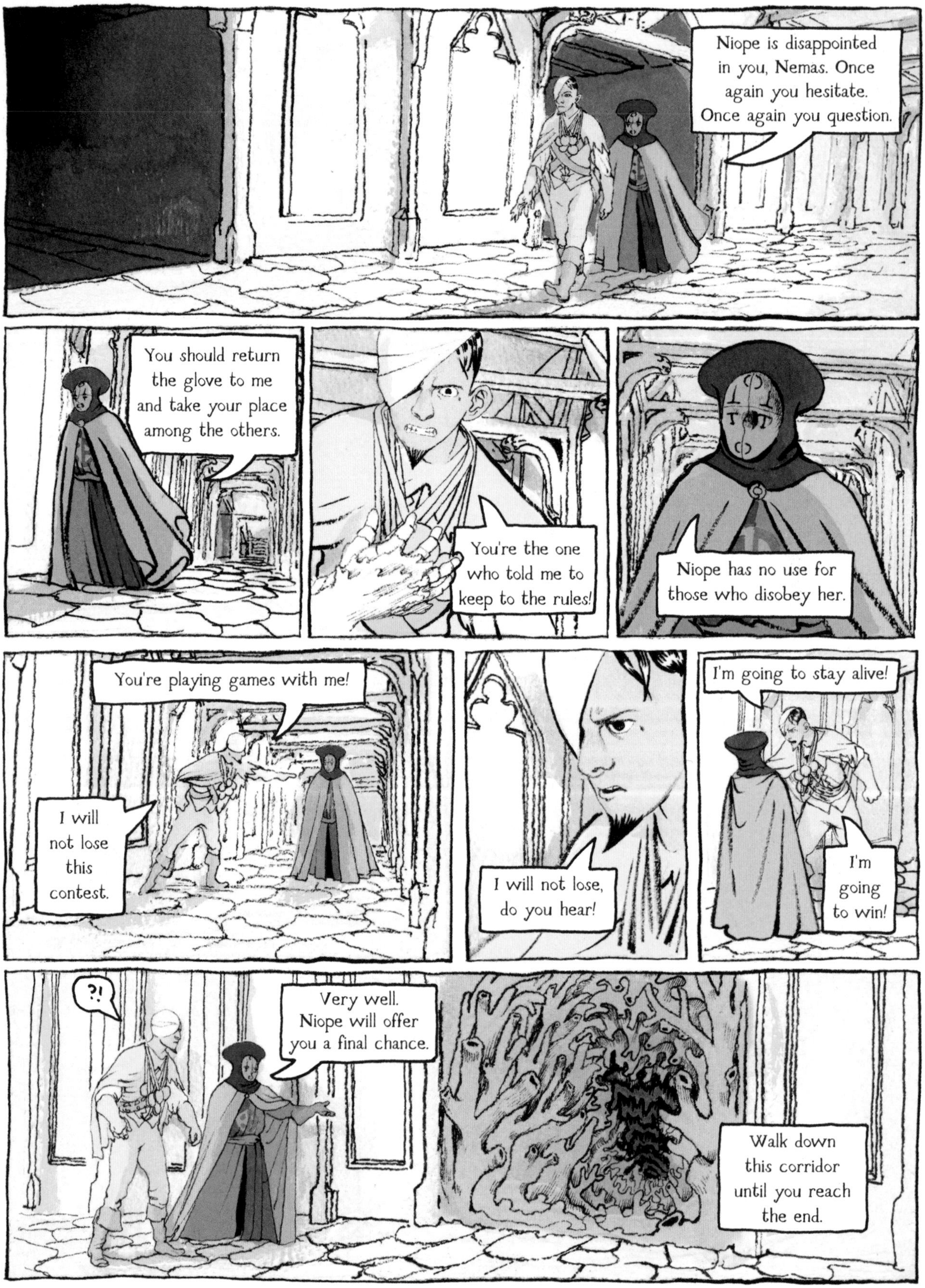
Niope is disappointed in you, Nemas. Once again you hesitate. Once again you question.
You should return the glove to me and take your place among the others.
You're the one who told me to keep to the rules!
Niope has no use for those who disobey her.
You're playing games with me!
I will not lose this contest.
I will not lose, do you hear!
I'm going to stay alive!
I'm going to win!
?!
Very well. Niope will offer you a final chance.
Walk down this corridor until you reach the end.

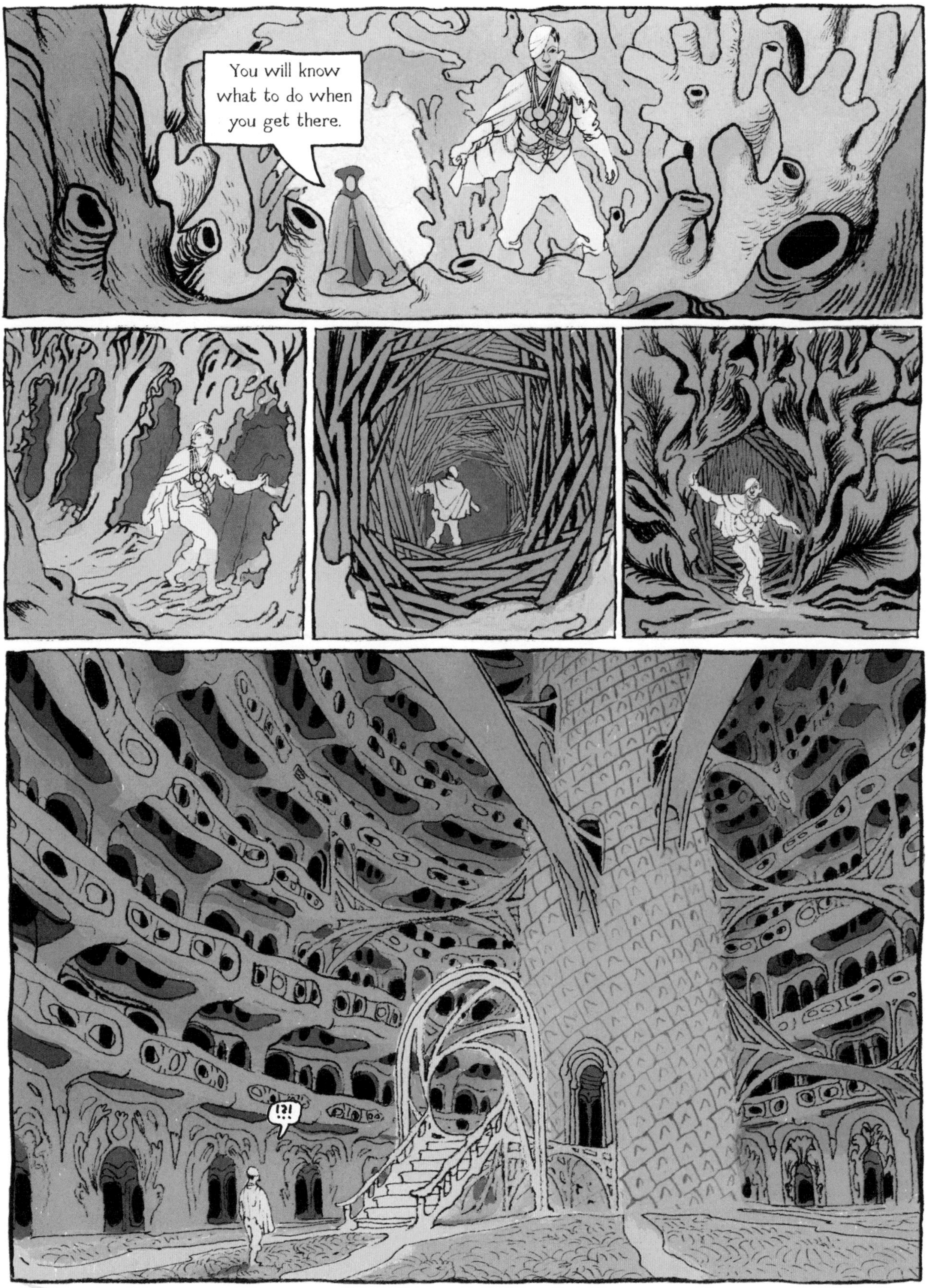
You will know what to do when you get there.
!?!
...

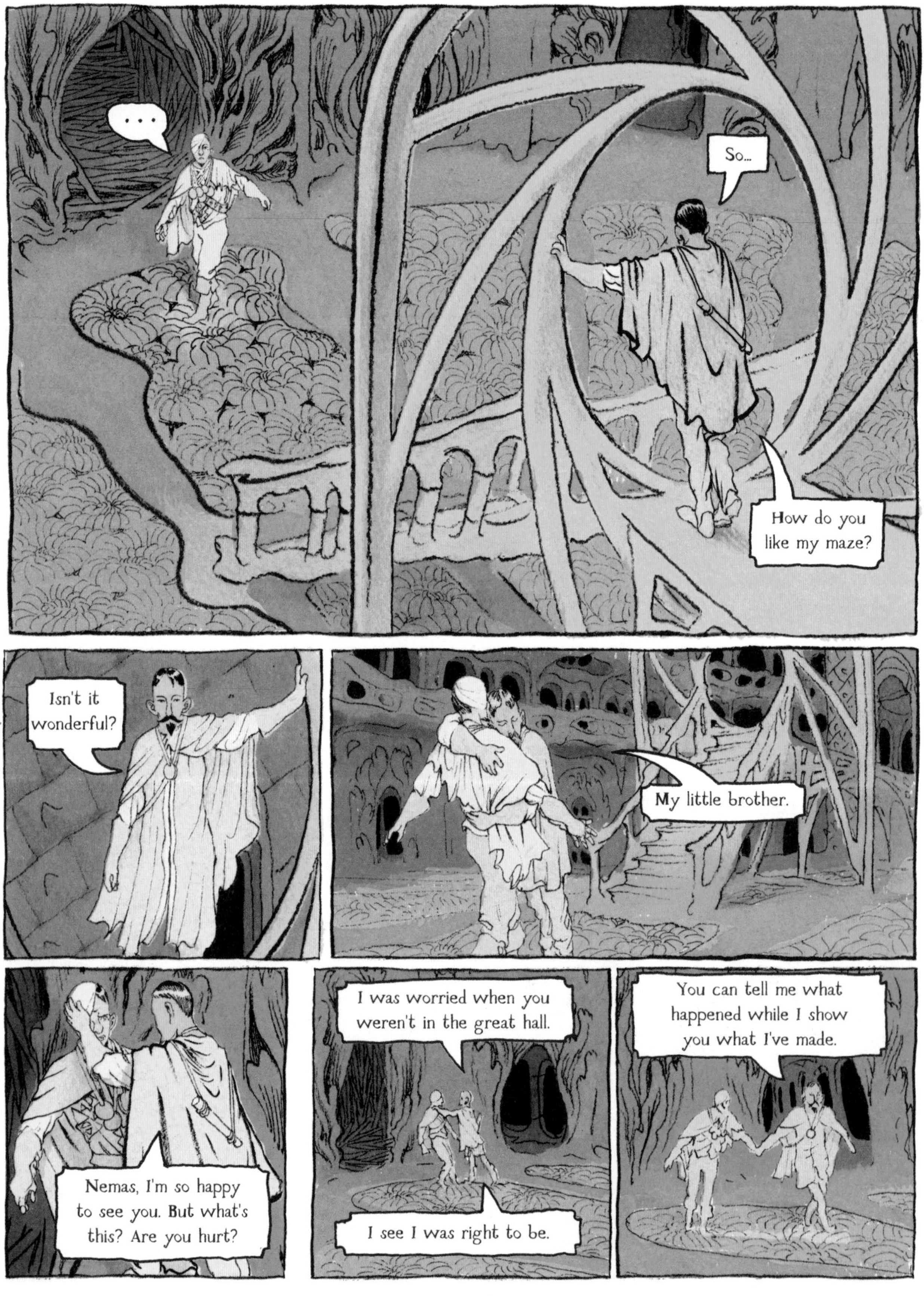
...
So...
How do you like my maze?
Isn't it wonderful?
My little brother.
Nemas, I'm so happy to see you. But what's this? Are you hurt?
I was worried when you weren't in the great hall.
I see I was right to be.
You can tell me what happened while I show you what I've made.

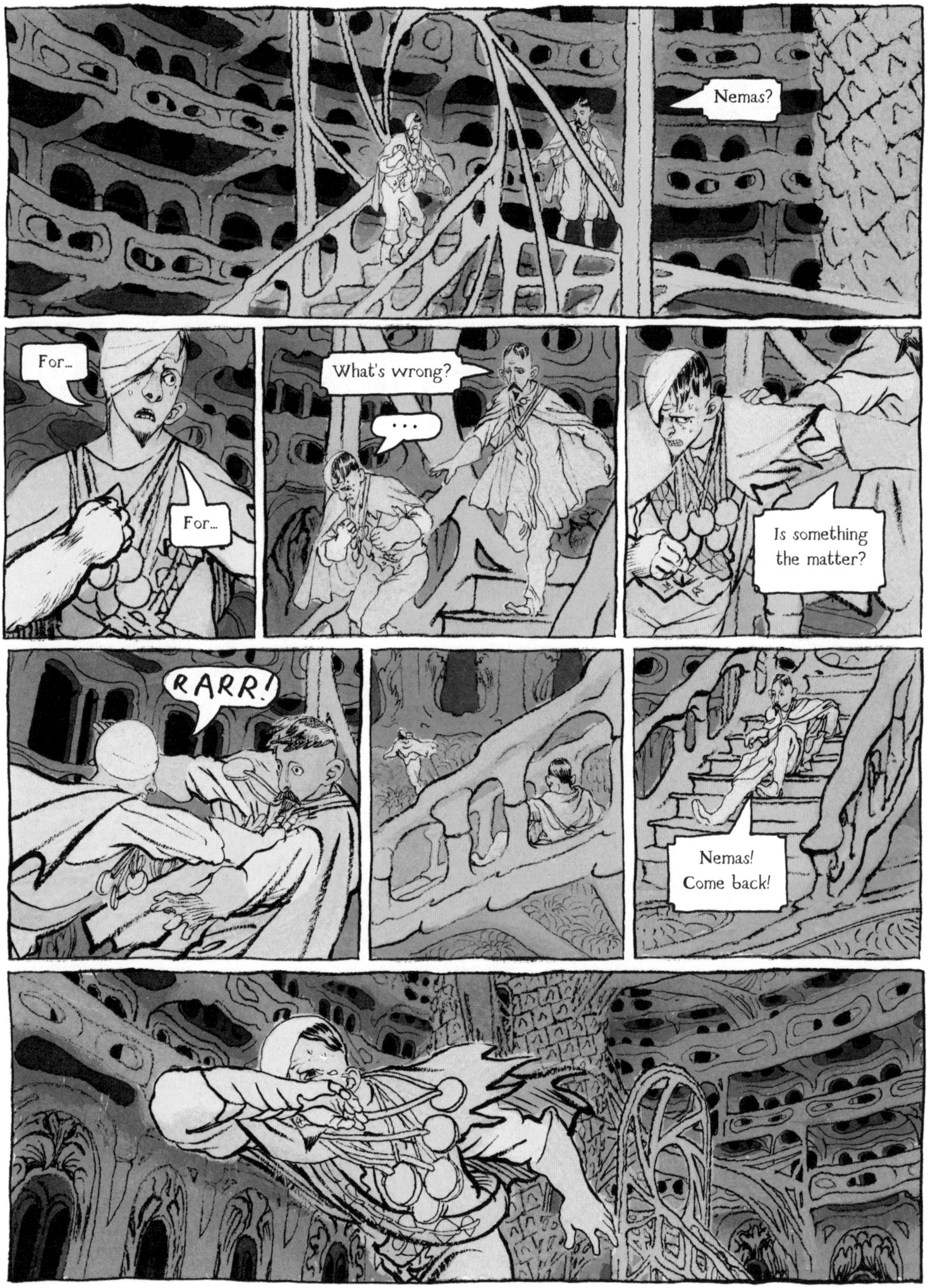

Nemas?
For...
For...
What's wrong?
...
Is something the matter?
RARR!
Nemas! Come back!

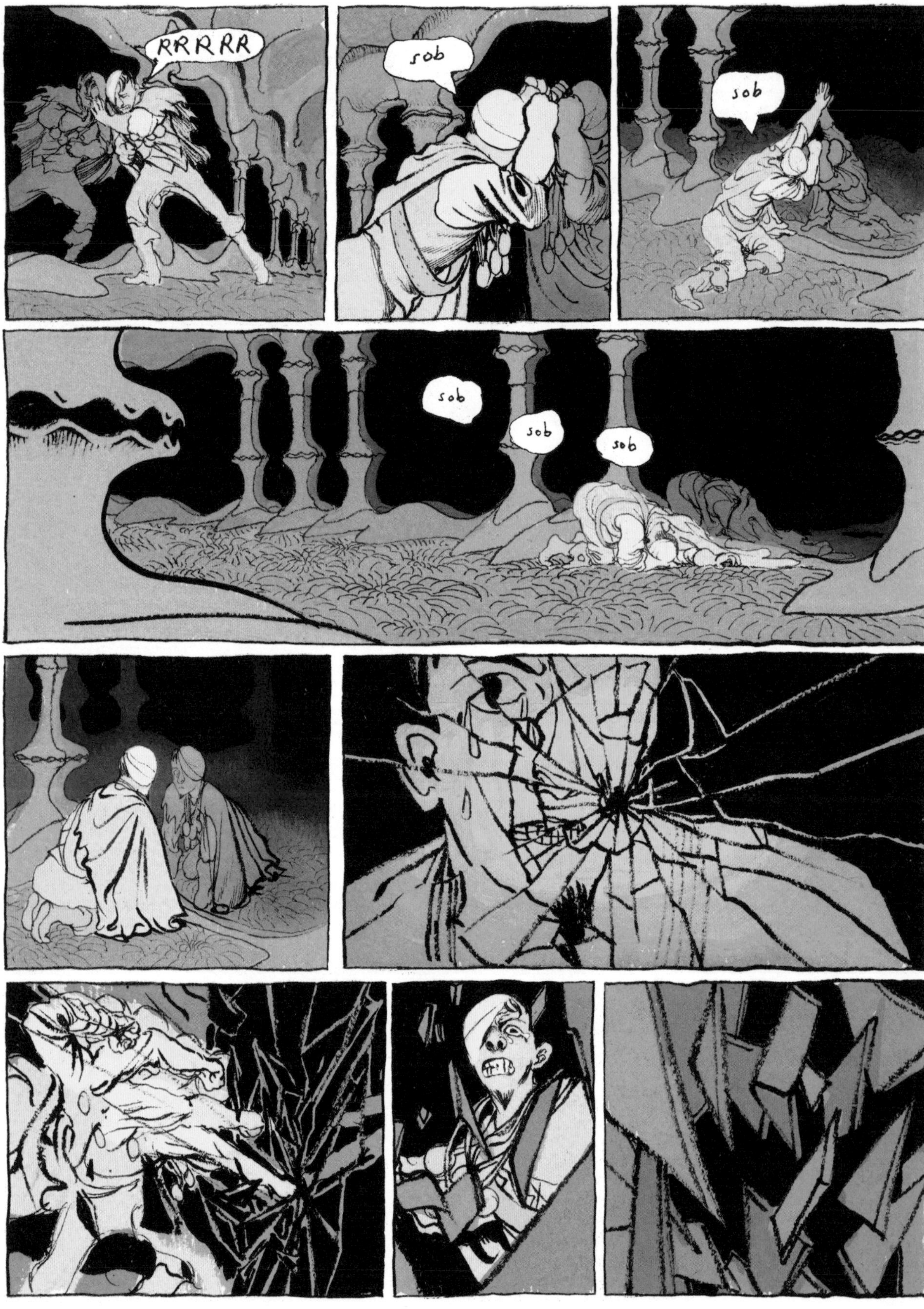
RRRRR
sob
sob
sob
sob
sob

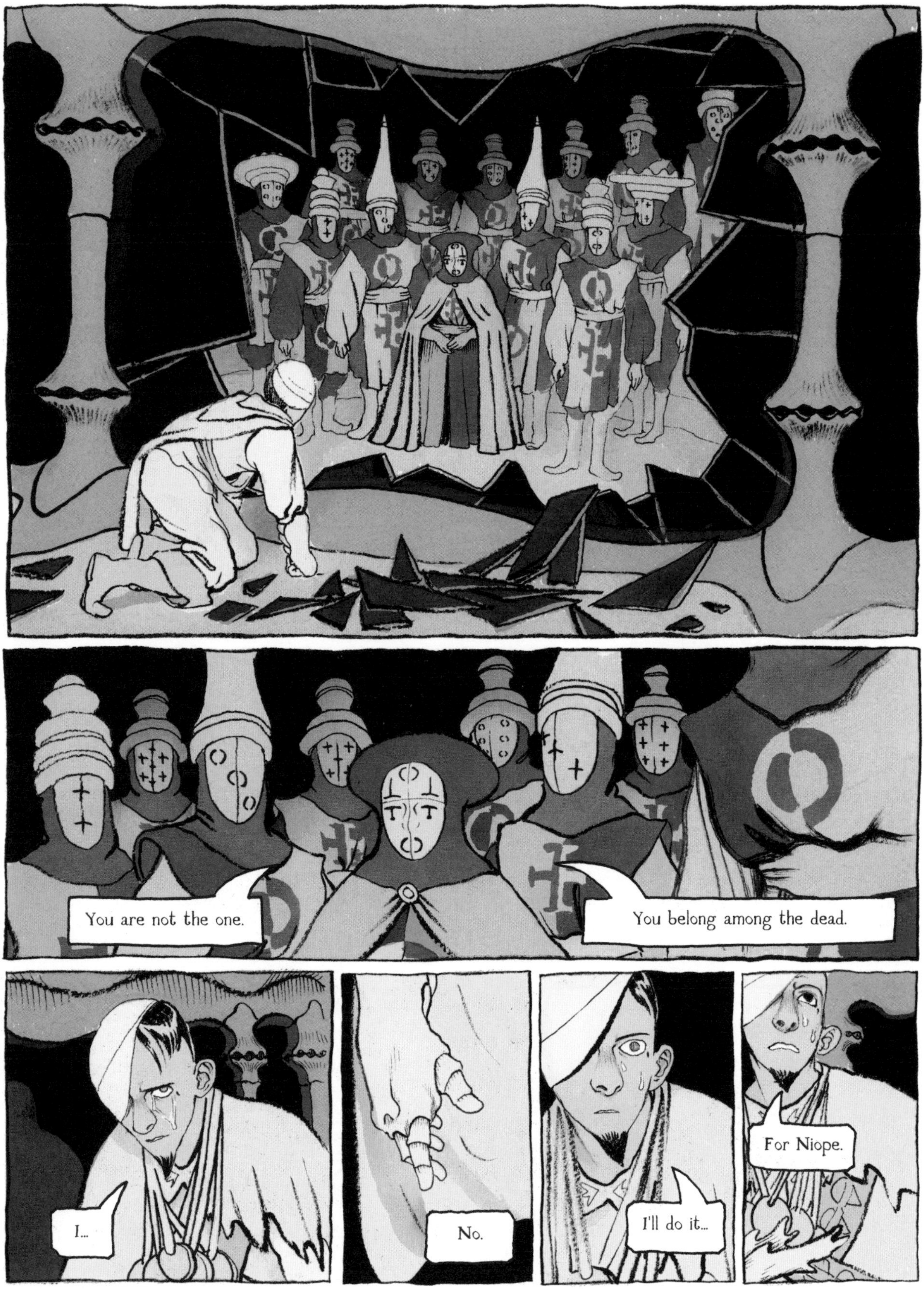
You are not the one.
You belong among the dead.
I...
No.
I'll do it...
For Niope.

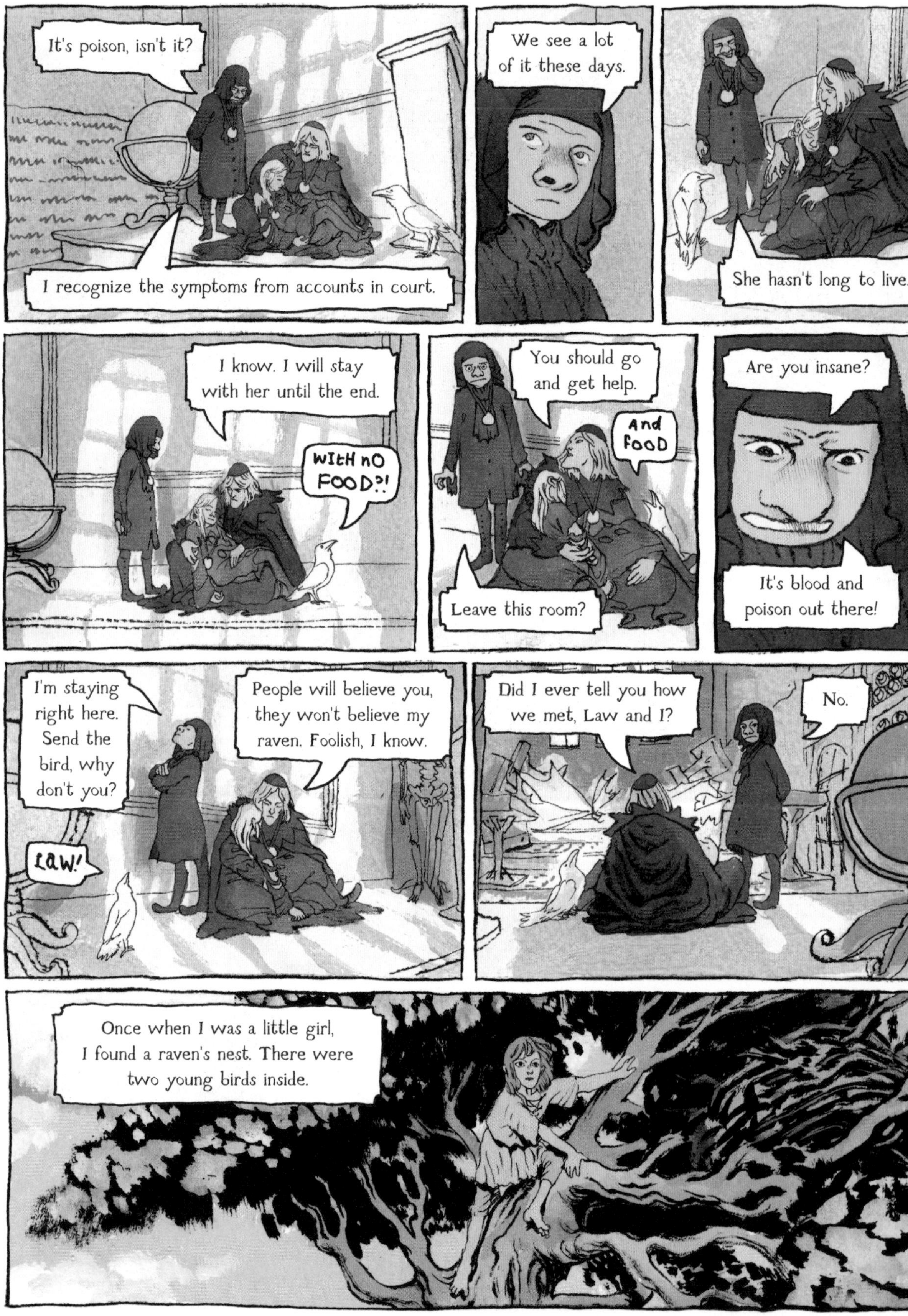
It's poison, isn't it?
I recognize the symptoms from accounts in court.
We see a lot of it these days.
She hasn't long to live.
I know. I will stay with her until the end.
WITH NO FOOD?!
You should go and get help.
AND FOOD
Leave this room?
Are you insane?
It's blood and poison out there!
I'm staying right here. Send the bird, why don't you?
People will believe you, they won't believe my raven. Foolish, I know.
LAW!
Did I ever tell you how we met, Law and I?
No.
Once when I was a little girl, I found a raven's nest. There were two young birds inside.

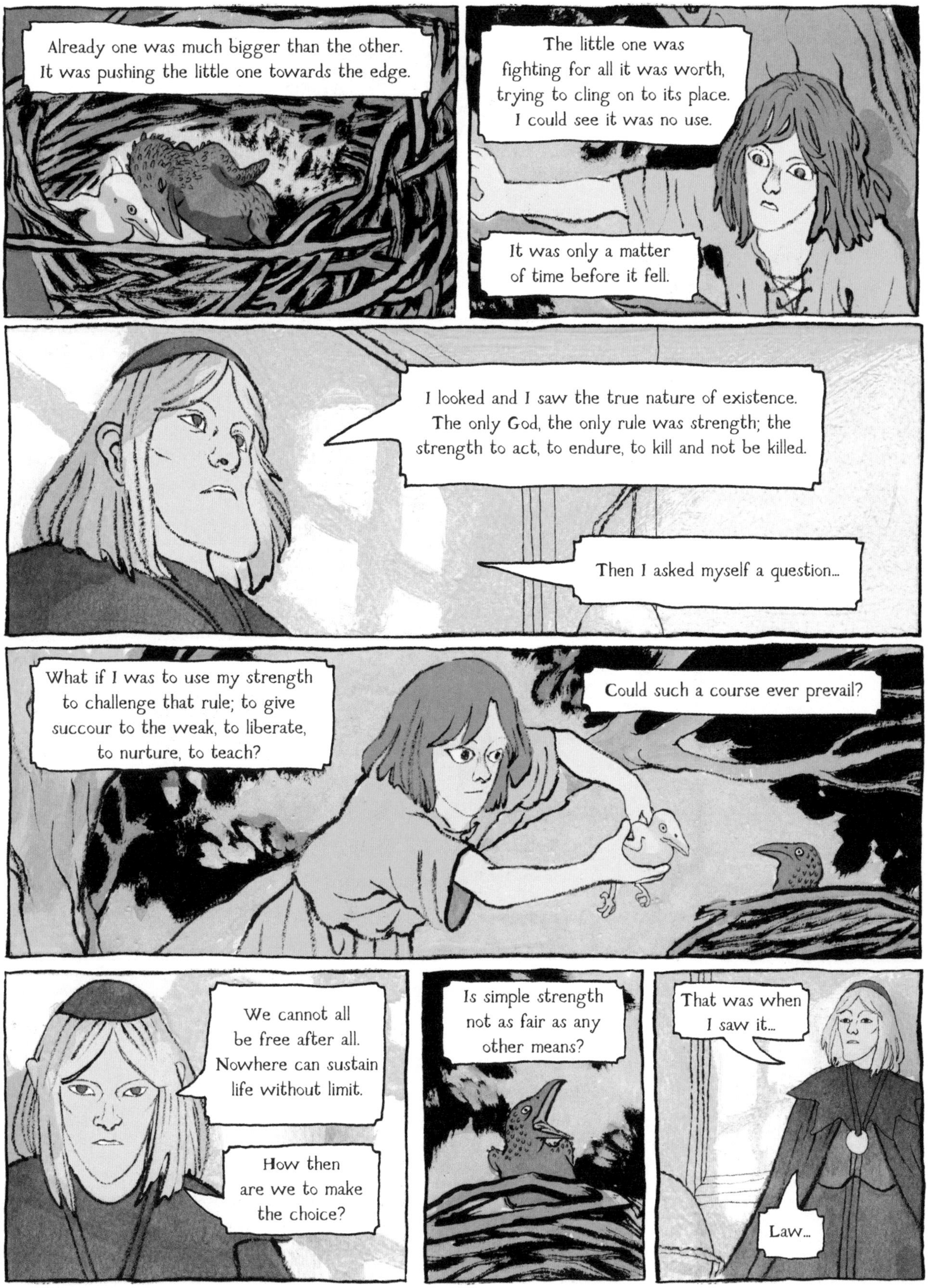

Already one was much bigger than the other. It was pushing the little one towards the edge.
The little one was fighting for all it was worth, trying to cling on to its place. I could see it was no use.
It was only a matter of time before it fell.
I looked and I saw the true nature of existence. The only God, the only rule was strength; the strength to act, to endure, to kill and not be killed.
Then I asked myself a question...
What if I was to use my strength to challenge that rule; to give succour to the weak, to liberate, to nurture, to teach?
Could such a course ever prevail?
We cannot all be free after all. Nowhere can sustain life without limit.
How then are we to make the choice?
Is simple strength not as fair as any other means?
That was when I saw it...
Law...

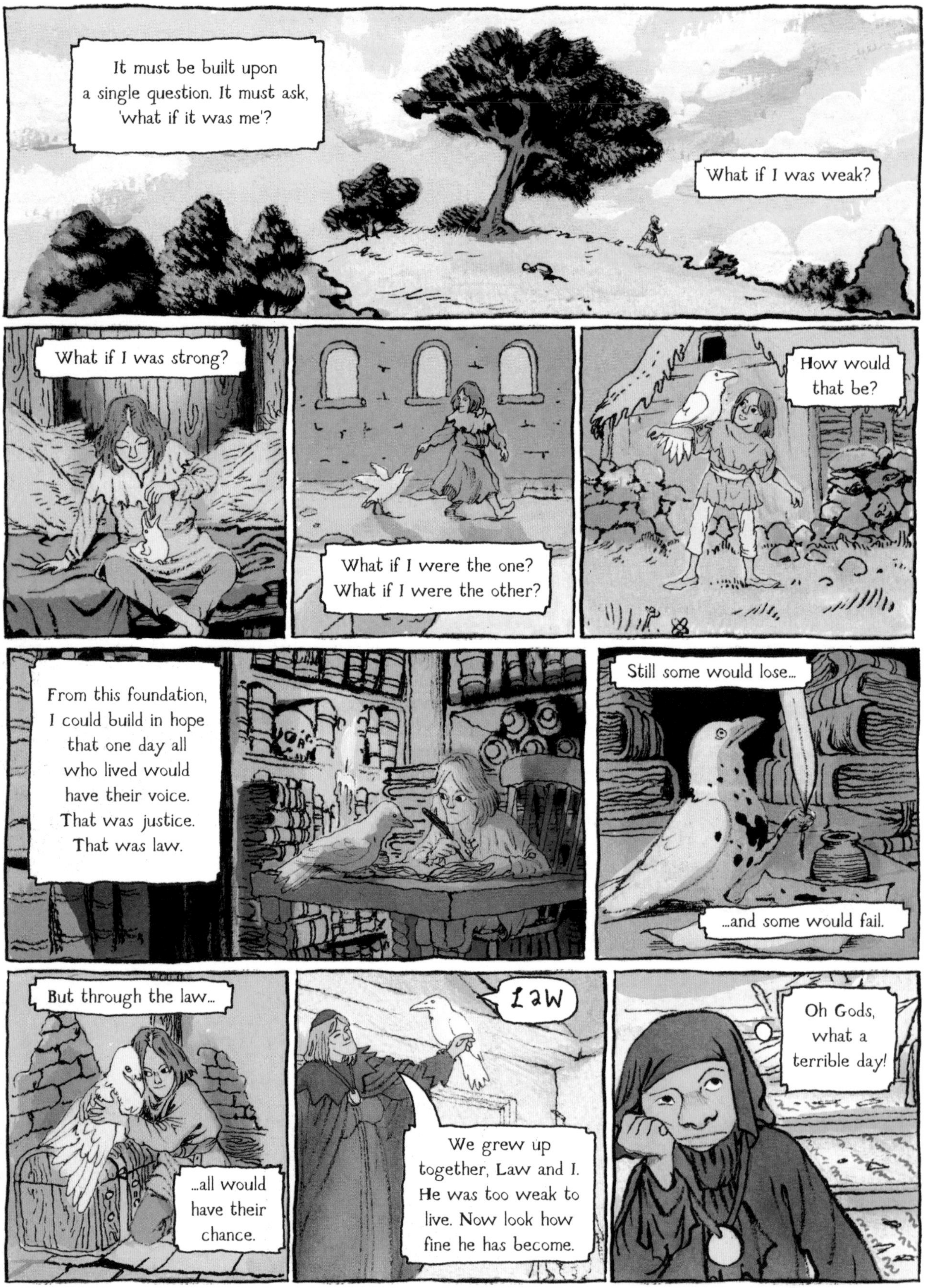

It must be built upon a single question. It must ask, 'what if it was me'?
What if I was weak?
What if I was strong?
What if I were the one? What if I were the other?
How would that be?
From this foundation, I could build in hope that one day all who lived would have their voice. That was justice. That was law.
Still some would lose...
...and some would fail.
But through the law...
...all would have their chance.
LAW
We grew up together, Law and I. He was too weak to live. Now look how fine he has become.
Oh Gods, what a terrible day!

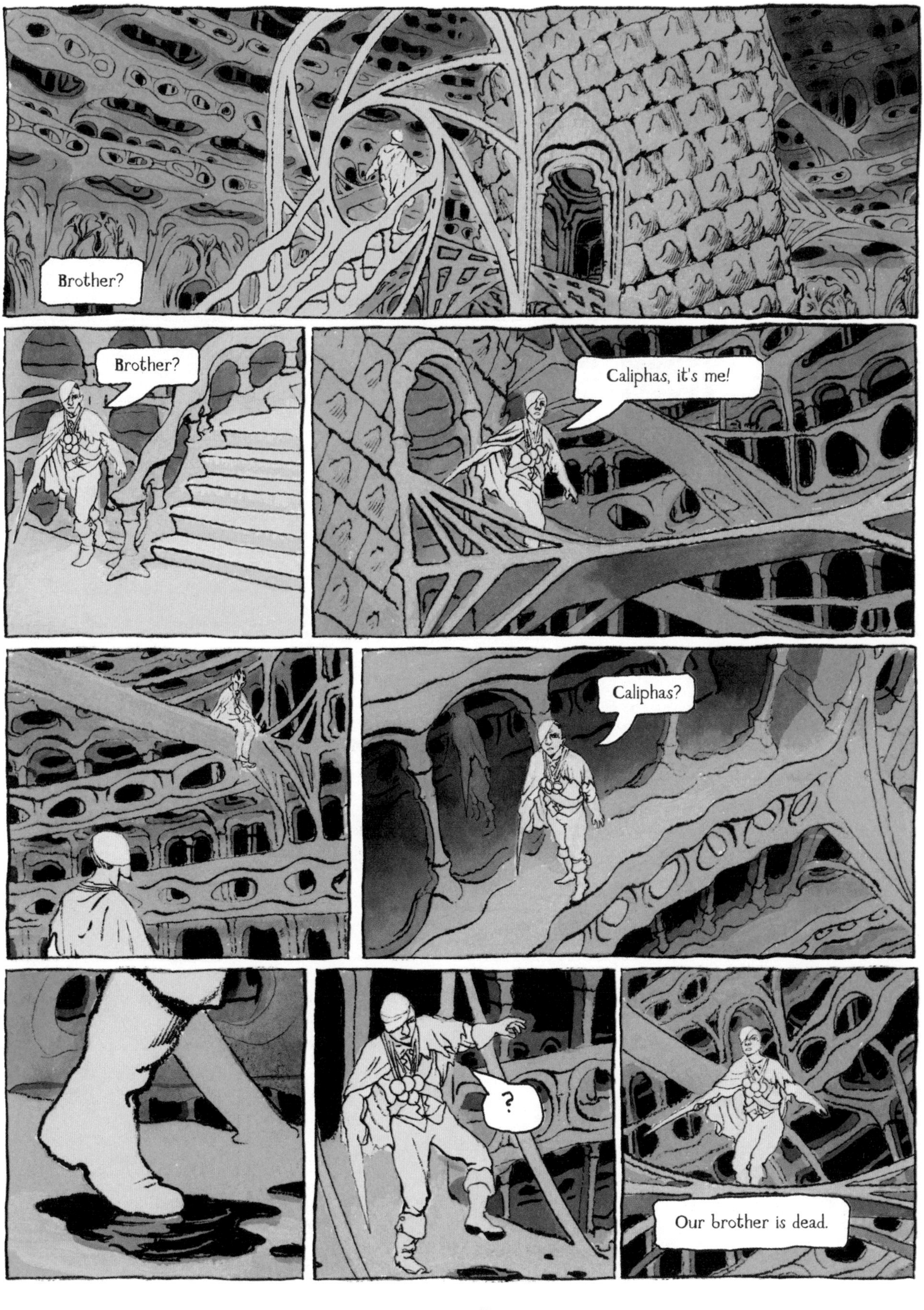
Brother?
Brother?
Caliphas, it's me!
Caliphas?
?
Our brother is dead.

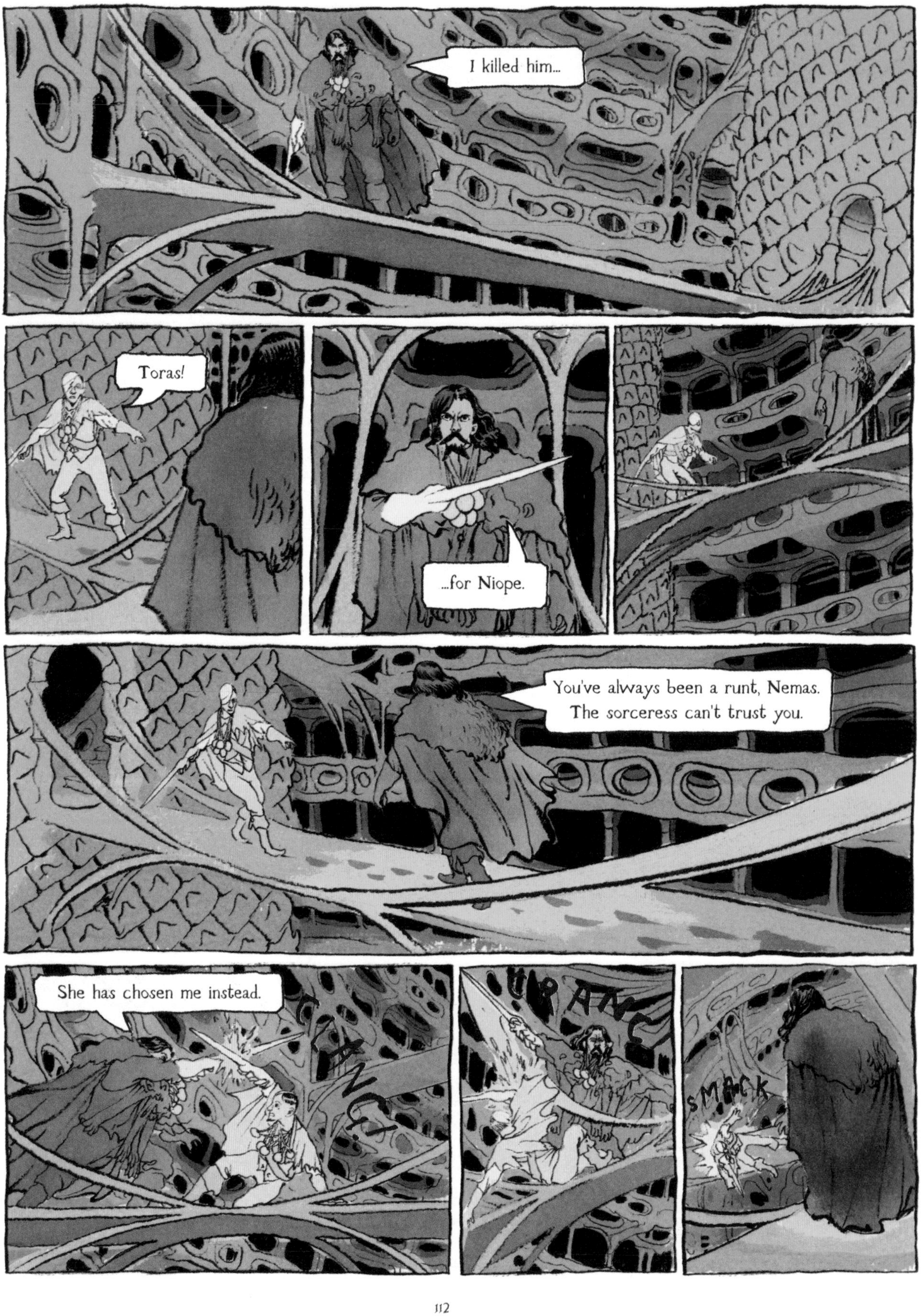

I killed him...
Toras!
...for Niope.
You've always been a runt, Nemas.
The sorceress can't trust you.
She has chosen me instead.
CLANG!
KRANG!
SMACK

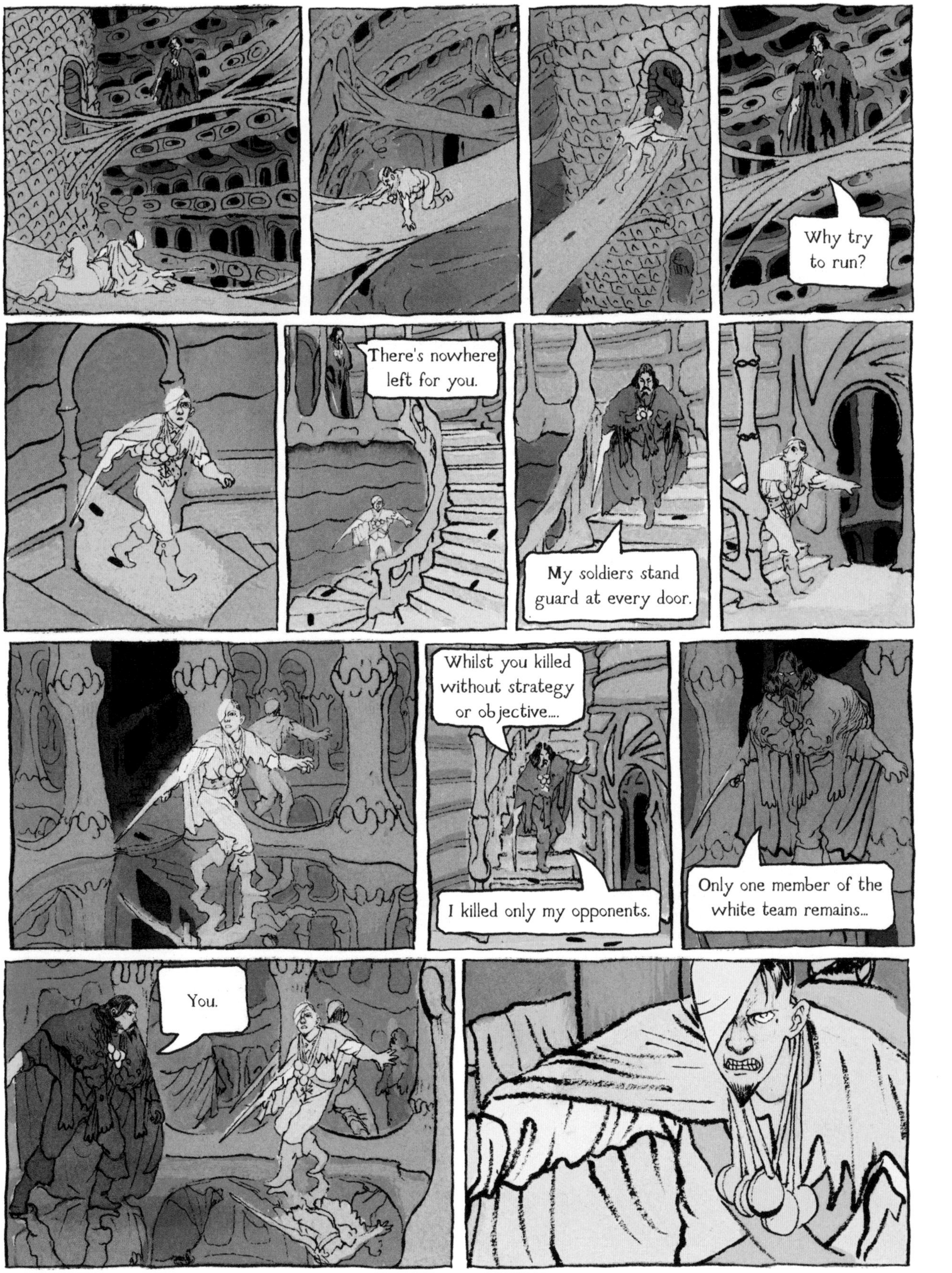
Why try to run?
There's nowhere left for you.
My soldiers stand guard at every door.
Whilst you killed without strategy or objective....
I killed only my opponents.
Only one member of the white team remains...
You.

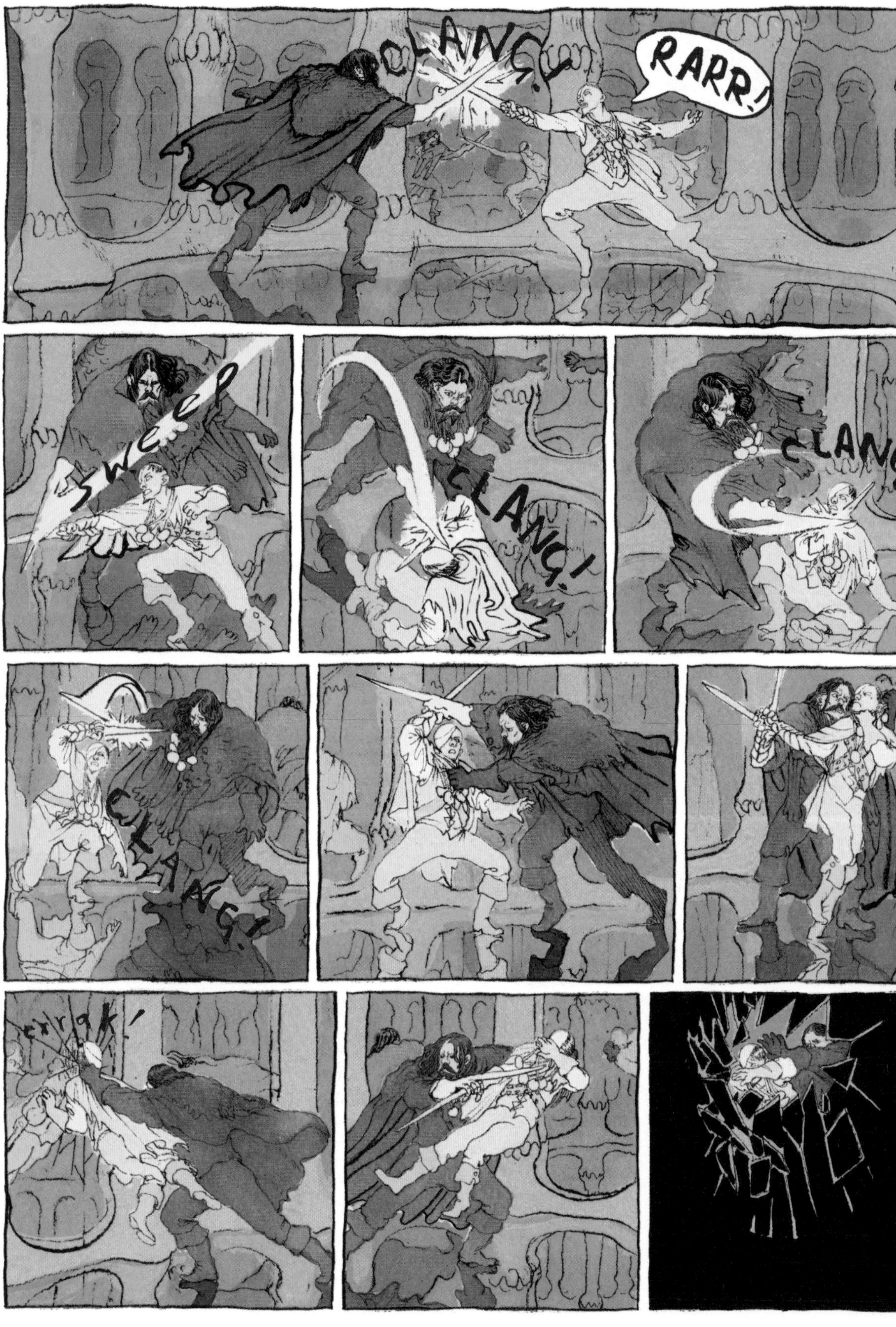
CLANG!
RARR!
SWEEP
CLANG!
CLANG!
CLANG!
CLANG!
crrak!

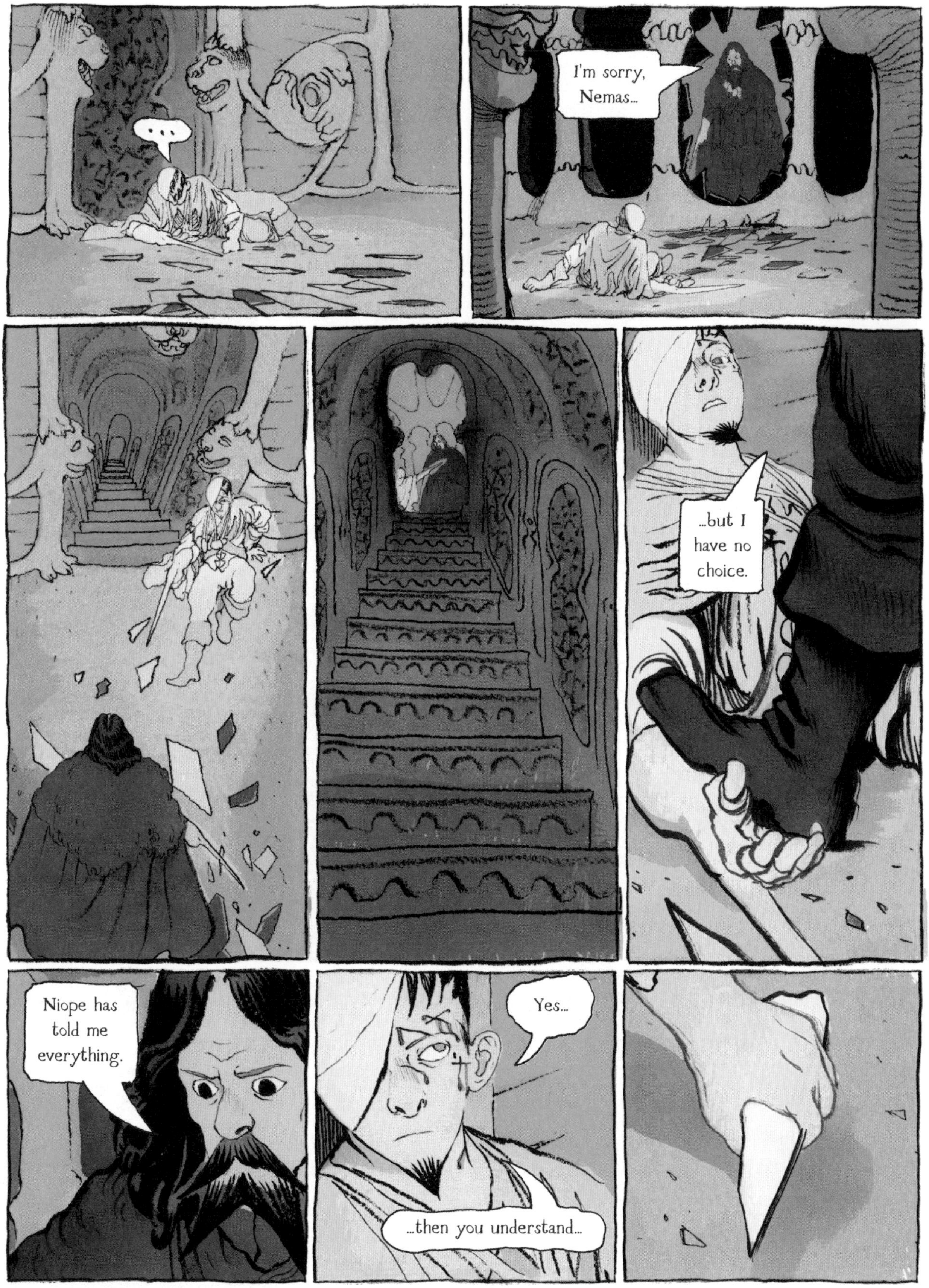

...
I'm sorry, Nemas...
...but I have no choice.
Niope has told me everything.
Yes...
...then you understand...

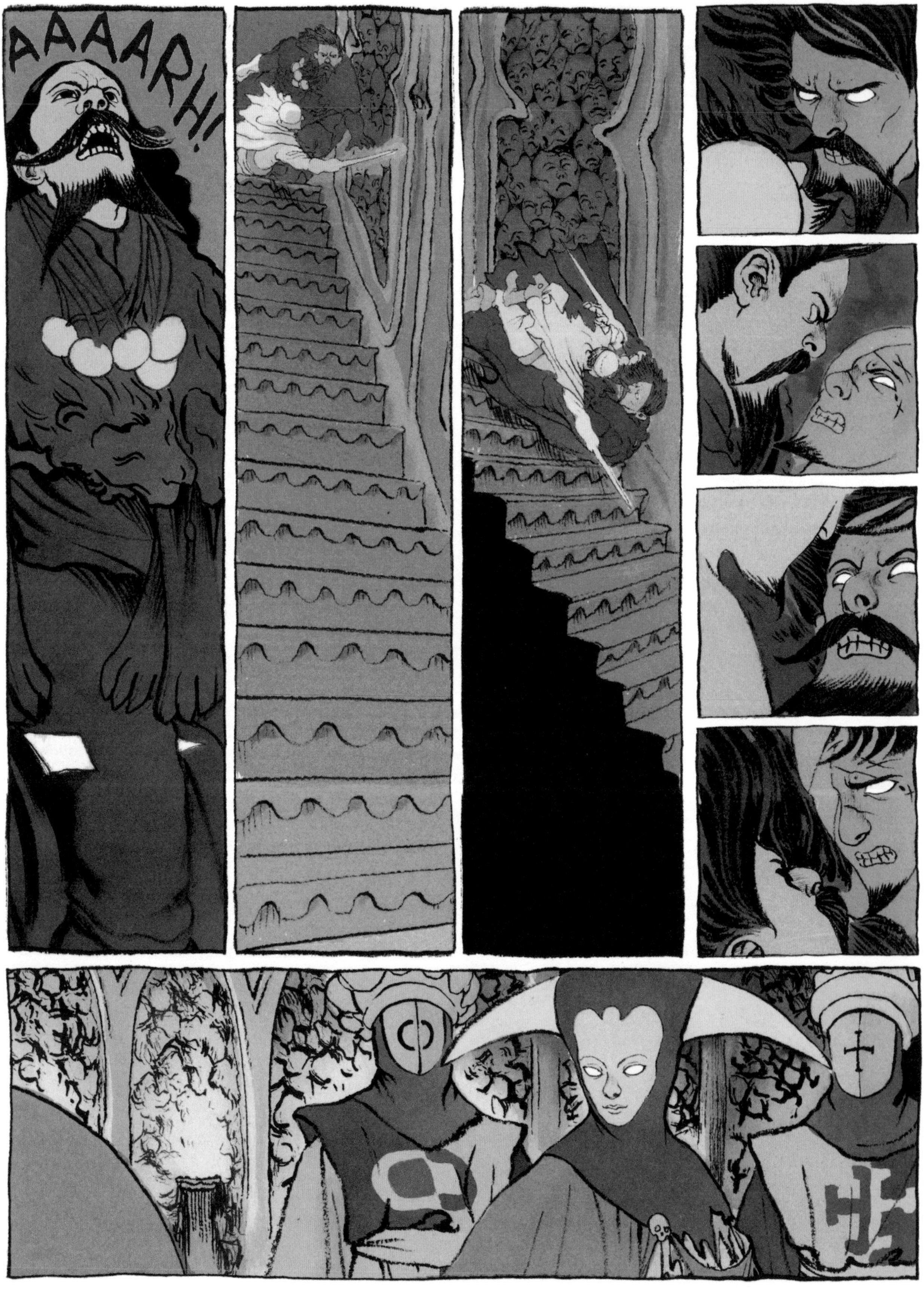
AAAARH!

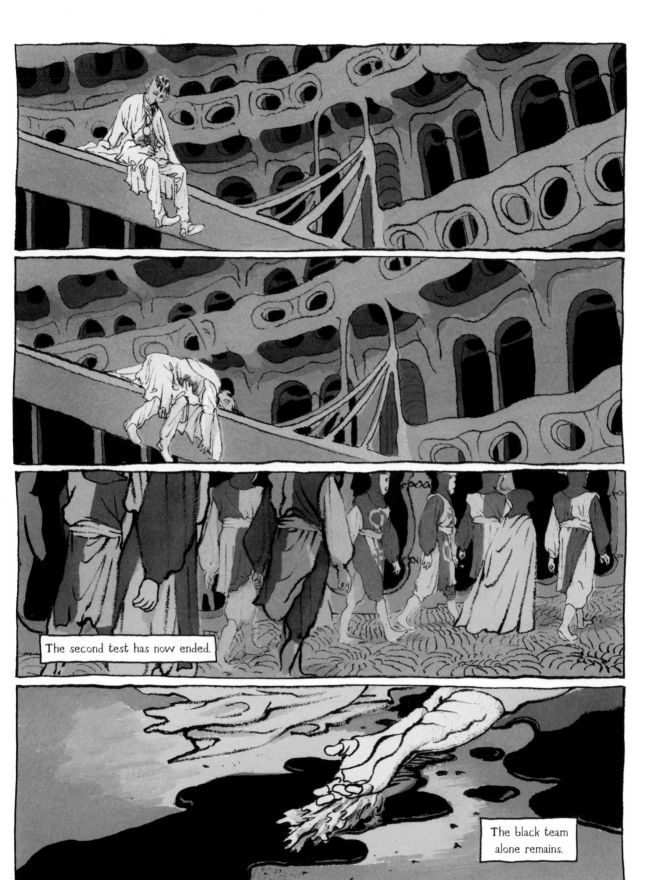

The second test has now ended.

The black team
alone remains.

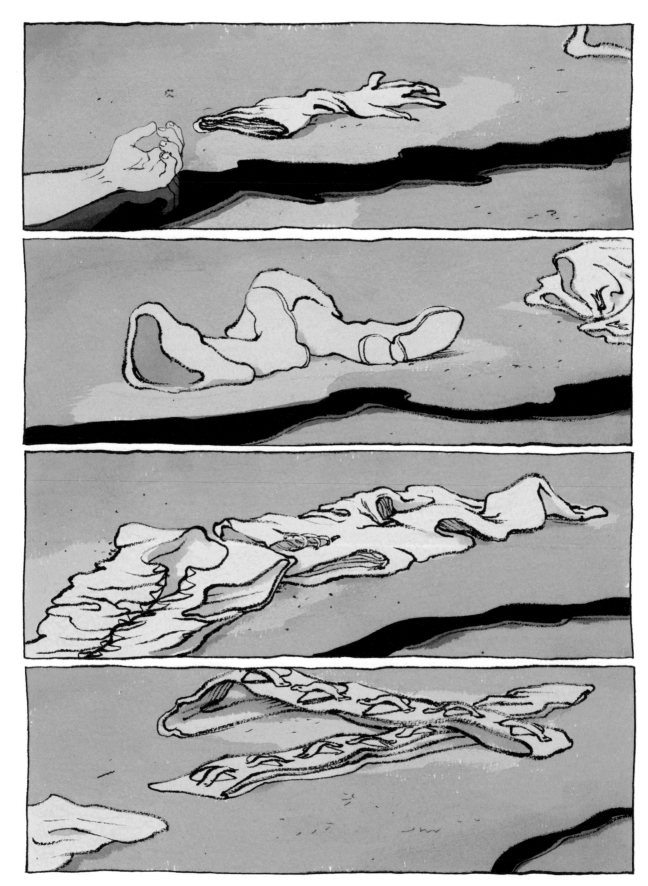

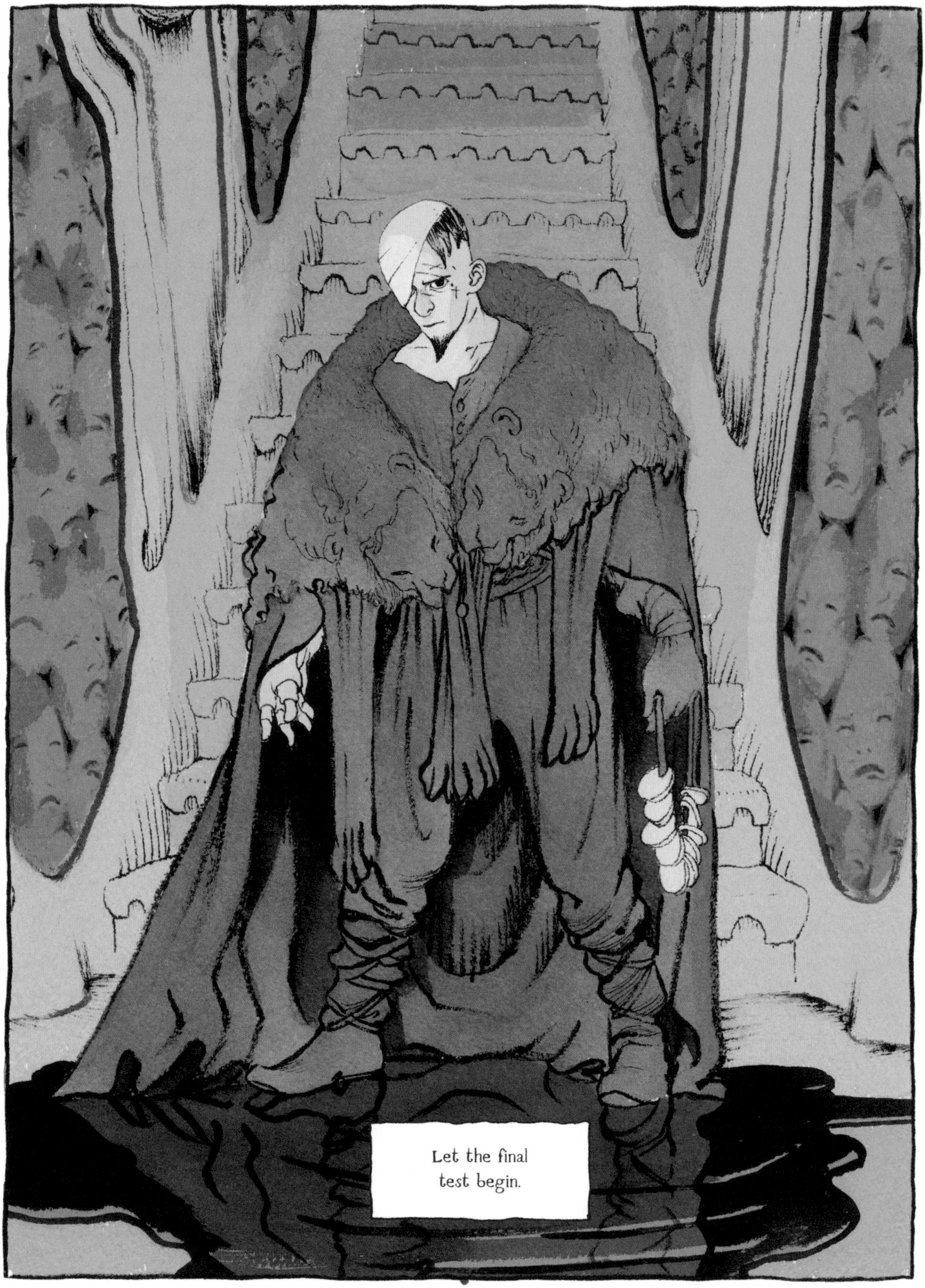
Let the final
test begin.

Thanks to Hannah Hayward, Frances Currie, Isabel Greenberg,
Ash McDow, Goksin Erdemli for their help making this book.

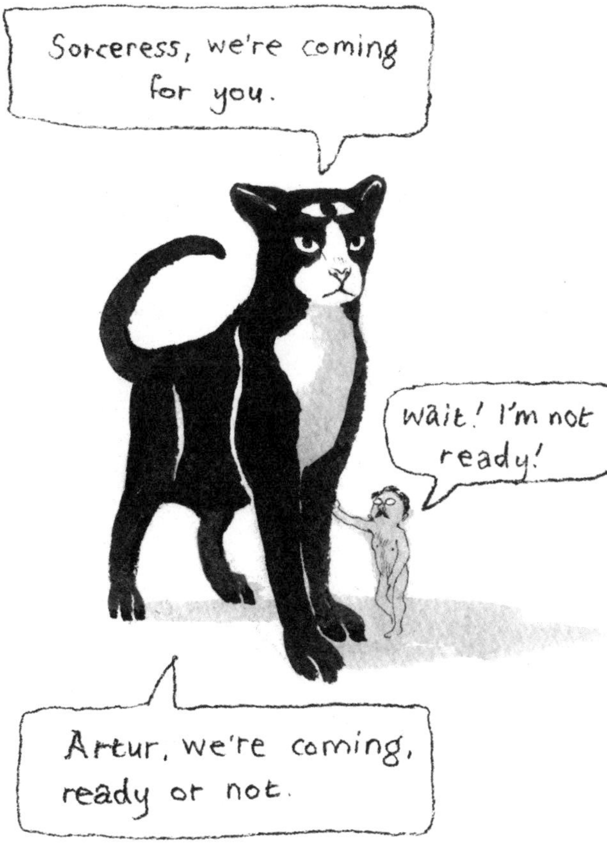
Sorceress, we're coming for you.
Wait! I'm not ready!
Artur, we're coming, ready or not.

Geis continues in Book Three,
The Will That Shapes the World...
COMING SOON.

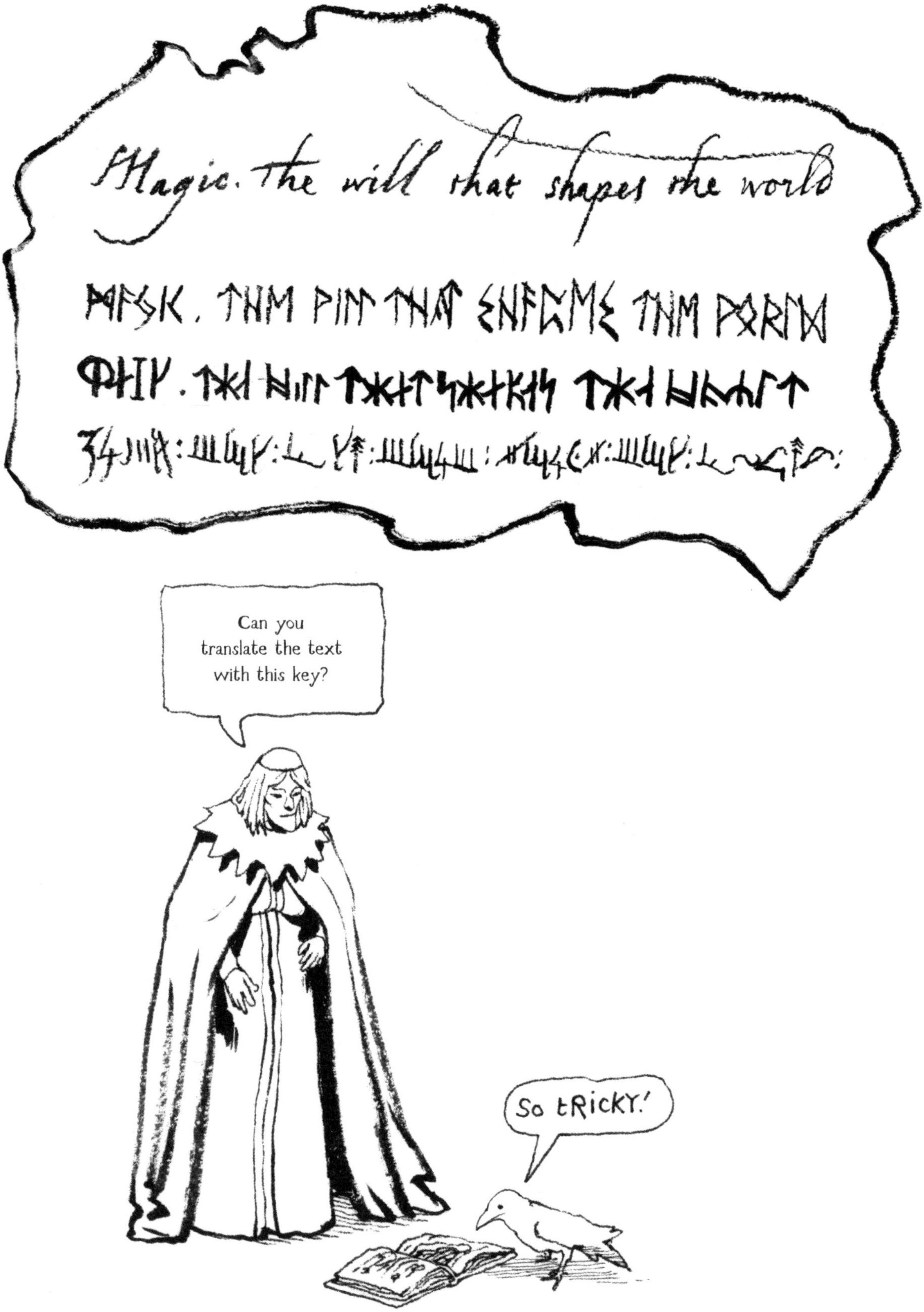
Magic. the will that shapes the world
Can you translate the text with this key?
So tRICKY!

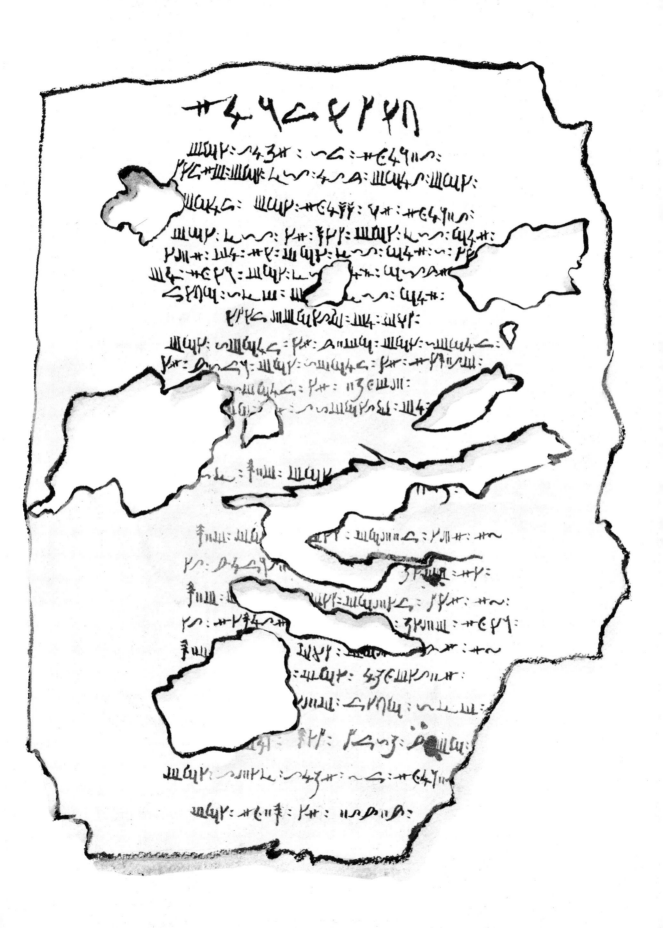

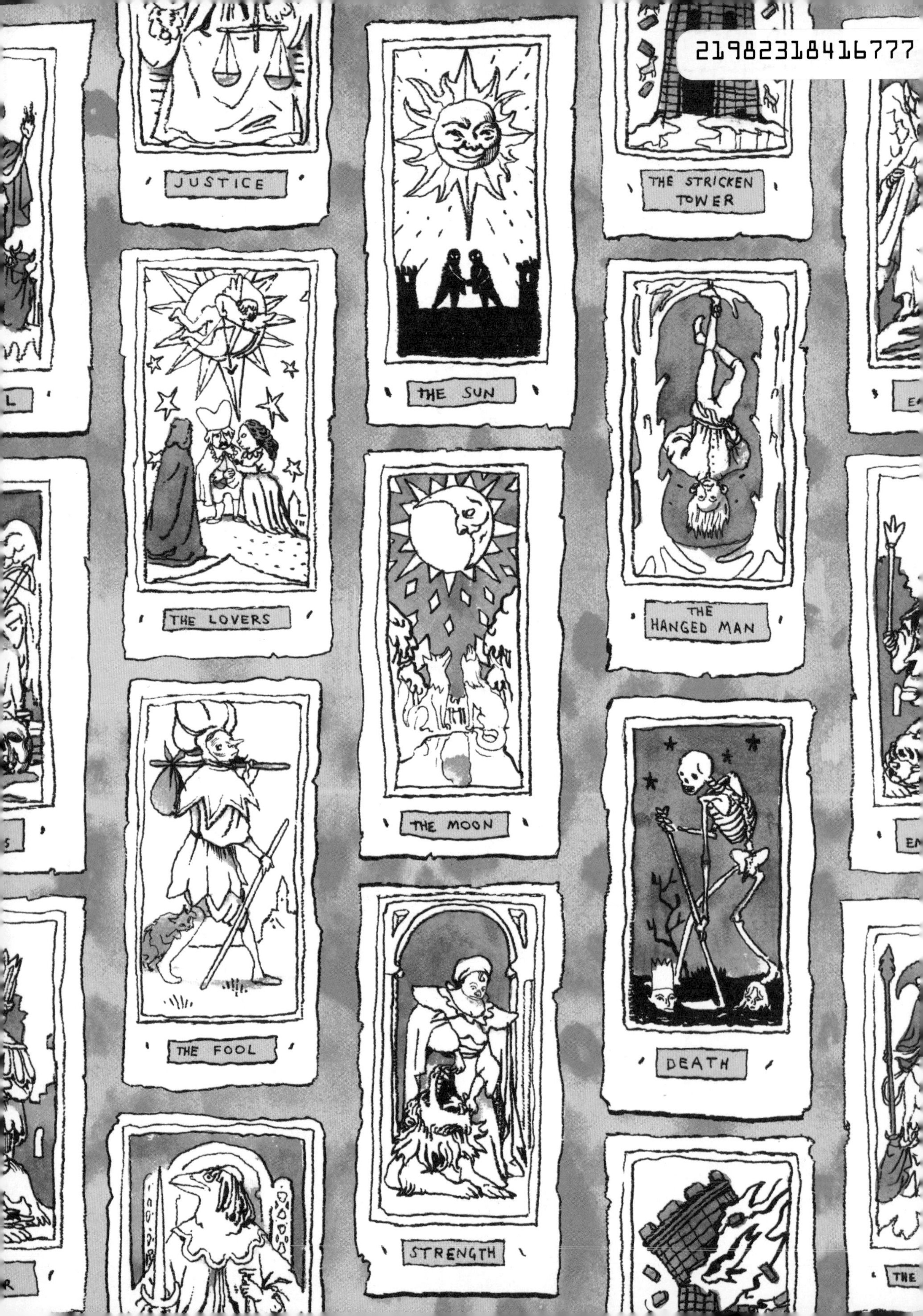
JUSTICE
THE SUN
THE STRICKEN TOWER
THE LOVERS
THE HANGED MAN
THE MOON
THE FOOL
DEATH
STRENGTH